THE ENEMY
IN THE HOUSEHOLD

Family Violence
in Deuteronomy and Beyond

Caryn A. Reeder

Baker Academic
a division of Baker Publishing Group
Grand Rapids, Michigan

© 2012 by Caryn A. Reeder

Published by Baker Academic
a division of Baker Publishing Group
P.O. Box 6287, Grand Rapids, MI 49516-6287
www.bakeracademic.com

Printed in the United States of America

Library of Congress Cataloging-in-Publication Data
Reeder, Caryn A.
    The enemy in the household : family violence in Deuteronomy and beyond / Caryn A.
    Reeder.
        p.   cm.
    Includes bibliographical references (p.   ) and index.
    ISBN 978-0-8010-4828-9 (pbk.)
    1. Family violence in the Bible. 2. Bible. O.T. Deuteronomy—Criticism, interpretation, etc.
3. Family violence—Religious aspects—Judaism—History of doctrines. Family violence—
Religious aspects—Christianity—History of doctrines—Early church, ca. 30–600. I. Title.
BS1275.6.V56R44 2012
222′.1506—dc23   2011042128

12   13   14   15   16   17   18   7   6   5   4   3   2   1

Contents

Acknowledgments

Many people have influenced the development of this book over the years, providing encouragement, offering criticism, and asking incisive questions that sharpened my thoughts and arguments in countless ways. The end result is the better for them (and needless to say, the weaknesses that remain are entirely my own).

This book represents a substantial revision of my doctoral dissertation at the University of Cambridge. I would like to thank James Carleton Paget, my supervisor, for his many helpful suggestions and in particular for his ability to ask the right questions at the right moments. Duncan Dormor at St. John's College was a valuable conversation partner, as were many colleagues at Tyndale House. Thanks are also due to my examiners, William Horbury and Steven Barton, for their comments and criticisms. In addition, friends and "family" at St. John's College, Tyndale House, and St. Mark's Church, Newnham, made the drudgery of doctoral research more than bearable.

My colleagues and students at Westmont College have encouraged me through the process of revising the original dissertation, providing sounding boards and fresh insight into the texts and traditions of family violence. In particular, Emily Thomas read and commented on the completed book; her thoughtfulness is much appreciated. I also want to thank Shirley Decker-Lucke at Hendrickson for her help in beginning the process of publication, Jim Kinney and the editors at Baker Academic for continuing to guide the book along, and Peter Enns for his careful reading and insightful comments and questions, all of which helped me deepen and tighten my arguments.

Special recognition is due to Emily Varner, John Walton, Craig and Kim Hovey, Zhang Ling, Helen Rhee, and Alicia Baker for their ongoing support, friendship, and cheerleading. Finally, my parents, Allen and Lynnette Reeder, and siblings, Megan, Ryan, and Sara, have provided constant support and encouragement: I would not be who I am today without them.

Abbreviations

'Abod. Zar.	'Abodah Zarah
Ag. Ap.	Josephus, *Against Apion*
Alleg. Interp.	Philo, *Allegorical Interpretation*
ANET	*Ancient Near Eastern Texts Relating to the Old Testament*
ANF	*The Ante-Nicene Fathers*
Ant.	Josephus, *Jewish Antiquities*
b.	Babylonian Talmud
B. Meṣi'a	*Baba Meṣi'a*
Bik.	*Bikkurim*
Cels.	Origen, *Against Celsus*
Cherubim	Philo, *On the Cherubim*
Comm. Matt.	Origen, *Commentary on the Gospel of Matthew*
Confusion	Philo, *On the Confusion of Tongues*
Contempl. Life	Philo, *On the Contemplative Life or Suppliants*
COS	*The Context of Scripture.* Edited by W. W. Hallo and K. Lawson Younger. 3 vols. Leiden and New York: Brill, 1997–2002.
Creation	Philo, *On the Creation*
Decal.	Philo, *The Decalogue*
Dial.	Justin Martyr, *Dialogue with Trypho*
Drunkenness	Philo, *On Drunkenness*
ET	English translation
Flight	Philo, *On Flight and Finding*
Fr. 1 Cor.	Origen, *Fragments on 1 Corinthians*
Giṭ.	*Giṭṭin*
Heir	Philo, *Who Is the Heir of Divine Things?*
Hom. 1 Cor.	John Chrysostom, *Homilies on First Corinthians*
Hor.	*Horayot*

Hypothetica	Philo, *Hypothetica: Apology for the Jews*
Joseph	Philo, *On Joseph*
J.W.	Josephus, *Jewish War*
Ketub.	*Ketubbot*
KJV	King James Version
LCL	Loeb Classical Library
Life	*The Life of Flavius Josephus*
LXX	Septuagint
m.	Mishnah
Ma'aś. Š.	*Ma'aśer Šeni*
Mak.	*Makkot*
Migration	Philo, *On the Migration of Abraham*
Moses	Philo, *On the Life of Moses*
MT	Masoretic Text
Names	Philo, *On the Change of Names*
NASB	New American Standard Bible
Nid.	*Niddah*
NPNF[1]	*Nicene and Post-Nicene Fathers*, Series 1
NPNF[2]	*Nicene and Post-Nicene Fathers*, Series 2
NRSV	New Revised Standard Version
PG	Patrologia graeca. Edited by J.-P. Migne. 162 vols. Paris, 1857–86, 1912.
Posterity	Philo, *On the Posterity of Cain and His Exile*
Qidd.	*Qiddušin*
Rewards	Philo, *On Rewards and Punishments*
Sacrifices	Philo, *On the Birth of Abel and the Sacrifices Offered by Him and by His Brother Cain*
Sanh.	*Sanhedrin*
Sipre Deut.	*Sipre on Deuteronomy*
Sipre Num.	*Sipre on Numbers*
Sir.	Sirach
Sobriety	Philo, *On Sobriety*
Spec. Laws	Philo, *On the Special Laws*
t.	Tosefta
Tg. Ps.-J.	*Targum Pseudo-Jonathan*
Unchangeable	Philo, *On the Unchangeableness of God*
Virtues	Philo, *On the Virtues*
Worse	Philo, *That the Worse Is Wont to Attack the Better*
y.	Jerusalem Talmud
Yebam.	*Yebamot*

1

Introducing the Enemy Within

Put no trust in a friend, have no confidence in a loved one; guard the doors of your mouth from her who lies in your embrace; for the son treats the father with contempt, the daughter rises up against her mother, the daughter-in-law against her mother-in-law; your enemies are members of your own household.

Mic. 7:5–6 (NRSV)

"Your enemies are members of your own household." This is a strong, emotionally laden statement, in the context of both ancient Israel and today. You can trust no one, not even your dearest friends and family. Your spouse is a spy in your arms, and your own children rebel against you. These people are your friends and kin, living and working by your side, but they have become your enemies, those who seek your harm, not your good (cf. Mic. 2:8–9; 7:8–10). Enmity here marks the people who should be your closest companions as outsiders who have infiltrated your very home. Enmity proves itself to be a question of identity.

For biblical Israel, identity is marked by loyalty. Identifying with the people of Israel requires being loyal to the God of Israel. Identifying with a family lineage means being loyal to that family, and identifying with a household means being loyal to the relationships and common life of the household. Members of God's people or a particular family should be loyal, obedient, and unified (e.g., Gen. 13:8; Exod. 19:3–6; Josh. 24:14–15; Ps. 133:1). Identity is fluid and changeable: when members of families are not loyal, obedient, and unified, as indeed they are not in Mic. 7:1–6, they show that they are outsiders. They do not truly belong to the people of God or the family. They are enemies disguised as kin.

Three laws in Deuteronomy address enmity in the household. A close friend, sibling, spouse, or child counsels rebellion against the God who saved Israel from Egypt (13:6–11 [7–12 MT]). A son disobeys and rebels against his parents (21:18–21). A husband slanders his wife, and a daughter and wife shames parents and husband by her sexual indiscretion (22:13–21). In each text, apparent insiders are revealed as enemies by their disloyalty to God and family. Their behavior threatens the identity of the family and of God's people. These enemies within are just as dangerous to Israel as foreign armies drawn up for battle.

In Mic. 7:1–7 enmity in the household is cause for lamentation and awaiting God's salvation. In Deuteronomy the response to the enemy within is rather different: the very family members who have been tempted to idolatrous worship or dishonored by a rebellious child bring the enemy—their own brother, wife, son, daughter, or dear friend—to judgment and execution. Emphasizing the household's role in the action taken against the enemy, in Deut. 22:20–21 the execution takes place at the door of the house, and in 13:9–10 (10–11 MT), the family member even throws the stone that begins the execution. For Deuteronomy, identifying a member of the household as an enemy has deadly consequences.

These laws can seem abhorrent to modern readers, who are perhaps more likely to see the enemy within as family violence rather than as an errant family member. How could a husband raise his hand against the wife who lies in his arms? How could a mother betray her daughter? How could a man take the life of his brother, or the friend who is like his own soul? These questions and concerns are not new. Ancient readers from the second century BCE to the rabbis of the second and third centuries CE also struggled to understand the kind of family violence represented in Deut. 13:6–11; 21:18–21; and 22:13–21. Clues in the way the laws are narrated in Deuteronomy suggest that even their producers recognized their inherent offensiveness. Though for modern readers these laws are horrifying because of the emotional and nurturing significance of the family and the value of individual freedom, for their earliest readers the family was the social, economic, and theological center and source of life. In this context, laws that require violence against a family member are ever more troubling.[1]

The demands of these texts sound a harsh, discordant note in ancient and modern ears alike.[2] Considering the value of family in the Hebrew Bible and

1. Though ancient readers do not address this issue, for modern readers the troubling nature of these laws is exacerbated by their association with God (cf. Deut. 4:5–8; 6:1; etc.). Due to the focus of this study, the larger question of God and violence will be approached through the ethical problem of reading these laws as directives for the life of the community of faith rather than on its own.

2. By "ancient," I mean readers and interpreters from the time of Deuteronomy to the early Tannaitic rabbis. I will use "ancient" and "antiquity" throughout this book as shorthand for the

ancient Israel, how should the legislation of the execution of family members in Deut. 13:6–11; 21:18–21; and 22:13–21 be understood? Given a modern understanding of family violence itself as the enemy within, how should—perhaps simply, *should*—these texts be read today? In this book, I seek to answer these questions through an intensive study of the three laws in Deuteronomy and their ancient interpretations, adaptations, and applications. I read these texts critically, recognizing the serious ethical questions they raise, but also faithfully, recognizing their place as sacred Scripture in the traditions of Judaism and Christianity. This study of family violence in Deuteronomy and beyond is an exercise in the practice of a hermeneutic of trust.

Preliminary Matters: Working Definitions

Three major topics are brought together in this book: family, violence, and reading. Each of these areas has spawned its own growing library of research. Before we begin the specific study of family violence in Deut. 13:6–11; 21:18–21; 22:13–21 and beyond, it will be helpful to set out basic guidelines for understanding each of these topics. What does "family" mean in the biblical, Second Temple, and rabbinic periods, and equally important, what does it not mean? What is violence? Can legislated punishment be properly called violence? Finally, how do we read difficult texts? What method of reading is most appropriate, in light of the power of texts to influence and even determine belief and behavior?

Finding the Family and Families in the Ancient World

Because of the ubiquity of family life in our world, it is easy to interpret ancient texts based on our own understandings of real and ideal families. Before we begin the study of violence in the family in the Bible and other ancient texts, then, it is quite important to survey the contours of the ancient family and families encountered in the texts.[3] "The family" in the biblical worlds has become a major area of research in recent years, drawing on ancient texts, archaeology, economic and sociological models, and comparative anthropology to reconstruct the ideals and realities of family life.[4] While I am not engaged

---

earliest readers of the texts. By "modern," I mean readers and interpreters of the Bible today, including people of faith and those who are uncommitted to the text, scholars and "ordinary" readers untrained in academic exegesis.

    3. Despite its presence in human society across time and space, "family" does not have a single, persistent definition. Rather, family, kinship, and the household develop naturally within and are constructed by each society in response to its needs. See further Goody 1983, 2; Casey 1989, 1; Bourdieu 1996, 19–21; R. Schwartz 1997, 78.

    4. For a representative sampling, see Meyers 1988; Cohen 1993; Barton 1996; Moxnes 1997; Perdue et al. 1997; King and Stager 2001; Balch and Osiek 1997; 2003.

in reconstructing the social history of the family at the time of Deuteronomy or later interpreters, I will draw on the insights of this field to understand the practical function and theological significance of households in the focus texts. As a brief, general introduction, the following survey outlines three basic assumptions regarding what family is and is not in antiquity.

First, a family in antiquity was not a mother, father, two kids, and a dog. Ancient families were household units that could incorporate relatives, slaves, and otherwise unattached people.[5] The life cycle of a household, the needs of the wider community, and economic status would shape the particular configuration of a household at any one time, as is obvious from the range of families pictured in the Bible (Gen. 13:1–12; Exod. 20:10; Lev. 18:6–18; Mark 1:29–30; John 11:1; Eph. 5:21–6:9; etc.). In general, households were patrilocal, centered around a male lineage and inheritance. They were often multigenerational, incorporating grandparents, parents, and children. They were connected to local communities and the nation through widening circles of kinship (cf. Josh. 7:16–18).[6] Households in the biblical worlds included much more than nuclear families or blood relations.[7]

Second, a family in antiquity was not solely nor even primarily concerned with nurturing and emotionally supporting its members. Households were focused on and dedicated to subsistence. In ancient agricultural and market-based societies, it was essential for all members of a household to work together to provide for their common life. Everyone capable of working, from the oldest to the youngest, would have responsibilities in the house, fields, or family business.[8] Texts like 2 Kings 4:18; Prov. 10:5; Matt. 21:28–31; and Luke 15:25 reflect this persistent reality. The necessary sharing of the burden of providing for the household has important implications. For one, childhood in the biblical world was not all fun and games; children were expected to do their part for the family. Second, the needs of the group took priority over an individual's desires or personal freedoms. Third, the contributions of wives and children to the household would balance patriarchal power and its potential abuse: a man would find life difficult if he alienated his coworkers.[9] Household life depended on the participation of all its members.

---

5. The understanding of "family" as members of a household is based on the definition of house societies in Gillespie 2000, 1; Chesson 2003, 82; see also Porter 1967, 9. Note that "house" and "household" (בַּיִת [bayit], οἶκος [oikos], οἰκία [oikia], οἰκεῖος [oikeios]) and "house of the father" (בֵּית אָב [bêt 'āb], ὁ οἶκος τοῦ πατρός [ho oikos tou patros]) are frequent identifiers for families in the Bible (Gen. 12:1; Exod. 1:21; Num. 25:6; Deut. 12:7; Judg. 6:15; Mark 6:4; Acts 10:2; 1 Tim. 3:4–5; 5:8; etc.).

6. The idea of nested households is helpful: an individual household fits into its larger kinship group, which is part of the state as a much larger kinship group, which is then part of the household of God; cf. King and Stager 2001, 4–5; Schloen 2001, 65–67.

7. Cf. L. Stone 2001, 1, 6.

8. See esp. Meyers 1997, 24–31; Peskowitz 1993, 28–30; Chesson 2003, 85.

9. Cf. Abu-Lughod 1986, 99.

Finally, family life in the ancient world was not private and personal, hidden away in a house surrounded by a lawn behind a hedge. Families lived, worked, and aired their dirty laundry in public.[10] Because of the importance of individual households to the functioning of society as a whole, the public was aware of families. In the biblical worlds, the family was the foundation of society and economy. It was understood to be a microcosm of the state and, for Israel, of the national relationship with God.[11] Households that reflected social order and lived according to traditional social expectations supported the life of broader society and were rewarded with honor; households that failed to do so were identified as threats and subjected to dishonor. The family was a public entity.

Families centered life in the ancient biblical worlds. They were the social, economic, political, and theological cornerstones of existence. Their importance is emphasized by their omnipresence in ancient narratives, laws, and other texts. The significance of family life in antiquity makes violence against members of the household in Deuteronomy and other biblical texts more surprising, but it also provides a framework for understanding this violence.

Understanding Violence in the Hebrew Bible and Today

Perhaps unsurprising in light of all that has happened around the world since September 11, 2001, interest in defining, identifying, and interpreting violence in the Bible has burgeoned over the past decade.[12] Modern scholars have categorized a range of acts and words in the Bible as violent: in addition to the obvious culprits (rape, fighting, murder, war), everything from sacrifice and circumcision to warnings of eschatological judgment and even sowing and harvesting crops has been called violent.[13] In this study, I define violence more narrowly as action taken against a person in order to cause their injury or death.[14] This definition is simple and flexible, able to cover a variety of situations (or perhaps a multitude of sins?), but also limited enough to keep the study helpfully focused.

My working definition of violence is broad enough to include the use of punitive force in Deut. 13:6–11; 21:18–21; and 22:13–21.[15] Beatings, executions,

10. House and city design in ancient Israel and Greco-Roman Palestine are indicative of the lack of family privacy; see, e.g., Stager 1985, 11, 18; Wallace-Hadrill 1988, 46, 50–52; Botha 1998, 40–45; Holladay 2009, 63, 68–71.

11. See esp. Sir. 3:1–16; King and Stager 2001, 4–5; Schloen 2001, 65–67.

12. For Bernat and Klawans (2007, ix), violence in the Bible is "perhaps the most pressing issue facing biblical scholarship today."

13. See, e.g., Desjardins 1997, 71–78, 82–90; Aichele 1998, 76; J. Collins 2004, 3, 24; Avalos 2005, 149–50; etc.

14. My definition of violence is influenced by the work of J. Collins 2004, 2–3; Avalos 2005, 19–20; Zevit 2007, 16–17; Young 2008, 4. See also the discussion of definitions of family violence (and their cultural variance) in Pilch 1997, 310–12.

15. On legislated punishments as violence, see Avalos 2005, 19; Kirk-Duggan 2006, 2; esp. Talstra (2005, 70–71) and Zevit (2007, 16–17, 21–22, 26–27), who both specifically address Deut. 13.

or other uses of physical force demanded by law as punishment for certain crimes are not always considered violence, which would consequently be limited to illicit activities. In the Hebrew Bible, violence is almost entirely the purview of the unrighteous. The words used for "violence" refer primarily to physical action and sometimes speech associated with oppression, injustice, and wickedness.[16] Rarely is the punishment of the wicked or other injury or harm justified by the demands of God described as violence, and when it is, the punishment is on a large scale (e.g., the destruction of cities and nations).[17] As a general rule in biblical thought, just or holy war, beating, or stoning and other forms of legal execution are not identified or described as violent acts.[18]

I have chosen to include legislated punishment in my definition of violence for several reasons: (1) the recognition that there can be coexisting interpretations of an act as violence and as a use of legitimate force, (2) the reactions of ancient and modern readers to the demands of the three focus texts in Deuteronomy, and (3) the connection of violence with identity in modern research. First, identifying an act as violent depends on one's viewpoint. There are multiple sides to every story (is a suicide bomber a terrorist or martyr? Is Abraham in Gen. 22 the ultimate example of devotion to God, or is he a child abuser?). What is violence from the perspective of the victim may look very different from the perspective of the perpetrator, and a third party may have a different perspective altogether (cf. 2 Sam. 18:9–15, 32; 21:1–14). The problem of perspective is exacerbated by our own distance from the texts. For modern Western readers in particular, the value of personal freedom influences our understanding of Deuteronomy's laws.[19] It is assumed that an individual has the right to choose what gods to worship, when and with whom to engage in sexual intercourse, or to be independent of parental authority, and this assumption of individual rights increases readers' discomfort with the laws that deny them. The laws can be classified as examples of violence because the reader sympathizes with the oppressed victim of the system.

Second, while the concern with individual rights is not an issue in ancient interpretations developing within cultures that valued the group over the individual, ancient readers also struggled with these three texts and others like

16. See, e.g., חָמָס (ḥāmās) in Gen. 6:11; Judg. 9:24; Ps. 7:17; Prov. 4:16 (17 MT); or Isa. 53:9; פָּרִיץ (pārîṣ) in Ps. 17:4; Ezek. 18:10; שֹׁד (šōd) in Prov. 21:7; Isa. 16:4; Ezek. 45:9; etc.

17. See שֹׁד (šōd) in Isa. 13:6; שָׁדַד (šādad) in Jer. 47:4; 51:55; etc.; and פָּרַץ (pāraṣ) in Exod. 19:22; 2 Sam. 6:8; etc.

18. Of course, not every instance of violence in the Hebrew Bible is labeled as such (cf. Zevit 2007, 19). Stories like Cain's murder of his brother, Abel (Gen. 4:1–16), and the rape of Tamar (2 Sam. 13:1–22) clearly fit the understanding of "violence" in biblical texts, even though the words of violence do not appear. Other stories, including Abraham's sacrifice of Isaac (Gen. 22), Absalom's murder of Amnon (2 Sam. 13:23–39), and the Levite's dismemberment of his concubine and the ensuing war against the Benjamites (Judg. 19–20), are less easy to categorize by biblical standards.

19. Cf. Minkoff 2003, 48, 52.

them. In the early first century CE, Philo's commentary on Deut. 21:18–21 (*Spec. Laws* 2.232) reveals his disquietude with the demands of the law. For parents to initiate the execution of their son is a very serious, troubling matter. Several centuries later, the rabbis claim that Deut. 21:18–21 and 13:12–18 (13–19 MT) are laws that could never be put into practice (*t. Sanh.* 11.6; 14.1). More recently, John Calvin marks the severity of the three laws of Deuteronomy and admits that they sound cruel to readers (*Harmony of the Law* 2–3).[20] Modern scholars label these laws as "ritualized atrocity," child abuse, "disturbing," "abhorrent," and "draconian initiatives."[21] In my definition of violence, the inclusion of legislated punishment recognizes the reactions of ancient and modern readers to the demands of Deut. 13:6–11; 21:18–21; and 22:13–21.

Within Deuteronomy, these laws represent the just, legislated punishment and execution of errant family members; but according to many readers, the location of the punishment within the family makes the actions taken against the errant violent. The pervasive recognition of Deut. 13:6–11; 21:18–21; and 22:13–21 as violent texts across the millennia suggests that more is at work here than modern scruples. Readers' reactions to the demands of these laws can be taken into account in interpretation, and the witness of the centuries, accelerated in our own day but certainly not new, is that these laws are shocking, troubling, and potentially abusive. Deuteronomy legislates family violence.

Third, describing punishment in Deut. 13:6–11; 21:18–21; and 22:13–21 as violence develops from the connection of violence with identity formation.[22] Biblical texts are engaged in the construction of the identity of the people of God, and this process requires determining both what the people of God should look like and what they should not look like.[23] Constructing identity, in other words, involves defining the identity of the group and of "others": the Israelites are defined in opposition to the Canaanites, Egyptians, Greeks, or other people groups.[24] In Deuteronomy, this process is apparent in the laws forbidding behavior that imitates "the nations," including idolatry, polytheism, child sacrifice, divination, and other practices (cf. 12:2–7, 29–31; 18:9–14). The people of Israel instead find their identity in living according to the ways God has commanded: "Keep silence and hear, O Israel! This very day you have become the people of the LORD your God. Therefore obey the LORD your God, observing his commandments and his statutes that I am commanding you today" (27:9–10 NRSV).

20. Calvin 1950, 2.81–82; 3.15–17, 92.
21. See, respectively, J. Wright 2002, 28; Minkoff 2003, 48; Brenner 2004–5, 12; Hamilton 1998, 12; Dion 1991, 206.
22. This understanding of identity and violence is part of a larger academic discussion of the sociology, anthropology, and psychology of violence; see esp. Sen 2006, 1–2, 175–76.
23. Forming identity is not the only function of a text, but in the case of Deuteronomy it is a particularly important function, and particularly effective for the purposes of this study.
24. Cf. Sparks 1998, 224, 236–39, 257–60; Wills 2008, 6, 12–14.

In addition to obeying God's law, the people of Israel are instructed to destroy other nations. "You shall annihilate them—the Hittites and the Amorites, the Canaanites and the Perizzites, the Hivites and the Jebusites—just as the LORD your God has commanded, so that they may not teach you to do all the abhorrent things that they do for their gods, and you thus sin against the LORD your God" (Deut. 20:17–18 NRSV; cf. 7:1–6). The destructive violence of war and the ban (חֵרֶם, *herem*) becomes part of the process of defining Israel's identity. It is a tool used to create and protect identity by radical separation from others.[25]

Identity is fluid. Definitions of identity change through time and across texts, and identity can change within a single text. Those who are the "other" can become part of Israel, keeping the ways of Israel instead of the ways of the nations, as in the case of sojourners (גֵּר, *gēr*) or captives of war (Deut. 5:14; 10:19; 16:11; 20:10–14). Likewise, Israelites can become the other when they fail to keep the ways of God. As enemies within, they would thus face the destructive violence of separation. As we will see, the laws of Deut. 13:6–11; 21:18–21; and 22:13–21 use physical force, beating, and execution to protect Israelite identity from internal corruption. Within the larger association of violence with the construction of identity, the legislated, punitive, judicial action against family members in Deuteronomy is as violent as the annihilation of the Canaanites.

In recognition of the disconnect between the biblical view of violence and my own definition, I have adopted Robert R. Beck's term "constructive violence" to describe the use of violent acts to punish covenantal transgressions in Deuteronomy. In *Nonviolent Story: Narrative Conflict Resolution in the Gospel of Mark*, Beck explores what he identifies as the myth of constructive violence in the stories of the American frontier. According to this myth, to defeat oppressive, hostile forces (the "bad guys"), the "good guys" must use violence. Any other response would be useless. Violence becomes a weapon of redemption, "civilizing" the Wild West and making it a habitable land.[26] Constructive violence is, paradoxically, violence that intends good.

Beck contrasts this myth with the nonviolent response to oppressive powers he finds in Mark's Gospel. I am instead taking over the idea of constructive violence to describe the punishments legislated in Deut. 13:6–11; 21:18–21; 22:13–21; and similar texts. The actions demanded by and narrated in the texts are violent, intending the injury of a family member, but they are also motivated by the need to protect communal identity from threats.[27] The "violence" in

25. See further Niditch 1993, 21–22; Sparks 1998, 235; J. Collins 2004, 11–12, 15, 17–18; Biezeveld 2005, 57. For R. Schwartz 1997, 5, the connection between violence and the formation of identity is so deep that the two can be identified as the same thing: violence *is* the formation of identity (cf. Kille 2007, 12–14; Frankfurter 2007, 114–15).

26. Beck 1996, xiv, 4–9.

27. Cf. Blount 2009, 2, on constructive violence in Revelation.

constructive violence recognizes readers' reactions to the texts; "constructive," in turn, recognizes the presentation of this violence as useful for the community within the texts. Constructive violence is a term redolent with value judgments and actually holds two discordant value judgments together.[28] It gives the freedom to respect the place of these laws in Deuteronomy and the responses of readers to these laws through time. Both are necessary for responsibly reading the legislation of constructive family violence in Deuteronomy.

Reading Constructive Family Violence in Deuteronomy

The apparent mismatch between the biblical understanding of violence and the assessment of Deut. 13:6–11; 21:18–21; and 22:13–21 as violent texts by ancient and modern readers raises key questions concerning hermeneutics. A hermeneutic is a method of reading that determines how the reader will approach, understand, and interpret a text. We all have a hermeneutic when we read the Bible, whether we realize it or not, and it is possible to read deliberately and consciously according to a particular hermeneutic. So what hermeneutic is appropriate in approaching texts that present family violence as a legitimate, even required, response to particular situations?

The Hermeneutic of Suspicion

One compelling option for interpretation is the hermeneutic of suspicion. Scholars who read according to a hermeneutic of suspicion, including liberationists, feminists, womanists, and postcolonialists, among others, begin with the assumption that many, if not all, biblical texts were written and eventually granted authority as sacred texts in order to maintain particular social hierarchies. Generally the ancient writers and supporters of these biblical texts are identified as wealthy, powerful men, heads of households and key political or religious leaders, who used the text to protect and preserve their favorable positions. Words are powerful; texts, including sacred texts like the Bible, can become weapons. Elisabeth Schüssler Fiorenza, a feminist scholar who champions the hermeneutic of suspicion, warns that biblical texts are "rhetorical symbol systems" that, if readers are not careful, can create the symbolic world they describe and thus implant unjust power relations in the readers' societies.[29] A hermeneutic of suspicion keeps readers on the lookout for these systems, thus guarding against their potential for domination and abuse. Forewarned is forearmed.

Reading the three laws of family violence in Deuteronomy through a hermeneutic of suspicion foregrounds the unequal power structures in the household and wider society. The patriarch, the male head of the family, is given complete

28. Cf. Beck 1996, xiv–xv.
29. Schüssler Fiorenza 1999, 60–64, esp. 92–94.

authority over the members of the household, even to the point of executing them without trial in Deut. 13:9–10. The wives, children, siblings, and others are nearly voiceless in these texts. When they do speak, their voices support the patriarch's voice (21:20), or they are heard through the patriarch's words rather than their own (13:6–7 [7–8]). They are identified by their relationship to the patriarch, and they are seen from the patriarch's point of view (13:6 [7]; 21:18; 22:15–17). Reading with the hermeneutic of suspicion draws attention to these characters who might be overlooked, the voices that might be drowned out. In this study of family violence in the laws of Deuteronomy, I will use some of the insights of suspicious reading to draw attention to the experiences of the apparently powerless in the texts.

Another advantage of the hermeneutic of suspicion is the necessary reminder that reading is not a neutral event. How we read matters, especially when the text is accepted as an authoritative sacred book. Readers must recognize the potential for using biblical texts to harm, as in the cases of child abuse, spouse abuse, and "sacrificial" murder that have been attributed to biblical texts (or at least interpretations of biblical texts). The potentially harmful implications of reading warn us that readers need to be careful as they interpret, teach, or embody biblical texts.[30] In the case of Deuteronomy, reading with a hermeneutic of suspicion insists on the possible use of the texts to motivate or justify domestic violence, abuse, or oppression, whether intentionally or not. As Schüssler Fiorenza suggests, texts like these should come with a warning: "Caution, could be dangerous to your health and survival."[31] In this study of legislated family violence, the need to interpret with care to avoid abusive consequences will be kept firmly in mind.

The hermeneutic of suspicion is not wholly advantageous, however. It can itself be dangerous and do violence to a text, especially when it is used to predetermine the potential or even nature of each and every biblical text to oppress. As Carol Smith reminds us, many biblical texts speak on behalf of victims of oppression in often vehement critiques of unjust social hierarchies and violent power.[32] With respect to family violence, the commands to punish family members to death are balanced by outrage over and critiques of family violence in other texts: Jephthah and his daughter (Judg. 11:34–40), the murder of Abel (Gen. 4:8–16), the rape of Tamar and subsequent murder of Amnon (2 Sam. 13), child sacrifice (Deut. 18:10; Jer. 7:31), and so forth. This intrabiblical tension provides a check on power in the family and, taken seriously, could prevent abusive reading practices by directing attention to the purposes, motives, and contexts of family violence. In addition, checks on seemingly absolute power arise naturally in family life. A patriarch may nominally hold the power of life and death over the members

30. Cf. Phillips and Fewell 1997, 2–3; Schüssler Fiorenza 1999, 28.
31. Schüssler Fiorenza 1999, 14; see also, among others, Fontaine 1997, 86–87; Phillips and Fewell 1997, 1–3; J. Collins 2004, 1–2, 16–19, 32; Young 2008, 1, 4.
32. Smith 2001, esp. 109–10; see also Kille 2007, 8.

of his household by law, but his wife and children have their own power as contributors to their common life. The power of a wife and mother in a patriarchal society is obvious in the stories of many biblical women, including Rebekah and Tamar in Gen. 27 and 38, Samson's mother in Judg. 13, Abigail in 1 Sam. 25, and Jezebel in 1 Kings 21. As several ancient commentators observe, the necessary involvement of the mother in Deut. 21:18–21 and 22:13–21 balances the patriarch's power. Reading with a stringent hermeneutic of suspicion runs the risk of minimizing or missing these key elements of biblical texts.

Another danger of the hermeneutic of suspicion represented in several recent studies of violence in biblical texts lies in the ultimate rejection of the text.[33] If oppression, suppression, and abuse lie behind and within biblical texts, and if these texts have the potential to teach and encourage oppression, suppression, and abuse among their readers, one response is to abandon the Bible. For some, the Bible as it has come down to us is virtually unreadable, and reading it as sacred Scripture is not a viable option. Regina M. Schwartz, Carol Delaney, and Hector Avalos represent this developing trend when they identify the Bible as a danger to humanity, a violent book that teaches violence and oppression. Avalos argues that the Bible should, therefore, have no authority or value in the modern world.[34] Both Schwartz and Delaney issue rousing calls for the creation of a new canon—a new set of "biblical" traditions that will teach "an ideal of plenitude and its corollary ethical imperative of generosity" for Schwartz, and "caring relationships" within the family for Delaney.[35]

Rejecting the Bible as an authoritative text is a seductive option, but it is not an option I am willing to embrace. The claim that a text presenting elements of violence or oppression causes violence and oppression among readers is an overstatement. Texts do not "do" things on their own; readers are the parties responsible for using texts for good or ill.[36] Interpretations that fail to account for biblical and social balances or to counteract potentially abusive readings are the problem, not the texts themselves. The Hebrew Bible and the Christian Bible, moreover, are sacred texts for Jewish and Christian communities of faith around the world. This heritage should not be abandoned lightly but should rather be struggled with as a witness to the faith of the past and an inheritance for people of faith. In this study, therefore, the hermeneutic of suspicion will be used to uncover suppression, oppression, and violence in the texts, but it will not be the only or the primary guide to interpretation.

33. Rejecting the text is not demanded by the hermeneutic of suspicion (cf. Schüssler Fiorenza 1999, 57), but it is arguably a logical progression.

34. Avalos 2005, 115.

35. See R. Schwartz 1997, 175–76; Delaney 1998, 47.

36. In the terms of Fowl (1998, 64, 72–73) and A. Adam (2006, 68–71), texts do not have ideologies; readers do. Readers are therefore responsible for the effects of their reading and must guard against reading in such a way as to breed oppression or injustice in the world (Fowl 1998, 61, 74–75). Cf. M. Adam 1998, 221; J. Collins 2004, 1–2, 29–33; Kille 2007, 9.

A Hermeneutic of Trust

The hermeneutic taken in this study is a hermeneutic of trust.[37] A hermeneutic of trust begins with the assumption that these texts have something to teach about what Eep Talstra calls the "family history" of God and God's people.[38] The story is not only of antiquarian interest; it is also our story when we allow ourselves to be challenged by the text.[39] It is a struggle to read texts in which violence against family members is enjoined and even celebrated, but the effort is worthwhile.[40]

A hermeneutic of trust requires reading sympathetically rather than antagonistically. For Deuteronomy, a sympathetic reading begins by accepting the book's thought world and theology as the primary context for interpreting the function and purpose of constructive family violence. This method of reading does not, however, mean uncritically accepting violence as an appropriate response in particular situations. Learning from practitioners of the hermeneutic of suspicion, I will read cautiously as well as sympathetically, balancing the recognition of potential inequalities or injustices with faith in the biblical story.[41]

A number of previous studies provide examples of sympathetic, cautious readings of troubling texts. Two that have been particularly helpful to me are Jon D. Levenson's *The Death and Resurrection of the Beloved Son: The Transformation of Child Sacrifice in Judaism and Christianity* and Susan Niditch's *War in the Hebrew Bible: A Study in the Ethics of Violence.* Levenson addresses child sacrifice in the Hebrew Bible and the interpretations and renarrations of the Aqedah, the sacrifice of Isaac in Gen. 22, in later traditions. Levenson's study is a practical exercise in the redemptive reading of disturbing stories. His model of careful, generous reading, exploration, and recognition of the narrative art and theology of such texts will be followed in this study.

Niditch traces the complex, multifaceted ideologies of war and related acts of violence across the texts of the Hebrew Bible. Her study uncovers tensions in and among the texts between an implicit (and sometimes explicit) recognition of the horrors and guilt of war and a straightforward acceptance and celebration of violence. For Niditch, these tensions do not mean that the Hebrew Bible offers a critique of warfare, but they do allow modern readers space for critical reflection.[42] In this study I also engage in reading between the lines to find potential internal tensions in Deuteronomy's laws and critiques of constructive family violence in other texts of the Hebrew Bible.

37. Cf. Hays 2005, 192, and also the hermeneutical stance of "provisional sympathy" in R. Barrett 2009, 12–13.
38. Talstra 2005, 82–83; see also E. Davis 2003, 177.
39. Hays 2005, 191, 197–98, suggests approaching the Bible with trust and using the hermeneutic of suspicion on ourselves, to critique our own fallenness on the basis of its "message of grace."
40. Compare esp. Trible 1984, 2; E. Davis 2003, 178.
41. As E. Davis 2003, 178, comments, interpreters must recognize that texts are ethically troubling, but also that a "difficult text is worthy of charity from its interpreters."
42. Niditch 1993, 136–37, 152–54.

These critiques become more vocal in postbiblical interpretations of Deut. 13:6–11; 21:18–21; and 22:13–21. Ancient interpreters of biblical texts are engaged in the balancing act of reading critically and faithfully. The history of interpretation of these texts in antiquity can thus provide guidance for their faithful, critical interpretation today. The practice of reading difficult biblical texts through the eyes of their earliest interpreters is not new. My work in this book builds on the example set by John L. Thompson, who surveys interpretations of texts that "people would just as soon avoid" from antiquity through the Reformation.[43] He notes that premodern readers, including the earliest readers of some of the texts, struggled to understand difficult texts too; their struggles are, for Thompson, an important check on our own reaction to difficult texts as well as examples of careful interpretation. The interpretations given "may make the problems in such texts even harder and more painful, but they don't turn a blind eye."[44]

The history of the interpretation of constructive family violence in antiquity demonstrates that enlightened modern readers are not the first to question constructive family violence in Deuteronomy or the broader tradition it represents, or to be concerned with their potential for violence in the real world. Ancient readers from the early Second Temple to the early rabbinic periods recognized the problems with the kind of violence required by the laws of Deuteronomy. They struggled to understand and interpret these texts from the standpoint of faith. There is much for us to learn from their approaches to, interpretations of, and uses of the biblical traditions of constructive family violence.

Rewriting Deuteronomy

Beyond the Hebrew Bible, the texts covered in this study date from the second century BCE to the early third century CE. Different kinds of interpretation and application are represented, including relatively straightforward commentary on Deut. 13:6–11; 21:18–21; and 22:13–21, allusions to or adaptations of these texts, and narratives that incorporate the themes of constructive family violence. The interpretations covered here thus provide the opportunity to see a range of responses to and uses of biblical constructive family violence, illuminating both the interpretation of the focus laws from Deuteronomy and the developing tradition of constructive family violence in Second Temple Judaism.

The texts included in this study can be placed on a continuum of interpretation ranging from explicit exegesis of Deuteronomy's laws to the uses of the vocabulary and themes of the laws in different settings.[45] At one extreme, echoes of Deut. 13 appear in the New Testament's concern with false teachers.

---

43. See J. Thompson 2007, 2; also J. Thompson 2001.
44. J. Thompson 2007, 5.
45. On the definitions and purposes of biblical exegesis, allusion, influence, and echoes, see Sommer 1998, 10–31.

These echoes do not necessarily interpret Deut. 13; they rather provide a way for the reader to connect the New Testament texts with earlier traditions.[46] At the opposite end of the continuum, Philo of Alexandria and the Tannaitic rabbis write commentaries on Deut. 13:6–11; 21:18–21; and 22:13–21 in which they seek to interpret these laws for their audiences. Their exegesis shows how they read Deuteronomy and also reveals their assumptions regarding the value or use of constructive family violence.

The other texts covered in this study fall between the two extremes. In the *Jewish Antiquities*, Josephus incorporates Deuteronomy's laws into his retelling of biblical and Jewish history. While he uses the laws for his own literary purposes, his presentation is also somewhat exegetical, showing how he read and understood Deuteronomy. The vocabulary and themes of Deuteronomy's laws appear in new contexts in Josephus's *Jewish War*, Sirach, and 1 Maccabees. These allusions are used primarily to support the arguments of the books, but in so doing, they become part of the interpretation of the traditions of constructive family violence.[47]

The influence of Deuteronomy's constructive family violence can be seen in *Jubilees* and several New Testament texts, including Matthew, Mark, and 1 Corinthians. These texts do not explicitly comment on Deuteronomy: they rarely quote or borrow words from Deuteronomy. The themes of Deuteronomy's laws and of constructive family violence in general are apparent, however. *Jubilees* and the New Testament thus participate in the ongoing development of the practice of constructive family violence, reinterpreting and at some points challenging biblical tradition in new settings.[48]

As Michael Fishbane warns, allusions and influence are not always easy to identify.[49] A text may use common words and ideas independently, with no attempt to interpret or respond to earlier texts in which the same themes appear. Throughout the current study, I take care to explore the possible connections of the focus texts with Deuteronomy's laws. Whether they exegete, allude to, or simply use ideas similar to Deuteronomy, each text is part of the tradition of constructive family violence. They thus implicitly interpret, use, modify, and challenge the practices and purposes of family violence present in Deuteronomy; in so doing they give us models to follow in our own reading of these troubling texts.

Moving Forward

The journey through ancient traditions of constructive family violence begins in chapter 2 with a careful study of the three laws in Deuteronomy along

46. Cf. Sommer 1998, 31.
47. See further Sommer 1998, 18, on the convergence of allusion and exegesis.
48. Cf. Sommer 1998, 25–29; also Hays 1989, 18–21.
49. Fishbane 1985, 10–13; cf. Hays 1989, 29–32.

with their echoes through the Hebrew Bible. The laws will first be contextualized within Deuteronomy's instructions for family life. The theological importance of the family helps explain the violence in 13:6–11; 21:18–21; and 22:13–21: the family in Deuteronomy is given the weapon of violent punishment of wrongdoers precisely because it is the primary agent of the covenant and the embodiment of Israelite identity. This analysis will be supported by surveying the use of the imagery of these laws in the Prophets and Proverbs.

The study will then turn to the interpretations and applications of constructive family violence in antiquity. Chapter 3 covers three early Second Temple period texts: Sirach, 1 Maccabees, and *Jubilees*. These texts do not explicitly comment on Deuteronomy's laws but rather make use of constructive family violence within their narratives and instructions. Sirach is a book of wisdom much like Proverbs; its model for the violent disciplining of sons and daughters can be read as a method for avoiding the use of Deut. 21:18–21 and 22:13–21. First Maccabees, a biased history of the Hasmonean dynasty, draws on Deut. 13:6–11 and related stories of constructive family violence to justify the civil war of the Hasmoneans against Jews who collaborated with the Seleucid government. *Jubilees*, on the other hand, an example of rewritten Scripture, can be read as a denial of the constructive nature of family violence. These three texts are in tension with each other on the use of constructive family violence.

The tension between these texts remains present in the first and second centuries CE. Chapter 4 looks at the commentaries of Philo and the Tannaitic rabbis and Josephus's rewritten biblical narratives and explanations of Jewish life. Each source supports some uses of constructive family violence while denying others. Their evaluations of Deut. 13:6–11; 21:18–21; and 22:13–21 reveal their discomfort with violence against family members; their choice to reinforce the use of violence in some situations indicates its importance to their constructions of Judaism.

Finally in chapter 5 we turn to the New Testament. There are few explicit references to Deut. 13:6–11; 21:18–21; and 22:13–21 or general constructive family violence in the texts of the New Testament, but the few that are present show two developments in the use of the traditions. Jesus warns the disciples that they will be subject to constructive family violence on account of their witness to him. These teachings in the Gospels provide a unique look at constructive violence from the perspective of its victims. The victims then adapt the practices of constructive family violence for their own use within the church. Once again, identity is key in understanding the presentation of constructive family violence in the texts of the early church.

The concern with understanding the constructive nature of family violence is present through the entire study, along with the question of how to read texts that demand violence against family members. Some basic conclusions on these underlying issues are broached in the last chapter. This chapter also addresses the implications of the biblical tradition of constructive family violence for the biblical view of the individual, the family, and the community. The final question to be raised is the significance of this study for modern readers. Do the laws of Deuteronomy in the end have an abiding message?

2

Understanding Constructive
Family Violence in Deuteronomy

Deuteronomy tells the story of the last days of the forty years spent in the wilderness before the people of Israel enter Canaan. Moses, who will not be going with them on the final journey, gathers his people together to exhort them once again to be obedient to the covenant. He calls on each of them, from the leaders of the people to their children to the aliens in their midst, to keep faith with their God (Deut. 29:10–13). The covenant therefore concerns the people as a whole and also every individual Israelite. In Deuteronomy, Moses is forming the group that stands before him into the united people of God.

The family has a central place in Deuteronomy. Families keep the covenant together. They weave the covenant into the life of the household. They teach the covenant to new Israelites. To some extent, families are responsible for embodying and passing on Israel's identity as the people of God. To protect this responsibility, many laws in Deuteronomy address the proper functioning of the family, including three laws that demand the life of an errant family member. The law about a member of the household who tempts others within the household to worship idols (13:6–11 [7–12 MT]), the law about the disobedient son (21:18–21), and the law about the slandering husband and foolish daughter (22:13–21), as shocking as they are, support the book's overarching goal of creating and inculcating the identity of God's people.

In this chapter I examine these three texts within Deuteronomy and reread them in light of their echoes in the Hebrew Bible. The depiction of family life in Deuteronomy provides one context for interpreting constructive family violence. This context receives support from Deuteronomy's understanding of Israelite identity. For Deuteronomy, the centrality of the household in society and religion is not a good in itself, but serves the greater good of the covenant community, a state of affairs sustained by the use of the language of Deuteronomy across the Hebrew Bible. By reading Deut. 13:6–11; 21:18–21; and 22:13–21 within Deuteronomy's construction of Israel as the people of God, we can understand these laws as a distressing but also unsurprising outworking of the covenant.

Introducing Deuteronomy

In canonical context, Deuteronomy brings the story of the exodus and wilderness wanderings in the Torah to a close.[1] The people of Israel stand on the banks of the Jordan River, looking across at Canaan, the goal of their long journey (1:5). The forty years of the exodus are at an end, and the era of the conquest is about to begin. This shift is accompanied by a change in leadership as Moses passes his authority to Joshua. The narration of Israel's story in Deuteronomy, through a series of speeches that Moses gives the people, emphasizes the sense of transition. Moses reminds the people of their recent past and of the covenant, the way of life given to them by God. He looks ahead to instruct them in the methods of conquest and how to live in the land. He also warns them of the consequences of their eventual disobedience. The final chapters of the book stress the uncertainty of the future. Will Israel remember God's law, given to them by Moses? Will the promises made to Abraham, Isaac, and Jacob finally be fulfilled? Or as Moses foresees, will the people fail and therefore suffer the punishment of the covenant curses?

The people of Israel in Deuteronomy stand at the crossroads of identity.[2] As they prepare to settle in God's land, they have a choice to make.[3] They can turn away from Yahweh, becoming the faithless idolaters that Moses fears they will eventually be, or they can be Israel, God's faithful, obedient, blessed people (30:15–20). In the transitional place on the banks of the Jordan,

1. This discussion focuses on the literary context and content of Deuteronomy. Historically, Deuteronomy is most often associated with the reforms carried out by Josiah, king of Judah, in 2 Kings 22–23 (Tigay 1996, xxi; Sparks 1998, 225; Wilson 2005, 122; etc.). Alternatively, G. Wenham (1985a, 16–19; 1985b, 15–17) argues for a much earlier date reflecting the narrative time established within Deuteronomy, and others (Blenkinsopp 1995, 50, 86; Seters 1997, 359–60; and Noll 2007, 344) suggest that Deuteronomy, though based on earlier traditions, was only completed in the postexilic Persian period.

2. Nasuti 1986, 19–20, addresses the formation of identity through law codes; on identity in Deuteronomy specifically, see Blenkinsopp 1995, 87, 115; Sparks 1998, 228–42; esp. Cohn 2004, 134–35; and Wills 2008, 28–31, 40–41.

3. Cf. C. Wright 1996, 9; and Millar 1998, 47.

between wilderness and promised land, the laws of Deuteronomy form the identity of the ideal Israel as a community of people who fear Yahweh, even as the retelling of Israel's story with a focus on the people's failings and the prediction of future failures implicitly establishes the antithesis of the ideal. In a sense, because of the liminal setting of the narrative, Deuteronomy is timeless: supported by the authority of Moses's voice, this is the identity of Israel.[4] The vividly depicted consequences of obedience (divine blessing) and disobedience (disruption and destruction) encourage the Israelites in Moses's audience and, through them, the real-world audience to implement the book's vision for the life of Yahweh's covenant people.

The Family in Deuteronomy

At the heart of Deuteronomy's vision for Israelite identity lies the family.[5] Households are the epicenter of the covenant, the arenas in which Israel's national identity is instituted and taught. The members of a household speak about the law and worship together. Their interrelationships are a living metaphor for the relationship between God the Father and the people of Israel, God's children. In its historical particularity and theological significance, Deuteronomy's Israelite family is the embodiment of Israel, the people of Yahweh.

The Family in the Covenant

In Deut. 29, Moses calls Israel into covenant with God. The heads of the tribes, the elders, the officials, and all the men of Israel with their wives, children, servants, and sojourners—entire households, in fact—are involved (vv. 9–10; cf. 31:12–13). Furthermore, the people present at that moment in Deuteronomy's story represent their fathers—Abraham, Isaac, and Jacob—and also Israelites yet to be born (29:13–15). "The revealed things belong to us and to our children forever, to keep all the words of this law" (v. 29): Deuteronomy, the book containing the revelation of God through Moses, is an inheritance for all the people of Israel. The inclusion of all members of the household in the covenant ceremony gives every Israelite the responsibility of keeping the law, now (within the narrative) and forever.[6]

The household's involvement in the covenant with Yahweh in chapter 29 is perpetuated by the family's responsibility for passing on the covenant to each new generation. Parents teach their children to fear Yahweh by telling them the

4. Compare Blenkinsopp 1995, 87; Miller 1990, 3; and C. Anderson 2004, 215–17. Notable also is McBride 1987, 229–36, who follows Josephus in describing Deuteronomy as the constitution (or polity) of Israel.

5. See also Miller 2008, 54–55.

6. Cf. McConville 2002, 27.

stories of their salvation from Egypt and the giving of the law at Horeb (Deuteronomy's name for Sinai; 4:9–10; 6:20–25). When the people keep the law as instructed by Moses, their children will learn to keep the law as well (6:1–2).[7] According to the Shema in Deut. 6:4–9, the law should be part of the sights and sounds of a household: the words of the covenant are to be inscribed on the heart, taught to children, spoken of in the home and on the road, bound on the hand and forehead, and written on the doorposts of houses and gates (cf. 11:18–21).[8] For Deuteronomy, the covenant is preserved by being woven into the daily life of the family, firmly placing Israel's relationship with God at the very center of social existence.

The Family in the Cult

The household provides the context for regular and special cultic activities. The fourth commandment allows rest on the Sabbath for "you," your son and daughter, your male and female servants, your ox and donkey, and the sojourner with you (5:14).[9] When sacrifices are made to Yahweh, the head of the family, sons and daughters, servants, and resident Levites all share in celebrating and eating (12:12, 18; cf. "you and your household" in 14:26; 15:20). All these people and any additional strangers, widows, or orphans in the community also celebrate the Feast of Weeks and the Feast of Tabernacles together (16:11, 14). The various festivals commemorate Israel's salvation from slavery by their faithful God (see 5:12–15; 16:1–8, 12): by participating in these celebrations, family members live out the central message of the covenant. As they rest, sacrifice, feast, and celebrate together, the family embodies "Israel."

The Family in Society

Along with the list of offenders in Deut. 13:6 (7 MT), the lists of those who celebrate the Sabbath and the festivals together are indicative of the parameters of the family for Deuteronomy. These families are patrilocal (centered around the husband's ancestral lineage and home). They are composed of a patriarch, his wife (or wives, in 21:15), children, and brothers. These families also include the slaves of the household and those in the community who are

7. Cf. *Targum Neofiti I* Deut. 5:17–21, explaining that parents who keep the commandments teach their children not to sin.

8. Moberly 1999, 143, suggests that writing texts at the transition points of social geography marks private and public space with allegiance to Yahweh (see also Römer 2000, 224).

9. An explicit reference to wives is strangely absent from this law (as well as the others discussed in this section). Wives are present in Deut. 29:10–11 and are implicitly addressed in the laws that directly concern their place in Israel, though, so they are likely included as an extension of the addressee (אַתָּה ['atâ], second-person singular, in 5:14; 12:18; 14:26; and 15:20; אַתֶּם ['atem], second-person plural, in 12:12). See further Frymer-Kensky 1996, 59; McConville 2002, 21, 26–29.

without family or land: widows, Levites, and sojourners. In Deuteronomy, identification with a family does not depend primarily on blood but on location. Those who share living space are family.[10]

This shared space in ancient Israel would not have been expansive (more like downtown apartments than sprawling suburban homes). The traditional Israelite four-room (or pillared) house was built around a common courtyard; adjoining households were likely kin. These houses had no private bedrooms, possibly not even space reserved for single nuclear family units. Members of households worked, ate, and slept side by side, and local households interacted with each other in shared courtyards, public space, and fields.[11] What modern Westerners think of as private life was public in ancient Israel.[12] Family life in Deuteronomy reflects this sociocultural context.

In addition to the involvement of the household in enacting and teaching the covenant, Deuteronomy includes legislation to regulate the relationship of parents and their children (5:16; 27:16), identify proper marriage partners and divorce procedures (7:3–4; 24:1–4; etc.), control sexual relationships (22:22–30; 27:20–23), and guide inheritance practices (21:15–17). The obedient, faithful family is key to the covenant in Deuteronomy, and these laws establish and protect the structure and life of the ideal family to ensure the continuity of the covenant.

The Family, God, and Israel

The centrality of household life within ancient Israelite society and in the social and theological vision of Deuteronomy is reflected in and sustained by the family metaphor used of the relationship between God and Israel. Moses's song of witness in Deut. 32 describes God as a father who has created (or purchased, קָנָה, *qānâ*),[13] made, and established Israel (v. 6). God bore and gave birth to Israel (like a mother, though this word is not used; v. 18). Yahweh found Israel in the wilderness and cared for the people as an eagle cares for its young, feeding them on the fat of the land (vv. 10–14).

The description of Yahweh's parental care echoes the metaphor of God's relationship with Israel as that of a man caring for his son in Deut. 1:29–31;

---

10. Cf. Schloen 2001, 123–26, 135.

11. On kinship in relation to settlement design, see Schloen 2001, 106–12. The form, function, and even theology of the four-room house has been extensively studied; Hardin 2004, 73–83, presents a very informative study of an Iron Age house at Tel Halif. See also Meyers 1997, 21–31, on daily life in these households.

12. Cf. Beebe 1968, 57; Kamp 2000, 84–92; Holladay 2009, 65–71.

13. Both meanings are possible ("purchasing" lives in Exod. 21:2 and Lev. 22:11; "creating" life in Ps. 139:13 and Prov. 8:22). Translating קָנָה (*qānâ*) as creation in Deut. 32:6 is supported by the use of "making" and "establishing" in the same verse and the later reference to God's birthing of Israel (v. 18; cf. 2 Sam. 7:24 ; Isa. 44:2; 51:13).

8:2–5. God's people, however, fail to trust their divine parent to keep them safe, and their resultant fear and disobedience lead to their punishment (1:32–36). Moses's song in chapter 32 likewise warns that Israel's future rebellion will endanger the nation's status as child of God, identifying them instead as faithless sons and daughters (vv. 5, 19–20).

Characterizing God as a parent who cares and provides for a child heightens the dramatic tension of Israel's rebellion. This imagery also superimposes the significance of the divine relationship with the nation on the human family, thus providing a meta-incentive for keeping the proper balance of care, authority, and obedience within the household.[14] The interdependence of family and nation is made clear in Deut. 32 when Moses instructs his audience, the children of God, to ask their fathers and elders to tell the story of Israel (v. 7), reminds them that their God is the God of their fathers (v. 17), and warns them that disobeying their divine parent will bring suffering to all the members of the household, young and old (v. 25). As the reflection of God's relationship with Israel in human society, the family will together suffer the curses consequent upon breaking the covenant (graphically portrayed in Deut. 28:15–68).

The Family as Protector of the Covenant

In Deuteronomy, the family has a key place in the life of Israel. The family is an agent of the covenant, and so also of Israelite identity. Families teach, preserve, and enact the covenant together, and they embody the symbolic relationship of God as parent with Israel as child. Because of these factors, families are in part responsible for guarding against infractions of the covenant, a serious responsibility in recognition of the punishments that follow disobedience: when the family of God fails, Israelite families suffer the consequences.

Several measures proposed in Deuteronomy protect the ideal community from internal disruption. The threat of divine punishment provides a stark introduction and conclusion for the book (chaps. 1–4, 27–28, 32), and fines, corporal punishment, and execution are consequent upon the transgression of various laws (as in 17:5, 12; 22:18–19; and 25:2–3). While priests and Levites, judges, and elders often take a leading role in judging and determining restitution for wrongdoing (17:8–13; 21:1–9; etc.), the community as a whole is sometimes involved in carrying out sentences. In this general context of the judgment of covenantal transgressions, the laws of Deut. 13:6–11; 21:18–21;

14. See further Strawn 2008, 118–34. Did the family household gain its central position in the covenant and Israelite society because God's relationship with Israel was described with family language, or was God's relationship with Israel described with family language because of the central place of the family in society and covenant? It is a chicken-and-egg question; King and Stager (2001, 4–5) and Schloen (2001, 1, 45–46) argue that the two moves are so interdependent as to be impossible to separate.

and 22:13–21 give the family power to punish serious transgressions committed by the members of the household with death.

In light of Deuteronomy's emphasis on the significance of Israelite family life, these three laws demanding the accusation of family members and acts of violence against them can seem discordant. However, for the same reason they are also comprehensible. The close living situations and companionship of the household give family members privileged information concerning the behavior of each member of the household. The ancient Israelite family was nearly always together. No single member could easily hide a particular infraction against the covenant, and other family members would therefore be in the position to accuse the individual of wrongdoing (whether they would want to make such an accusation, knowing the potential consequences, is another matter). Deuteronomy's use of the family as agent of the covenant increases the household's responsibility for maintaining the purity of the covenant for the common good. In recognition of the primary importance of the family in teaching, keeping, and guarding Israel's identity, Deuteronomy's laws ordaining violence against family members are both unthinkable and only to be expected.

Deuteronomy 13:6–12: Executing the Idolater

According to Deuteronomy, Yahweh is a just, impartial, righteous, loving God (e.g., 10:17–18). Yahweh is also a jealous God who demands absolute loyalty from the people who have been saved from slavery (4:20, 24; 5:9; 10:20–21; etc.). The foundation of Israelite identity is devotion to Yahweh alone. God saves the people from Egypt precisely in order for them to be a holy people in a holy land, reflecting God's own holiness (7:6; 26:19; 28:9; etc.). Within this construction of identity, idolaters, be they Canaanites or errant descendants of Abraham, are automatically identified as outsiders simply because they do not fear Israel's God.[15] Idolatry becomes the besetting sin of Israel.

The specter of idolatry hovering over the narratives, laws, and covenant curses of Deuteronomy issues forth from the narrative setting. As Israel stands on the edge of the Jordan, the people are nearing contact with the idols of the nations of the land. The fear of their failure in the face of temptation undergirds the warnings against idolatry throughout the book. The first laws of the Decalogue prohibit following gods other than Yahweh and making or worshiping idols (5:6–10). To motivate obedience, Moses reminds his audience of their idolatrous indiscretions at Baal of Peor and Horeb and their subsequent punishment (4:3; 9:12). To prevent further opportunities to learn idolatry from pagans, he instructs them to completely

---

15. Cf. Cohn 2004, 140–43. Stulman (1990, 614–16) offers an insightful discussion of insiders and outsiders in Deuteronomy; see also Nelson 1997, 49–51; Wills 2008, 29–30.

destroy the peoples of Canaan and their cultic sites, avoiding contact with either (7:1–6; 12:2–3, 29–31). And he warns that, despite these measures, their children, those who should learn the covenant from them, will worship false gods, and as a result the nation will suffer the wrath of God (4:25–28; 29:14–28; 31:16–18).

Deuteronomy is, as C. J. H. Wright has said, "uncompromisingly, ruthlessly monotheistic."[16] To maintain the holiness of God's people, all things abhorrent, including idols and their worshipers, must be eradicated from the land. By divine command, the idolatrous Canaanites are to be completely and utterly destroyed, and if God's people worship the gods of the nations, they will be treated as these nations are (as the reversals of the blessings and curses in chap. 28 suggest). This is the danger that Moses in Deuteronomy tries to avert through instructing the people in the covenant, remembering the story of Israel's relationship with Yahweh, commanding the annihilation of the idolatrous Canaanites, and legislating the prevention and punishment of idolatry.

According to the absolutes of Deuteronomy, the only option for idolatrous Canaanites and Israelite lawbreakers is destruction. Their impurity must be purged from among the holy people (cf. 13:5 [6 MT]; 17:7; 19:19; etc.), and when the entire people become abhorrent instead of holy, they must be purged from the holy land (11:16–17; 28:20, 63). The rhetoric of destruction surrounding the disobedience of Israel, however, is tempered by a hope of future forgiveness (4:25–31; 30:1–10; 32:36, 43; etc.).[17] Individuals are clearly connected with the nation in Deuteronomy; individual offenders are punished for the sake of the nation. If the inverse holds true, the possibility that individual offenders may be forgiven, as the nation is, must likewise be considered. The grace of eventual forgiveness for repentant idolaters running through Deuteronomy provides a key, if contrary, context for interpreting the violent punishment of idolatry within the family in chapter 13.

Deuteronomy 13

The household's joint participation in the cult of Yahweh is accompanied by the family's presence in Deuteronomy's anti-idolatry legislation. Since the family sacrifices and celebrates together, it also has a lead role in the fight against the worship of foreign gods in Israel. Chapter 13 addresses three situations in which missionaries of idolatry arise within Israel itself, first as false prophets or dreamers; second, within the household; and third, as "children

16. See C. Wright 1996, 10; also McBride 2006, 147–49; R. Barrett 2009, 50–55.
17. Cf. Hamilton 1998, 15; R. Barrett 2009, 88. Rahab's family and the Gibeonites provide Canaanite parallels: in Joshua, the absolute destruction of the Canaanites, carried out to fulfill the commands of Moses (cf. 1:7; 10:40, etc.), leaves these Canaanites alive and part of the Israelite community (6:22–25; 9:21, 27).

of Belial" who mislead an entire city. Their words and actions show that these idolaters are foreigners masquerading as Israelites. In each situation, the response of true Israelites should be violent and total. Those who counsel rebellion against Yahweh must be utterly destroyed lest the nation as a whole be led astray and in turn suffer divine punishment.

The NRSV translates the Hebrew word סָרָה (sārâ) in Deut. 13:5 (6 MT) as "treason."[18] The traitors in this chapter are national enemies by virtue of tempting others to rebel against Yahweh by worshiping idols. The treason of this act is emphasized by the succinct definition of an Israelite given in verses 3–4 (4–5): being an Israelite means loving God with all one's being (heart and soul, לֵבָב [lēbāb] and נֶפֶשׁ [nepeš]; cf. 4:29; 6:5; 11:13; etc.). This all-encompassing love is expressed in obedience. The lover of God walks after God, fears God, keeps God's commands, listens to God, serves God, and clings to God (see also 10:12; 26:16–17). God saved the people from Egypt (13:5 [6]), and in response they owe God their fealty.[19] Idolatry and the temptation to idolatry are high treason, and those who commit these acts of unfaithfulness are the enemies of God's people.[20]

Deuteronomy 13:1–5, 12–18 (2–6, 13–19)

The first act of treason described in Deut. 13 involves prophets and dreamers. Not all prophets are true prophets of Yahweh. Deuteronomy 18:20–22 warns of just such a presumptuous person who only pretends to speak in Yahweh's name. Deuteronomy 13:1–5 (2–6 MT) is concerned with another kind of false prophecy. If prophets or dreamers teach Israelites to serve other gods, even if the message is supported by signs, they are a test from Yahweh to determine if the people will be obedient (vv. 1–3; cf. 8:2). The people must not listen to them but must kill them. In this way, the evil in Israel's midst—the foreigners among them—will be uprooted (13:5).

The third section of Deut. 13 broadens the scope of the idolatry to include an entire city (vv. 12–18 [13–19 MT]). If the Israelites learn that "children of Belial" have seduced a city in the land to follow other gods, the report

---

18. On treason in Deut. 13, see esp. R. Barrett 2009, chap. 5.

19. Cf. *Sipre Deut.* 86.

20. We can profitably compare Deut. 13 with the seventh century BCE Neo-Assyrian Succession Treaty of Esarhaddon, which requires the vassals of the king of Assyria to be loyal to, love, and serve his heir (lines 1–10, 266–68, 283–301, 385–96). Lines 108–22 warn of the possibility of rebellion against the heir arising from his family, the vassals and their families, prophets, ecstatics, dream interpreters, and others. In lines 130–46, if anyone "instigates" the vassal to rebel, they should report the rebellion, seize and kill the rebels, and "eradicate their name and descendants from the country" ("The Vassal-Treaties of Esarhaddon," trans. D. J. Wiseman [*ANET* 535–36]). Comparing this treaty with Deut. 13 emphasizes the problem there as treason against Yahweh, king of Israel (cf. Dion 1991, 197–204; Levinson 1995, 38–40, 58–60; Tigay 1996, 128; R. Barrett 2009, 146–50).

must be investigated.[21] If it is true, then all living creatures in the city—men, women, and animals—must be killed. The city should be burned. The city, its inhabitants, and their material possessions are put under the ban (חֵרֶם, herem, vv. 15–17 [16–18]), utterly destroyed because the city and everything in it belong to Yahweh.[22] This treatment resembles the annihilation of the Canaanites and their cultic objects, carried out in part to prevent the potential corruption of Israel's worship through proximity to idolatrous practices (7:2–5, 23–26; 12:3). In Deut. 13:12–18, Israelites are clearly turned away from pure devotion to Yahweh, and the apostate city faces the destruction enacted upon Canaanite idolaters. Perhaps more important, the city that should be holy to Yahweh has become abominable on account of its idolatry (cf. תוֹעֵבָה, tôʿēbâ, in v. 14 [15]). Just as the land is to be cleared of the abhorrent idolatrous practices of the Canaanites in order for God and God's people to take possession, so also this nominally Israelite city must be destroyed to maintain the holiness of the land.

The judicial process outlined in Deut. 13:12–18 resembles the investigation of charges that an Israelite serves other gods in 17:2–7.[23] In that law, on the evidence of two or three witnesses, the guilty person is taken out to the city gate and stoned to death, an act that, like the death of the prophet in Deut. 13:5 (6), rids Israel of evil. As in chapter 13, the idolater of chapter 17 can be identified as an outsider, doing what Moses has not commanded (17:3). The distinction between the idolaters of chapters 13 and 17 lies in their influence. The idolater of chapter 17 apparently commits idolatry alone; the attempt to preach idolatry to other Israelites in chapter 13 makes the prophet or dreamer and the children of Belial all the more dangerous.

The outsiders in Israel's midst in Deut. 13:1–5 (2–6), 12–18 (13–19) are indistinct people, a faceless prophet, or even more impersonally, a nameless city full of nameless foreigners. The central section of chapter 13, however, identifies the other as someone "you" know, someone you are very close to: your brother, your child, your wife, your best friend. In the Hebrew Bible, these relationships have their own sanctity. They should not be broken; when they are broken, the resulting chaos depicts the worst that can happen in life

21. The children of Belial, בְּנֵי־בְלִיַּעַל (bĕnê-bĕlîyaʿal), "worthless" people (NASB) or "scoundrels" (NRSV), are of Israelite descent, though they are clearly set in opposition to the ideal Israelites as the children of God. They can be compared to the sons of Eli, children of Belial who disrupt the proper functioning of Yahweh's cult (1 Sam. 2:12–17, 22–36).

22. Note also the ban in Deut. 2:34; 3:6; 20:16–18; esp. see Niditch 1993, 62–68 (and all of chaps. 1–2); Nelson 1997, 44–52. The city of Deut. 13 is explicitly identified as a gift of God (13:12 [13 MT]); like the promised land (4:1; 8:10; etc.), this city rightly belongs to God's faithful people (cf. Benjamin 1983, 116–17).

23. Weinfeld (1983, 92n2) suggests that Deut. 17:2–7 originally preceded 13:1 (2); Levinson 1997, 118, identifies Deut. 17:2–7 as a late revision of chap. 13. Whether one of these theories is correct or not, the points of dissimilarity between the two passages noted by Levinson indicate that the two texts are not about the same thing at all (see esp. Levinson 1997, 108; cf. Dion 1991, 162).

(see Deut. 28:53–57; Mic. 7:5–6). Deuteronomy 13:6–11 calls for these close ties to be sacrificed for the cause of the covenant.

Deuteronomy 13:6–11 (7–12)

6 If your brother, the son of your mother,[24] or your son, or your daughter, or the wife of your bosom, or your friend who is like your own self, urges you secretly, saying, "Let us go and worship other gods,"[25] gods whom you and your ancestors have not known,

7 gods from the nations surrounding you,[26] the nations near you or the nations far from you, from one end of the earth to the other,

8 do not give in to her.[27] Do not listen to him. Do not let your eye pity her. Do not spare and do not conceal him.

9 Rather, you will indeed kill her.[28] Your hand should be against him first to kill him,[29] and the hand of all the people after.

10 You will stone[30] her with stones until she dies, for he sought to turn you away from Yahweh, your God, who brought you out from the land of Egypt, from the house of slavery.

---

24. Several versions read "son of your father or your mother" (4Q30 22–23, LXX, and Syriac; see also *Sipre Deut.* 87 and *Tg. Ps.-J.* Deut. 13:7). The evidence for the variant is strong. If the longer description of the brother is accepted, the text would emphasize that all brothers are included in the law.

25. The quotation of the tempter's words may extend through verse 8. Clearly, however, the description of the gods is given from the perspective of a faithful worshiper of Yahweh, not an idolater (see Bartor 2007, 246–47). The reader is not given the opportunity to interpret the invitation positively.

26. Most pronouns and pronominal suffixes in these verses are second-person masculine singular, but "the nations surrounding you" takes a second-person masculine-plural suffix, perhaps in order to refer to all Israel. The shift from second-person masculine singular to plural is common in Deuteronomy (see McConville 2002, 27–35).

27. The pronouns and suffixes referring to the tempter in verses 7–9 (8–10) are all third-person masculine singular. I have alternated masculine- and feminine-singular pronouns in my translation to preserve the multiplicity of the possible referents identified in verse 7 in their individual identities.

28. In 13:9 (10) the LXX reads, "You will indeed report about him," ἀναγγέλλων ἀναγγελεῖς περὶ αὐτοῦ (*anangellōn anangeleis peri autou*; reading נָגַד [*nāgad*, "to announce"] for הָרַג [*hārag*, "to kill"]), bringing this law into line with Deut. 17:4–5 (see also *m. Sanh.* 7:10). Reporting the attempted idolatry before carrying out the sentence makes sense judicially and also matches the order of events in 13:8 (9) and 14 (15). On the other hand, immediate execution emphasizes the judgment pronounced in verse 9 (10). Philo understands the announcement in the LXX to be an announcement of an execution, not a trial (*Spec. Laws* 1.315). See further Dion 1991, 154; Levinson 1995, 40–54; Aejmelaeus 1996, 20.

29. To kill here is first הָרַג (*hārag*) and then מוּת (*mût*). When used together, these words are interchangeable, referring to accidental killing, willful murder, and punitive execution (see, e.g., Exod. 21:14; Lev. 20:15–16; Josh. 10:11).

30. The verb is second-person masculine singular in the MT, but plural in the Syriac and Targumim; in the LXX, it is third-person plural.

11 And all Israel will hear and fear, so that they will not again do anything
   like this evil thing in your midst.[31]

The introduction of this section of Deut. 13 sets the scene with the detailed
identification of some of the parties involved. The language of verse 6 emphasizes the intimacy of the addressee's connection with the one who encourages
the worship of other gods.[32] It is your full brother, son of your father and your
mother, a person with whom you have an especially close bond (as in Gen.
43:29; Judg. 8:19).[33] It is your own child, either your son or your daughter. The
tempter may be the wife you hold in your arms, a description that also appears
in the horror of husband and wife turning against each other in the covenant
curses of Deut. 28:54–56 (cf. Mic. 7:5). Finally, the tempter may be the friend
who is like your own self. This person can be seen as part of the family (Ps.
35:14; Prov. 17:17), sometimes even as better and closer than a family member
(Prov. 18:24; 27:10). Such a friend deserves the utmost loyalty (2 Sam. 16:17).

The relationships highlighted in Deut. 13:6 are privileged. They are the
most intimate relationships a man would have, as the extended descriptions
of the brother, wife, and friend indicate. These are the people with whom a
man tells the stories of the ancestors, recites the covenant, keeps the festivals,
and embodies Israel. In verse 7, however, these closest relationships are redefined as nonexistent: your brother, your wife, your child, and your friend
are just like the mass of nations that are not Israel. The marker of identity
here is worship. The nations that surround Israel worship gods of wood or
stone or heavenly host (4:19; 28:36), gods that neither the addressee of Deut.
13:6–7 (7–8) nor his ancestors ever knew (cf. 13:2, 13; 32:17), and they worship in ways abhorrent to Yahweh (12:31; 18:9–12; 20:18). When any one of
Yahweh's people turns aside to follow other gods, that Israelite becomes like
the other nations, and Israel as a whole may be infected with the evil (13:11)
and in consequence suffer loss of identity and divine punishment. Once again,
idolatry endangers Israel.

The third party involved in Deut. 13:6–11 is the addressee, a man with
wife and child. Since no parents are mentioned, it is possible this man's father has died, and he has become the patriarch of the household. As the head
of a household, he would have a particular responsibility to ensure that the
members of the family remain true to the covenant.[34] The patriarchal focus
could indicate that the patriarch has absolute power over his household. He
is empowered to execute them without trial, but they have no power over him:

31. The pronominal suffix is second-person masculine singular in MT but plural in the
majority of LXX manuscripts, and also in the Syriac and *Tg. Ps.-J.* Cf. Deut. 13:5 (6); 17:7;
19:19; 21:21; etc.

32. Rhetorically, the descriptors in Deut. 13:6 (7) recall Gen. 22:2.

33. Cf. Levinson 2001, 241.

34. Compare Dion 1991, 173.

the patriarch's own actions are checked only by his brother or dear friend. A suspicious reading would highlight the power structures that subject the members of the household to patriarchal control, which has no bounds.[35]

Perhaps, though, the text need not be read so suspiciously. The first section of Deut. 13, after all, undermines the power of a prophet or dreamer as an authority in the community. This limitation of power structures provides an important context for reading verses 6 to 11. Furthermore, as noted above, ancient Israelite living conditions entailed nearly continual family togetherness. The accountability engendered by working and living in the presence of others would necessarily control the patriarch and limit his opportunities to engage in and proselytize for secret idol worship as much as those of the rest of the family. Since these family members can keep other laws, they may also be able to kill the patriarch, even if that contingency is not made explicit.[36] The "secret" nature of the temptation, finally, would naturally allow for letting the situation slide: who would ever know? Rather than the danger of patriarchal abuse of this law, the question may instead concern its "enforceability," to borrow from Chaya Halberstam. For Halberstam, a law like this, especially in light of the secrecy of the invitation, is not about power but about faithfulness.[37] Deuteronomy 13:6–11 calls Israelites to be faithful to God by guarding the covenant even when no one would know that it has been broken.

The list of people and the descriptions of the other gods and nations in Deut. 13:6–7 provide a gentle, slow introduction to the law, contrasting sharply with the staccato clip of 13:8. The quick succession of prohibitions in this verse resembles the second half of the Decalogue. In Deut. 7, another series of do-nots calls on the conquering Israelites to destroy the Canaanites, not making a covenant with them, showing them mercy, intermarrying with them, or serving their gods (vv. 2–3, 16). Like the prohibitions in chapter 7, Deut. 13:8 protects Israel from compromising with foreign idolatry. Deuteronomy 7, however, concerns those who are outsiders by virtue of birth, ethnicity, and geography as well as cult. Chapter 13 commands similar behavior toward those who should be insiders. The intensely personal nature of the relationships listed in verse 6 increases the dramatic and emotive tension of prohibitions in verse 8: do not listen to your brother; show no mercy or pity to your child; make no attempt to save your wife.

35. It is sometimes argued that Deuteronomy limits patriarchal power (so Clements 1989, 65; Steinberg 1991, 163–65; Stulman 1992, 55, 57, 60–61; Dion 1993, 73–74, 81; see further on Deut. 21:18–21 and 22:20–21 below). The demand that a patriarch initiate the execution of a member of the household without trial in Deut. 13:6–11 (7–12) challenges this thesis.

36. Whether they would take this opportunity or not is another question. Because the life of the household depends at least to some extent on the presence and social power of the patriarch, perhaps other members of the household would be reluctant to accuse the patriarch of wrongdoing.

37. Halberstam 2007, 347, 359; cf. R. Barrett 2009, 139.

The prohibition of listening or obeying echoes Deut. 13:3, protecting Israelites from the dangerous power of a tempter's words. The remaining three prohibitions in 13:8 would shock the social sensibilities of the ancient reader (a point highlighted in *Sipre Deut.* 89). First, the offender must not be pitied nor spared (cf. 7:16; 19:13, 21; 25:12). "To pity" (חוּס, *ḥûs*), and "to spare" (חָמַל, *ḥāmal*), are often found together in the Hebrew Bible, and their associated contexts provide an indication of normal Israelite expectations of pity. David spares Mephibosheth because of an oath made to Jonathan, his good friend (2 Sam. 21:7). The Medes will show no mercy on young men or infants nor pity children (Isa. 13:18). In Mal. 3:17, God promises to spare the faithful just as a father spares the son who serves him. In other words, the relationships highlighted in Deut. 13:6 would, in normal circumstances, be the proper arena for pity and mercy. The reversal of expectations here reflects the heinousness of the sin of idolatry in Deuteronomy.[38] Deuteronomy 13:6–11 involves God's faithful people in the merciless destruction of the idolatrous children of Israel, demanding that even nearest kin join in punishing false worship.

The final clause of Deut. 13:8 (9) prohibits covering (כָּסָה, *kāsâ*), the offender. Covering can mean keeping a secret or concealing a sin, as in Ps. 32:5; Job 31:33; Prov. 11:13; 17:9. Readers often take the meaning in Deut. 13:8 to be this: if someone secretly entices you to worship other gods, do not let the matter remain secret.[39] "Covering" could also be interpreted as forgiveness, as when God covers a sin (Ps. 85:2 [3]; Neh. 4:5 [3:37]).[40] Hiding the sin and forgiving the sin are perhaps not so very different. For Deut. 13:8, those who encourage an Israelite to worship other gods are beyond the hope of forgiveness. Their sin must not be hidden: it must be made public by the very act of their execution by stoning.

The verbal construct in verse 9 (10), "You will indeed kill him" (הָרֹג תַּהַרְגֶנּוּ, *hārōg tahargennû*) suggests the necessity and intensity of the action. Similar grammatical constructions in Deut. 7:2; 12:2; and 20:17 indicate the completeness of destruction (cf. 13:15). "You will indeed kill him" in 13:9 completes the picture of mercilessness begun in verse 8, and this mercilessness is emphasized again by the insistence that the first stone should come from the person—the husband, father, brother, or dear friend—tempted to idolatry. The rest of the people then join in. The close parallel with Deut. 17:7 identifies the protagonist of Deut. 13:6–10 as a witness against the offender.[41] The first stone confirms the accusation.[42]

38. Compare God's merciless punishment of idolatry in Ezek. 5:11; 9:5, 10; Jer. 13:14; 21:7; see also R. Barrett 2009, 140.

39. So most translations and *Sipre Deut.* 89; C. Wright 1996, 175; Biddle 2003, 224.

40. Levinson 1996, 603–18, argues vigorously for this reading of Deut. 13:8 (9).

41. A major difference between the two laws is the absence of the formal investigation and trial in Deut. 13 (see above, n. 28). The lack of a public trial in chap. 13 may be because the secrecy of enticement precludes formal investigation.

42. Girard (2001, 56–59) claims that the first stone is the hardest to throw (cf. John 8:7–9), so this demand in Deuteronomy would limit and control violence. The emphasis on the nearness of the relationship and the shock of violence within such a relationship in Deut. 13:6–11 (7–12)

The offense, secret enticement to worship foreign gods, is described in Deut. 13:10 as seeking to turn a true Israelite away from Yahweh (as is also the case in vv. 5, 13). A warning in Deut. 30:17–18 similarly states that if Israel turns away from God to worship other gods, they will be destroyed from the land (or be turned out, vv. 1, 4, from the same verbal root, נָדַח, *nādaḥ*). If, on the other hand, they remain faithful to Yahweh and keep the covenant, they will prosper in the land (30:19–20). The action taken against the offender in Deut. 13:6–11 reflects the serious consequences of compliance with and defiance of Israelite identity.[43]

The death of the tempter must also be read within Deuteronomy's understanding of the character of God.[44] In 13:10 the extended identification of Yahweh as "your God, who brought you out of the land of Egypt, out of the house of slavery," is a frequent refrain in the book (and throughout the Torah). This refrain reminds the Israelites of God's mercy and also that they were created to be God's people in order to worship God alone (Deut. 4:15–20; cf. 7:6–8). God's mercy and jealousy are both integral to God's character. As in the Decalogue, remembering that God has saved them from Egypt should prevent Israelites from worshiping other gods (5:6–10). The descriptions of God in Deut. 13:5, 10 remind the people that God has created them, has saved them, and continues to care for them. For Deuteronomy, breaking the bond between God and Israel requires the death of the offender who counsels rebellion against Israel's faithful God.[45]

In addition to punishing the crime and removing the immediate temptation to idolatry, the execution of the tempter acts as a warning for all Israel. The news of the death will make the people fear, and their fear will prevent them from committing the same wrong (13:11). This motivation (or justification) occurs alongside the punitive measures in Deut. 17:13; 19:20; and 21:21. Elsewhere, fearing Yahweh encourages Israel's faithfulness to the covenant (4:10; 5:29; 10:12–13; etc.); fear and obedience are distinguishing characteristics of a true Israelite in 13:3–4. Idolatry is an offense against Yahweh, and the execution of the tempter at the hands of a loved one provides a measure of Yahweh's holiness. Far more than the fear of death by stoning, fear of Yahweh should prevent Israel from repeating the offense of encouraging others to worship the gods of the nations.[46]

---

undermine Girard's suggestion. It may rather be that the witness in Deut. 13 would prefer to let the situation pass; as Tigay (1996, 131) says, violence would need to be encouraged, not limited.

43. Compare C. Wright 1996, 179. Finkelstein (1981, 26–28) and Tigay (1996, 133) associate stoning with acts of rebellion against communal and cosmic order.

44. See *Sipre Deut.* 86; Hamilton 1998, 15.

45. The references to God in Deut. 13 are not, as Dion (1991, 197) suggests, marginal or "mere motivating developments," but key presuppositions of the law (cf. Hamilton 1998, 13–15).

46. In this respect, Hamilton (1998, 13) identifies Deut. 13 as an extended reflection on 5:8–10 (cf. Braulik 1985, 261–62). Though the immediate problem in chap. 13 is leading others into idolatry rather than practicing idolatry, the correlation of the punishment or rewarding of

Deuteronomy 13 develops from and reinforces the book's focus on mono-theistic worship. It strongly supports destroying the cults of foreign gods and their worshipers. It also adds to the definition of an Israelite. In the ideal com-munity, an Israelite is not simply a member of the nation created by Yahweh to worship Yahweh. An Israelite must also be personally dedicated to the worship of Yahweh and the eradication of the worship of other gods from within and around Israel. The specification of the enemy within Israel as a member of a person's own family, from among the closest personal relationships possible, is jarring. The prohibitions in Deut. 13:8 paradoxically draw attention to the attitudes that should be characteristic of such a close relationship: love, pity, mercy, and care. In place of these expected attitudes, the Israelite is called upon to cast the first stone at this close relative or friend, to initiate his or her execution for idolatry. It is not a pleasant picture. It is likely that Deut. 13 sounded as horrific to its earliest audiences as it does now, perhaps even more so since verses 6–11 conflict with the values and customs of traditional Israelite society, in which the family engenders and centers life. In challenging merely human values, though, Deut. 13:6–11 claims that some values weigh more than the closest human relationships, and some requirements of life justify the violent sacrifice of all.[47]

Deuteronomy 13 in the Hebrew Bible

The danger of idolatry looms large across the Hebrew Bible, and several texts recall certain elements of Deut. 13.[48] A denunciation of God's people in Jer. 7 focuses on injustice and worshiping other gods (vv. 6, 9). In the midst of this accusation, the prophet is instructed not to pray for his people because they provoke God to anger (כַּעַס, ka'as, v. 19), just as Moses warns they will do in Deut. 32:16, 21. The specific provocation in Jer. 7:18 is the inversion of the family's cultic responsibility. Instead of celebrating the feasts and sacrificing to Yahweh, children and parents together worship the queen of heaven and other gods. As a result, God's people will be punished (v. 20).

The people are punished to death for false worship in several narratives in the Hebrew Bible, including Num. 25.[49] In the story of the Israelites' idolatry at Baal of Peor, Phinehas's murder of the Israelite Zimri and his Midianite paramour punishes sin, removes this threat of foreign influences from Israel,

---

households for disobeying or obeying the second commandment with the household focus of 13:6–11 (7–12) is particularly striking.

47. Cf. McConville 2002, 239.

48. According to Weinfeld (1983, 1), the Deuteronomic history is marked by the fight against idolatry for the establishment of a centralized cult. Among the texts discussed here, Jeremiah and 1 and 2 Kings are identified as Deuteronomic, and Exod. 32 is often associated with Deut. 9–10 and 1 Kings 12.

49. See also 1 Kings 18:40; 2 Kings 10:25–27.

and protects the cult of Yahweh from illicit forms of worship. This violence is described as an act of zeal that reflects God's own zeal, the zeal (or jealousy) that demands Israel's devotion to God alone (Num. 25:11; cf. Exod. 20:5; Deut. 4:24; etc.).[50] Numbers 25 has many points of contact with another wilderness story in which Israel's flirtation with idolatry is punished by priestly violence.[51] The story of the golden calf in Exod. 32 integrates the zealous violence of Phinehas with the constructive family violence of Deut. 13:6–11.

The Golden Calf and the Bloody Sword

As in Deut. 13:6–11, the story of the golden calf in Exod. 32 stops Israel's slide into idolatry by means of violence against family members.[52] In Exod. 24:12, Moses climbs Mount Sinai to receive the stone tablets inscribed with the law and commandments. In 32:15, he finally descends again, carrying the two tablets with him, only to find the people engaged in worshiping the golden calf. In response, Moses breaks the tablets of the law and destroys the calf. He forces the people to drink the dust of the destroyed calf.[53] He rebukes Aaron for his role in the story (vv. 20–24). Moses next calls on those who are "for Yahweh" (מִי לַיהוָה, mî lyhwh), who turn out to be the Levites (v. 26), to punish the transgression of God's law.[54]

When the Levites join Moses outside the camp of idolaters, he instructs them in the name of Yahweh, God of Israel, to take up their swords and slaughter the people all through the camp—this despite the fact that Moses has just petitioned Yahweh not to destroy them (vv. 7–14). The shock of the abrupt

50. Though Phinehas is not Zimri's relative, the murder occurs in Zimri's home (Num. 25:11). The LXX of Num. 25:6 emphasizes the family context of Zimri's sin (cf. the punishment of family members, οἰκεῖος [oikeios], decreed in v. 5). On the tradition of zealous violence against sinners or apostates in the Hebrew Bible, see further Hengel 1989b, 147–50; Seland 1995, 42–48.

51. Cf. *Sipre Num.* 131; *Sipre Deut.* 349; Hengel 1989b, 148; Milgrom 1990, xv, 211; Lutzky 1997, 546.

52. The narration of the golden calf story in Deut. 9–10 ends before the Levitical violence of Exod. 32 (but see Deut. 33:8–11). On the relationship between these texts, see Blenkinsopp (1999, 102–7), arguing for the priority of Deuteronomy; or Begg (1997, 475) and Hayes (2004, 48–49), arguing for the priority of Exodus.

53. This strange scene has been compared with Num. 5:11–31, in which a suspected adulteress drinks the words of a curse to make her guilt or innocence apparent. In Exod. 32, then, drinking would somehow mark those Israelites who engaged in worship of the calf (cf. Stern 2008, 504). However, there is no indication that this is the case in Exod. 32: nowhere does this story distinguish between the guilty and the innocent. According to Exod. 32, all Israel is guilty in this matter.

54. In the story line of the Pentateuch, the Levites are not introduced as servants of the cult of Yahweh until Num. 1:50, although Gen. 34:25–26 provides a foretaste of Levitical violence (cf. *Sipre Deut.* 349). For many scholars, the contrast between Aaron, who makes the calf, and the Levites who punish the idolaters is evidence of a historical conflict between the Aaronide and Levitical priesthoods (e.g., Propp 2006, 567; MacDonald 2007, 28). In Exodus itself, however, Aaron is a Levite, and despite their participation in punishing the sin, there is no indication that the Levites did not join in the worship of the calf.

notice of violent punitive measures against Israel in verse 27 is heightened by
the identification of the victims of the Levites as their brothers (and sisters?),
neighbors, and near ones (or relatives, קָרוֹב, *qārôb*, v. 27), and in verse 29 as
their sons and brothers (and daughters and sisters?).[55] Exodus 32:28 rather
baldly announces that the Levites actually killed about three thousand of "the
people." It is important to note that nowhere does the text limit the violence
to the guilty. In fact, there is no indication that only some of the Israelites
joined in the worship of the calf: "the people" are a united group in this story,
and they all are potential victims of the violence.

Violence consecrates the Levites (or following their action they must consecrate themselves; v. 29).[56] Moses literally says, "Fill your hands to Yahweh"
(v. 29), a phrase that parallels sanctification in the ceremony of priestly ordination described in Exod. 28:41 (cf. 29:9, 29; etc.). The Levites' ordination
as a result of killing the worshipers of the golden calf provides a foretaste
of their position in the cult.[57] It sits uneasily, however, with the expectations
placed on communal relationships in Exodus. The early chapters of the book
are particularly instructive. Moses reprimands two Israelites for fighting their
neighbors, that is, each other (2:13). When he murders an Egyptian who is
beating an unidentified Israelite, Moses protects his brother (2:11). The deaths
of the sons of the Israelites and the Egyptians are tragic (chaps. 1, 12–13).
The victims identified in Exod. 32:27–29 should not be objects of violence.

As in Deut. 13:6–11, the danger of idolatry in Exod. 32 overcomes normal
familial expectations. The very first verse of the story introduces the major

---

55. The victims in Exod. 32:27, 29 could be the people of Israel in general. "Each his brother"
and "each his neighbor" can signify each other (cf. 10:23; 21:18), and son and brother are also
used of the Israelites in general (1:1; 2:11; etc.). Thus Propp (2006, 563) argues that all the Israelites except the Levites are potential victims. However, the specificity of the two lists of victims
and the combination of sons and brothers in 32:29 suggest that specific family relationships
are intended: the Levites are killing Israelites, including their own family members (cf. Moberly
1983, 55). In light of the inclusion of women in Exod. 32:2, the absence of explicitly identified
women from verses 25–29 is curious. Are women included in the "brothers" and "sons" (both
of which can refer to men and women), neighbors, and near ones? In Deut. 33:9, a text that
may reference the story of Exod. 32, the Levites are said to disregard their mothers and fathers,
brothers (or siblings, אָח, *'āḥ*) and sons (or children, בֵּן, *bēn*).

56. There is some question over the meaning of this phrase. As it stands in the Masoretic
Text, the phrase is a second-person masculine-plural command: "Fill your hands" (מִלְאוּ יֶדְכֶם,
mil'û yedkem), that is, consecrate yourselves to God after committing these acts of violence
(cf. NASB). The verb can be repointed, however, as a third-person plural perfect: "Your hands
were filled." The latter is followed in the Septuagint (Ἐπληρώσατε τὰς χεῖρας ὑμῶν, *Eplērōsate
tas cheiras hymōn*), allowing the interpretation of the violence against family members as the
act of ordination (cf. NRSV).

57. Brisman (1999, 166) suggests that ordination means something else in Exod. 32:29 because the Levites' hands are filled with human blood rather than animal blood, a suggestion that
seems to come out of the moral qualms he has about the text (cf. Durham 1987, 432). Perhaps
instead the language of ordination in Exod. 32 sanctifies the violence as a sacrifice to Yahweh,
something also suggested in Num. 25 and 1 Macc. 2 (cf. *Num. Rabbah* 21.3 on Num. 25:13).

problem that the Levitical violence seeks to redress: Israel has forgotten precisely who brought them up from the land of Egypt. This phrase, "brought you [Israel] up from the land of Egypt," is repeated over and over in Exodus to identify God (6:13; 12:42; 20:2; etc.). A central goal of the narrative, getting Israel out of Egypt, is linked inextricably with the character of God. In Exod. 32:1, however, the Israelites say that Moses, not God, brought them up from Egypt. The shift from God to Moses as the savior of Israel introduces a distance between God and the people that is confirmed and strengthened when they acclaim the golden calf as the god who brought them up from Egypt (vv. 4, 8). God acknowledges the change in relationship by reporting to Moses what the people whom he, Moses, brought up from Egypt have done (v. 7). When Moses intercedes for his people before God, he reminds God that God is the one who brought Israel out of Egypt (v. 11), but in Exod. 33:1, it is again Moses who brought the people up. Significantly, this announcement is the final use of the phrase "brought up from the land of Egypt" in the book.

The beginning of the story of the golden calf, then, warns the reader that all is not well in the camp of Israel. In Moses's absence on the mountaintop, the people have forgotten who he is and what his role in their story has been; they have confused the God who saved them from Egypt with the man who has acted on God's orders. Since this forgetful, confused people do not know what has become of this man, their request for Aaron to make a god makes sense. The people need a replacement for Moses to lead them on their journey. Indeed, it could be that they are asking for a visible manifestation of Yahweh to go before them, just as Moses had done.[58] Their request, however, drives a major division between Yahweh and Israel.

Before Moses's ascent of Mount Sinai, he had instructed the people in the first installment of the law, including the Decalogue (Exod. 20–24). The very first commandments of the Decalogue, commandments that could be considered foundational for the entire law, demand that Israel have no god but Yahweh and prohibit the making, worshiping, and serving of images (20:3–4). This demand is based on the identity of God as the God who brought Israel up from the land of Egypt, from the house of slavery (v. 2). God is further characterized as a jealous God, punishing the disobedient up to the fourth generation and blessing the obedient by the thousands (vv. 5–6). In Exod. 24:3–8, all the people swear to keep the laws of God, thus accepting the basis of the law in the character of God, and they are sprinkled with blood as a sign of their covenant.

"The people" next appear in the narrative in Exod. 32, blatantly disregarding the God with whom they have covenanted and the commandments they

58. So Moberly 1983, 44–48. Ironically, as Moberly points out, on the mountaintop Moses is receiving the instructions for the tabernacle, a visible sign of God's presence that will go with Israel (Exod. 25–31); cf. MacDonald 2007, 25–27.

have promised to obey.[59] The divine summary of the Israelites' sin in verse 8 condemns the people for turning away from God's path by making the calf, worshiping it, sacrificing to it, and ascribing God's own saving acts to it. The golden calf represents abhorrence of Yahweh, the God who did bring the people up out of Egypt. In breaking the foundation of their covenant by worshiping in ways Yahweh has not commanded, "the people" bring punishment on themselves.[60]

In this light, Moses's wrath in Exod. 32:19 is more comprehensible. It is perhaps only surprising that Israel survives this crisis. Complete annihilation would be almost unremarkable in Exodus, a book that reeks of blood from beginning to end. The salvation of the Israelites from Egypt is accomplished through violence, including the plagues, the killing of the firstborn males of Egypt on the night of Passover, and the drowning of Egypt's army in the Red Sea. Divine violence can also be directed against Israel, as Exod. 5:3 and 22:24 (23 MT) warn. The violence in Exod. 32:25–29 is of a piece with the rest of the book. The identification of the victims as brothers, sons, and relatives along with neighbors in verses 27 and 29 is still surprising, though. Why are the Levites instructed to kill other Levites, those who are "for Yahweh"?

As with Deut. 13:6–11, the household context of the violence in Exod. 32 can be correlated with the household's role in passing on the covenant and traditions of Israel (Exod. 10:2; 12:26–27; 13:8, 14). The family participation in the cult of Yahweh expected in Exod. 10:9 and 20:10 is inverted in chapter 32. When the people ask Aaron for new gods, his instructions involve the entire family, fathers and mothers, sons and daughters, in making the image (v. 2). Presumably, the entire family also takes part in the sacrificing and feasting that occur on the day of the festival to Yahweh (vv. 5–6). This text goes beyond prioritizing loyalty to God over loyalty to the family.[61] Rather, violence against family members directly addresses the problem of Israel's sin: the family together has broken Yahweh's command, and so the family rightly bears the punishment.

The number of the Levites' victims in Exod. 32:28 is comparable with the deaths of vast numbers of Egyptians during the plagues and at the crossing of the Red Sea, but Exod. 32 pitches Israelite against Israelite, brother against brother, father against son. In a book that begins by denigrating violence against sons, brothers, and neighbors, the picture of the Levites murdering their nearest and dearest is appalling. However, it is not incomprehensible. The commendation of the Levites within the story and in Deut. 33:8–11 indicates that ancient readers understood the violence. Exodus as a whole justifies it: Israelite families have broken the cardinal rule of their covenant with Yahweh, and they get their deserts. In addition to the plague in Exod. 32:35 and the

59. As has also been proposed for Deut. 13, Brichto (1983, 42–43) suggests Exod. 32 is a commentary on the first two commandments.
60. Cf. Hayes 2004, 58.
61. So Durham 1987, 432; Brisman 1999, 166; Propp 2006, 563.

intercession of Moses in verses 11–14 and 30–34, the Levitical slaughter of relatives and neighbors reverses the wicked worshiping of the golden calf, wiping the slate clean for another attempt at worship of Yahweh alone in the ways the law commands.

Idolatry and the Family in Deuteronomy

Israelite families hold a central place in the covenant community in Deuteronomy. Family members together support the life of the household, keep the commandments, and embody Israel in relationship with God, the divine parent. When one family member tries to convert the others to the worship of foreign gods, the identity of the family as Israelite is threatened. When one family turns away from Yahweh, the covenant of the nation is threatened. For Deuteronomy, the most fundamental principle of Israel's life is the recognition of Yahweh alone as God. When this foundation is challenged by idolatrous family members, Israel's future hangs in the balance, a danger that justifies and even demands the death of the challenger, the enemy within the household.

Deuteronomy 21:18–21 and 22:13–21: Parents and Children

The law of Deut. 13:6–11 responds to a particular situation in which the identity of the covenant community as worshipers of Yahweh, carried out by families sacrificing, feasting, and celebrating together, is threatened. Two further laws in Deuteronomy, the law of the disobedient son in 21:18–21 and the law of the slanderous husband and foolish daughter in 22:13–21, address situations in which the passing on of the covenant is also endangered. In Deuteronomy, children inherit the covenant from their ancestors. The covenant is also taught as parents model the laws and tell the stories of Israel to their children. Israelite identity is formed in the context of household life, and the laws of Deut. 21:18–21 and 22:13–21 protect the covenant at the potentially perilous point of transition from one generation to the next.

The importance of good intergenerational relationships is reflected in the fifth commandment: "Honor your father and your mother as Yahweh your God commanded you, so that your days will be long and so that it will be well with you in the land that Yahweh your God is giving you" (Deut. 5:16). Honor entails respect, concern, and consideration. In demanding honor for fathers and mothers, the fifth commandment promotes obedience to parental instruction, an essential corollary to the teaching of the covenant in the household.[62] In addition, the fifth commandment has physical and economic ramifications for parents facing old age in an agricultural society, ensuring

62. See also Sivan 2004, 121.

that if mothers and fathers outlive their usefulness, their adult children will continue to care for them.[63]

The reward promised to the obedient in Deut. 5:16 echoes the book's frequent refrain that keeping the law brings long, blessed lives (e.g., 4:40; 5:29; 6:1–3). The resulting analogy between obedience to parents and to the law highlights the significance of parents in Deuteronomy's construction of Israelite society, a significance supported by the covenant curses in 27:15–26. According to verse 16, anyone who dishonors ("despises" or "shames," קָלָה, qālâ) a parent is cursed. The fifth commandment is further sustained by Deuteronomy's description of God as parent, Israel as child (1:29–31; 8:2–5; 32:6, 18). This metaphor imbues the relationship between parents and children with great significance: obedience to parents is demanded by and reflects obedience to Yahweh.[64]

The parent-child relationship and, consequently, obedience to God and the perpetuation of the covenant are threatened when parents misuse their power over their children, failing to care for them or even harming them (as in Deut. 12:31; 21:15–17). Likewise, children can refuse to accept their parents' authority, failing to learn from, obey, or care for them. God's care for Israel models correctives to these two disruptions of covenantal family life. God carried Israel in the wilderness like a man carrying his son (1:31; cf. 32:6, 10–14), and God also disciplines the people as a man disciplines his son (8:5). Loving care and discipline are fundamental parental responsibilities.

In Deut. 21:18–21 and 22:13–21, two particular examples of the recalcitrance of children are met with extreme measures of familial and communal discipline. These laws concern sons and daughters who are growing up, if not grown: the son has an established character as a rebellious, stubborn glutton and drunk, and the daughter is of an age to be married. Their growing maturity does not give them independence from the family. On the contrary, they have become members of the community responsible for the covenant, no longer innocent by reason of young age (cf. 1:39). The irresponsibility of the disobedient son and foolish daughter identifies them as threats to the community that must be redressed.

A Stubborn and Rebellious Son

According to Deut. 21:18–21, the parents of a stubborn, rebellious son should formally denounce him before the city elders. Since the accusation leads to the execution of the son, these parents are faced with the dreadful duty of putting their son to death. In Deuteronomy's vision of family life and in general Israelite

---

63. So Sir. 3:12–13; Matthews and Benjamin 1991, 224; Meyers 1997, 31; etc.; cf. Jungbauer 2002, chap. 3, on Exod. 20:12 and Deut. 5:16.

64. Cf. Sir. 3:1–16; Philo, *Decal.* 119–20; Josephus, *Ag. Ap.* 2.206, 217; Tigay 1996, 196; C. Wright 1996, 77; Brenner 2004–5, 3.

culture, sons are vital to the economy of the family, the inheritance of ancestral land, and the perpetuation of the national covenant. The disobedience of a son on whom such expectations rest is a serious problem for the household and wider community, and therefore the condemnation of this son protects the life cycle of the covenant. The unteachable son is destroyed so that the covenant will survive.

Deuteronomy 21:18–21

18 If anyone[65] has a stubborn and rebellious son[66] who does not listen to the voice of his father or the voice of his mother, and when they discipline him he will not listen to them,

19 then his father and his mother should seize him and bring him out to the elders of his city in the gate of his place,[67]

20 and they should say to the elders[68] of his city, "This son of ours is stubborn and rebellious. He does not listen to our voice. He is a glutton and a drunk."

21 All the men of his city will stone him with stones until[69] he dies, and you will destroy the evil from your[70] midst. And all Israel will hear and fear.

In Deut. 21:18–21, the mother and the father present their son for accusation and punishment. It is often assumed that only the patriarch has ultimate authority over family members, but the mother is equally involved in this law and the law of the foolish daughter in 22:13–21. Both parents try to discipline the son, both are ignored, and together they bring him before the elders. This situation reflects the concern with honoring father and mother throughout the Torah (Exod. 20:12; Lev. 19:3; Deut. 5:16).[71] According to early Jewish interpretation, the necessity for the joint intervention of the parents also limits the potential abuse of the law.[72]

---

65. Literally, "a man" (cf. Deut. 19:11; 21:15). Though some laws in Deuteronomy are addressed to only the male head of house, the mother is explicitly involved in 21:18–21. The beginning of this law follows the expected form of casuistic law (see Dion 1993, 75).

66. "Son" (בֵּן, bēn) often includes sons and daughters; Philo in *Spec. Laws* 2.224–48 and Josephus in *Ant.* 4.260–64 apply this law to both genders. In Deuteronomy, however, the wrongs listed are particularly relevant to sons, with their responsibilities to the covenant and family, and the context of the law also suggests that Deut. 21:18–21 addresses sons alone.

67. Meaning his hometown: "place" (מָקוֹם, māqôm) refers to a person's home in Gen. 18:33; Ruth 4:10; Job 7:10.

68. For "elders" in the MT, the LXX and Samaritan Pentateuch read "men" (cf. v. 21), and the Vulgate reads "them."

69. Or "so that" (וָמֵת, wāmēt), as in the KJV.

70. The pronominal suffix is second-person masculine singular in the MT, but plural in the LXX, Syriac, *Tg. Ps.-J.*, and Vulgate (the verb is second-person masculine singular in all versions). Cf. Deut. 13:11 (12).

71. Cf. Jungbauer 2002, 56–58.

72. So Philo, *Spec. Laws* 2.234; *m. Sanh.* 8:1–4; and *Sipre Deut.* 218–19. See further in chap. 4 below.

The fundamental problem with this son, emphasized by the repetition of key words from verse 18 in verse 20, is his stubborn, rebellious nature.[73] It is often remarked that this accusation is too general to be useful. Scholars therefore define the son's disobedience with reference to the basic expectation of honor of, obedience to, and care for parents implicit in the fifth commandment, along with the specific wrongs of striking, cursing, and dishonoring parents addressed in Exod. 21:15, 17; Lev. 20:9; and Deut. 27:16.[74] In the context of Deuteronomy's presentation of the family, though, the description of the son may be more exact than this modern interpretative tradition would suggest.

In the Hebrew Bible, the words translated here as stubborn (סָרַר, *sārar*) and rebellious (מָרָה, *mārâ*) are interchangeable terms that almost exclusively describe Israel disobeying Yahweh and, as a consequence, being punished.[75] In Isaiah, the people of Israel are even called the stubborn, rebellious sons of God (30:1, 9; 63:8–10). Often, as in Deut. 21:18, 20, the rebellion is explained as refusal to listen: the people will not hear God's words and commands or listen to the prophets, and therefore they do not do God's will (as is the case with מָרָה in Deut. 1:43; 9:23).[76] Moses warns his stubborn, rebellious people of exactly this danger in Deut. 31:27.[77] In Jer. 5:23, the people's stubbornness and rebellion are demonstrated by their refusal to fear God; instead they commit acts of social injustice (vv. 20–28). In Ps. 78:5–8, the example of Israel's stubborn rebellion in the past should encourage future generations, "the children yet unborn" (v. 6 NRSV), to remember God's acts and keep God's laws.

The use of "stubborn" and "rebellious" to describe God's people when they refuse to obey God explains the nature of the son's behavior in Deut. 21:18–21: by his refusal to listen to, learn from, and live according to the instruction of the parents, the son rebels against the covenant of Israel. He endangers the system by which the covenant is passed on; he rejects the identity he should be assuming. This son is a threat to the covenant, and thus Israel's identity, as it is in the process of transmission to the next generation.

The disobedient son specifically refuses to accept the parents' discipline. Discipline (יָסַר, *yāsar*) can refer to punishing wrongdoing, as in Lev. 26:18, 23,

73. Hagedorn (2000, 104) and Fleishman (2003, 312) reasonably suggest that an established behavioral pattern, rather than a onetime event, is intended by the description "stubborn and rebellious"; cf. Dion 1993, 77–78.

74. See, e.g., Callaway 1984, 342; Frymer-Kensky 1996, 58; Hagedorn 2000, 104; Fleishman 2003, 315–19.

75. See, e.g., סָרַר (*sārar*) in Isa. 65:2; Jer. 6:28; Hosea 4:16; 9:15; and מָרָה (*mārâ*) in Num. 20:10; Isa. 1:20; Hosea 13:16.

76. See also סָרַר in Zech. 7:11; Neh. 9:29; and מָרָה in 1 Sam. 12:15; Isa. 50:4–5; Ezek. 2:3–8. This tendency is particularly pronounced in the use of מָרָה in the hiphil stem, including Deut. 1:43; 9:23 (in Deut. 21:18, it is qal).

77. The rebellion in Deut. 31:26–29 may relate to idolatry (the evil that angers Yahweh is the "work" of the people's hands [v. 29], which is an idol in 4:28). Note that "rebellious," סָרַר, in Deut. 21:18 is related to "treason," סָרָה (*sārâ*), in Deut. 13:6.

28. This is the meaning of discipline in Deut. 22:18 as well, and it could be so for 21:18: the son's misbehavior is not corrected by his parents' punishment. Discipline can also indicate instruction, though, as in Ps. 94:12 and Jer. 31:18. In Deuteronomy, God as father disciplines his children by speaking to them, bringing them through the wilderness, testing them, and caring for their needs (4:36; 8:5). This discipline should result in obedience: "Keep the commandments of Yahweh your God, to walk in God's ways and to fear God" (8:6). It is likely, particularly in light of the metaphor of God as Father and Israel as son in 8:5, that the disciplining of the disobedient son in 21:18 involves parental care and instruction as much as or more than punishment. The son, however, rejects the discipline; he will not honor, fear, or obey his parents.

Faced with the son's ongoing rebellion, the parents should seize him and drag him before the elders. The parents' action here is akin to arrest (cf. תָּפַשׂ, tāpaś, "to seize," in 1 Kings 18:40; 2 Kings 25:6; Jer. 37:14), and the city's elders play the part of judges. The elders are heads of households recognized as authoritative in a community. They represent local inhabitants and determine matters of local concern.[78] In Deuteronomy, the elders hold judicial authority. They are involved with determining and avenging cases of manslaughter (19:12; 21:3–6; cf. Josh. 20:4). They witness the accusations against an adulterous wife and the case of levirate marriage (Deut. 22:15–16; 25:8; cf. Ruth 4:10–11). The elders are also given particular responsibility to preserve, teach, and enforce the covenant (Deut. 27:1; 31:9).

In the case of the rebellious son, the elders witness the parents' public accusation of stubbornness, rebellion, and refusal to listen. In 21:20, the parents also accuse their son of drunkenness and gluttony, an expansion of the initial description of the son in verse 18 that has raised many questions among interpreters. Some identify gluttony and drunkenness as a late addition to the original law.[79] For others, these extra descriptions indicate the exact nature of the son's disobedience.[80] Certainly in Prov. 23:20–21 and 28:7, gluttony and drunkenness are presented as foolish, dishonorable acts characteristic of those who disrupt social expectation.[81] According to Elizabeth Bellefontaine, to call the son a glutton and drunk marks him as "a 'bad lot,' . . . a non-productive, non-contributing parasite in the community."[82]

Paul Dion argues that the additional charges of gluttony and drunkenness in Deut. 21:20 make the case against the son public rather than limited to the privacy of the home. Though the elders have to accept the word of the parents

78. On the elders in ancient Israel, see Reviv 1989, esp. 8–11. Willis (2001) provides a full study of the elders in Deuteronomy specifically, covering 21:18–21 in chap. 5.
79. See, e.g., Dion 1993, 78–79; Hagedorn 2000, 103–4; Willis 2001, 170.
80. Compare Callaway 1984, 342; Fleishman 2003, 325.
81. Compare Isa. 56:12; Ezek. 23:42; Hosea 4:18.
82. Bellefontaine 1979, 20–21. See also Matthews and Benjamin 1991, 222–24; Fleishman 2003, 321–24.

concerning the son's rebellion against their teaching and discipline, habits of overeating and drinking would be known to the whole community.[83] For Dion, the accusation of gluttony and drunkenness thus mercifully limits the parents' authority over the son by allowing for members of the community to either support or deny the charges. The elders are truly judges in determining the strength of the parents' case rather than passive witnesses to the accusations.[84]

Although this reading addresses the concerns of ancient and modern readers with the potential abuse of Deut. 21:18–21, it misunderstands the inherently public nature of all life in ancient societies. Israelite families lived and worked in the public eye. Interactions between members of a household would be witnessed by the community at large, even when occurring in what modern readers would identify as the privacy of the home.[85] The son's misdeeds from stubbornness to drunkenness would be known in the community before the parents lodge their accusation.[86] In this respect, there is no suggestion that the parents could be in the wrong or that the elders or other community members would defend the son; the son is guilty. By charging the son before the elders as representatives of the community, the parents make his disobedience a newly official concern rather than a newly public one, inviting the community as a whole to join the parents in disciplining the son.

The communal discipline resolves the problem of the disobedient son with his execution by stoning at the city gate, the place also of his judgment. The location of the execution in public space draws attention to the communal nature of the problem. Though on the surface the son's behavior may seem to be problematic for his own family only, publicly trying and executing him shows otherwise.[87] Though stoning is a somewhat common method of execution in Deuteronomy, the identity of the people carrying out the sentence in 21:21 is rather unusual.[88] In 13:9–10 and 17:5, the witness of the offense is the first to throw a stone, and then the rest of the people (כָּל־הָעָם, kol-hā'ām) join in. By contrast, the parents of the disobedient son, the primary witnesses of his misbehavior and his accusers, are notably absent from the executioners

---

83. Dion 1993, 78–79.

84. Dion 1993, 81.

85. See Meyers 1997, 16–17, 21; Kamp 2000, 85–86.

86. Compare Willis 2001, 178–79.

87. Here J. Wright (2002, 20) identifies the gate of the city as a transition point from inside to outside the community boundaries. It is fitting, then, that the son, a presumed insider, is executed in this space, since his behavior has proved him to be an outsider. Wright adds that the location of the city government in the gate reinforces the location of the execution: the son who has threatened the local power structure is executed in the place of power.

88. The particular term used for stoning in Deut. 21:21, רָגַם (rāgam), is unique in the book. There seems to be no semantic difference between the two words for stoning (רָגַם and סָקַל [sāqal]); they appear together in Josh. 7:25, and also in 1 Kings (12:18 and 21:10–15). The choice of words has been used to date Deut. 21:18–21, but there is no consensus on whether the use of רָגַם makes it early or late (Hagedorn 2000, 106; Willis 2001, 173).

in 21:21. This absence may reflect the moral repugnance of parents' execution of their own child, though such an objection does not seem to affect 13:6–11. It may also be that their presence is assumed but simply not made explicit. In any case, the parents' overt responsibility in the case of the disobedient son ends with their official accusation. The duty of execution falls to the men of the city (כָּל־אַנְשֵׁי עִירוֹ, kol-'anšê 'îrô),[89] a group that would include the elders who have witnessed the accusation (cf. Deut. 22:21; 1 Kings 21:11–13). In light of the danger the son poses to the community as a whole, it is logical for representatives of the whole community to participate in killing him.[90] By their participation, they confirm their support of the accusation.

At the conclusion of the passage, the son's stubbornness and rebellion are described as an evil in the midst of the people. Other evil acts in Deuteronomy include idolatry and the temptation to idolatry, false witness, and adultery. In each case, as in Deut. 21:21, the evil is purged or cleansed by the death of the offender (13:6; 17:7; 19:19–20; etc.). The common element in these offenses is the threat they pose to the community.[91] For Deuteronomy's ideal society, individual participation in communal life is a prime factor in ensuring the survival of the covenant and covenant community. Conversely, one individual's offense, if left unpunished, could put the covenant-based community in danger of divine anger (as in 4:25–26; 9:18–19). The death of the disobedient son averts this possibility.[92]

The son's death also makes all Israel fear. In Deuteronomy, fear is an essential corollary to and motivation for covenant faithfulness (5:29; 6:2; 10:12; etc.). As in the case of the tempter in 13:11 and the false witness in 19:19–20, then, the death of the son will remind Israel of the need for obedience and the dangers of disobedience. Louis Stulman suggests that the dual motivation underlying the son's death, to cleanse the guilt of his offense and warn the community to be faithful, indicates the extent of the threat to the entire community.[93] The son presumably would inherit at least part of the ancestral land and become the patriarch of a family himself, responsible for embodying and teaching Israelite identity. His disregard for the values and traditions of the community could seriously damage this system.[94] The close of Deuter-

---

89. All the people? "Men" (אֲנָשִׁים, 'ănāšîm), often refers specifically to males in Deuteronomy (cf. 1:22; 2:14; 25:11; 31:12), though it could refer to the people in general in 1:35. All the "people" (עַם, 'am), presumably including women and men, are involved in carrying out an execution in Deut. 13:9–10 (10–11) and 17:7 (cf. Finkelstein 1981, 27).

90. Compare Pressler 1993, 18; Tigay 1996, 197.

91. For W. Brown (2005, 267), the son's evil (his rebellion) is "tantamount to treason." According to Finkelstein (1981, 26–27), stoning is the punishment for the most heinous crimes that threaten the community.

92. On this point, see esp. Bellefontaine 1979, 21–24; Willis 2001, 178–80.

93. See Stulman 1990, 625; 1992, 52–55.

94. Compare Bellefontaine 1979, 21–22; Miller 1990, 168; C. Wright 1996, 236; Willis 2001, 179–80.

onomy underlines the danger: Moses warns his people (yet again) that their
future disobedience, their stubbornness and rebellion, their evil in the sight of
Yahweh—all these will provoke Yahweh's anger and result in their punishment
(31:27–29). The son of 21:18–21 is an individual example of the potential
national disaster, and his behavior must be met with absolute judgment to
prevent the destruction of Israel.

The comparison of the disobedient son and the rebellious nation highlights
another level of interpretation for Deut. 21:18–21, one that has already been
introduced: the description of the son as stubborn and rebellious likens him
to the stubborn, rebellious child of God. In Deut. 32, Moses laments the foolishness of Israel, God's son, in turning away from the Father's care (vv. 5–6,
10–18). Israel is punished when God in turn abandons the child to destruction
(vv. 19–25). The prophets tell the same story. In Isa. 30:1–17, the stubborn sons
of Israel shift their allegiance from God to Egypt. They are rebellious, false sons
who refuse to hear God's words (v. 9), and their destruction is near. Again, in
Isa. 63:7–10, God cares for the children like a loving parent, and yet they rebel.
For Jeremiah, Israel's suffering is a result of their rebellion against the God
who fathered and birthed them (2:27–29). The people of Israel should listen
to, obey, and honor God; that their failure to do so is couched in the language
of a child's rebellion against a loving, caring parent only heightens the offense.
Rereading Deut. 21:18–21 in light of Jeremiah, Isaiah, and Deut. 32, the rebellious, stubborn son represents the entire nation, turning away from Yahweh to
their own destruction.[95] He embodies the evil disruption of the community and
endangerment of Israelite identity that the regulations of Deuteronomy guard
against: for Deuteronomy, his death is the one sure solution to the problem.

Several internal balances potentially mitigate the violence of this law. First,
the necessary involvement of father and mother, the elders, and the community
members as executioners could limit the possibility for abuse. This suggestion
is supported by the context of the law of the rebellious son, which immediately
follows a law protecting a son from being wronged by a father (21:15–17). Deuteronomy does not give parents unlimited rights over their children. Finally, while
the connection of the rebellious son with the rebellious nation provides some
justification for the harsh treatment of the son, it also provides some relief.[96]
As child of God, Israel is not utterly destroyed in the punishment for rebellion. A remnant is preserved, forgiven, and restored (e.g., Deut. 32:36–43; Isa.
30:18–26; and Jer. 3:11–18). This context of grace provides interpretive balance
and perhaps even an alternative for the harsh judgment on the rebellious son.

Within Deuteronomy, of course, the son's end is absolute. Since the disobedient son has broken the fifth commandment, his days are not long on the

95. So also Bellefontaine 1979, 18, 25–26; Pressler 1993, 18; Willis 2001, 182–85; Jungbauer
2002, 58.
96. Thanks to Peter Enns for pointing out the importance of this context.

land promised to Israel by God. This son has not listened to his parents and, in consequence, has not learned to fear Yahweh or keep his commandments. Faced with the repeated failure of their attempts to teach and discipline their son, the parents are given only one option: they must make a public accusation and thus turn their son over for execution. Although this situation seems abhorrent, in light of Deuteronomy's expectations for the role of the family in the covenant, the disobedient son receives his just deserts. His end is just because his behavior has been inconceivable.[97]

A Foolish Daughter

The female equivalent of the disobedient son appears in Deut. 22:13–21, which addresses the case of a bride accused by her new husband of not being a virgin at the time of their marriage. If the girl's parents can prove otherwise, the husband is punished. If no evidence of the daughter's virginity is available, however, she is judged guilty and stoned to death. This text comes first in a series of laws concerning rape and adultery, laws based on the expectation that a woman's first sexual partner would be her betrothed husband (vv. 22–29). This expectation reflects a concern with the honor and shame consequent upon male control of female sexuality. It also acts to ensure the paternity of any children, thus protecting the inheritance of the name and land of the man's family—the inheritance of Israelite identity.

The law of the foolish daughter resembles Deut. 21:18–21 in several respects.[98] The parents are involved, and the elders of the city judge the case. If guilty, the daughter is executed by stoning at the hands of the men of the city, and her death purges Israel of an evil. There are also significant differences between the two laws, resulting from the identity of the woman as daughter and wife. The role of the family in punishing the daughter is also more ambiguous than it is in the case of the son. What is made clear by the presence of these two laws in Deuteronomy is that sons and daughters are both able, though in quite different ways, to shame and distress their families and threaten the covenant community. Each is eligible to be killed for so doing.

Deuteronomy 22:13–21

13 If a man takes a wife and goes to her, but then hates her,

14 and accuses her of empty deeds[99] and gives her an evil name by saying, "I took this woman and lay with her,[100] but I did not find any evidence of virginity in her,"

97. See also Miller 1990, 166–67; and to some extent, Hagedorn 2000, 106.
98. Compare Epstein 1967, 206; Pressler 1993, 4; Rofé 2002, 179; Fleishman 2008, 200–207.
99. Literally, "places upon her deeds of words."
100. Literally, "came near to her" (וָאֶקְרַב אֵלֶיהָ, wā'eqrab 'ēlêhā).

15 then the father of the girl[101] and her mother will take and bring out the evidence of the girl's virginity to the elders of the city in the gate.

16 The father of the girl will say to the elders, "I gave my daughter to this man as a wife, but he hates her,

17 and behold, he has placed empty deeds [on her] by saying, 'I did not find evidence of virginity for your daughter.' This is the evidence of the virginity of my daughter." And they will spread out the cloth before the elders of the city.

18 And the elders of that city will take the husband and discipline him,

19 and they will make him pay one hundred pieces of silver, and they will give it to the father of the girl because he brought an evil name on a virgin of Israel. And she will be his wife; he cannot divorce her all his days.

20 But if this charge is true, and evidence of virginity is not found for the girl,

21 then they will bring the girl to the door of her father's house, and the men of her city will stone her with stones, and she will die because she has done a foolish thing in Israel to prostitute the house of her father. And you will destroy the evil from your midst.[102]

This passage describes two situations developing from a husband's accusation: the case of the slandering husband and the case of the foolish daughter.[103] The accused woman in this text goes from being a wife in the husband's speech to a girl (or young woman, נַעֲרָה, naʿărâ) to the narrator, to being a daughter in the father's speech. The shifting identity of the woman marks her confused place in society as a new wife, now linked to her husband's paternal household but also still a daughter tied to her own paternal household.[104] Like the son, the daughter has no voice of her own. Responsibility for her actions and character, even her very identity (based as it is on the identity of the speakers in this text), lies with the male authorities in her two households.[105]

101. Throughout Deut. 22:13–29, the MT is corrected from "young man" (נַעַר, naʿar), to "young woman" (נַעֲרָה, naʿărâ).

102. In the MT, a second-person masculine-singular pronominal suffix; second-person masculine-plural suffix in the LXX, Syriac, and T.Ps.-J. (cf. Deut. 21:21).

103. There is some debate over whether these are two separate laws or two potential outcomes of one law. See Ellens 2008, 224–26.

104. Compare Ellens 2008, 220. The involvement of two households may suggest that the husband's accusations cause social tension in the community (so Willis 2001, 228; Fleishman 2008, 197).

105. See Pressler 1993, 111. Stulman (1992, 62) argues that Deuteronomy gives women legal rights, taking "ownership" of them away from the men in their lives (so also Otto 2004, 136–37, on Deut. 22:13–21 specifically). These rights are not apparent in Deut. 22:13–21, where the voiceless woman is spoken for and about by her two patriarchs. While the case is public (Stulman 1992,

One of the most important distinctions between this law and the law of the disobedient son is the primary assumption that the accuser is lying.[106] In Deut. 21:18–21, the son has no opportunity to defend himself; no witnesses speak for him. In the case of the daughter, the parents are able to mount a defense. The first part of Deut. 22:13–21 describes the procedure for combating a false accusation of harlotry against a new wife. Just as Amnon hated Tamar once he had raped her (2 Sam. 13:15), a husband may hate his wife (אִשָּׁה, 'iššâ) once he has lain with her.[107] Because of his hatred, the husband accuses her of not having been a virgin at the time of her marriage. His accusation is described as an accusation of "deeds of words" (עֲלִילֹת דְּבָרִים, 'ălîlōt dĕbārîm, v. 14), which could indicate false behavior or equally a baseless accusation—deeds that are composed only of the husband's words. The parents' defense is a defense against slander and defamation.

Although based in the husband's attitude toward his wife rather than proof of unfaithfulness, the husband's slander is serious enough to threaten the wife with an evil name (שֵׁם רָע, šēm rā', v. 14). Names (or labels) are a serious business in the ancient world. How a person is known or identified in society can bring honor or shame to their family.[108] The law of levirate marriage in Deut. 25:5–10 provides a comparable example. The brother of an heirless dead man should beget a child with the dead man's wife in order to carry on the dead man's name in Israel. If the brother refuses to complete his duty, he receives a new name that would shame him and his household. So also the evil name given to the wife by her husband in 22:14 affects her family, thus leading to the public defense by the parents.

The involvement of the parents indicates the shame they would experience and the guilt they would bear for their daughter's empty deeds and evil name.[109] If the charge were true and the girl was not a virgin at the time of her marriage, the girl's paternal household would be shamed by her behavior, indicative of the parents' lack of control over her, and by their misrepresentation of her as a virgin.[110] Therefore it is the parents' responsibility to their own good name to retain the evidence of their daughter's virginity and to defend her character before the elders.[111]

The elders of the city first enter the story when the parents approach them to refute their son-in-law's slander. The audience of the husband's slander

---

57–58), the identification of the woman as wife and daughter indicates her dependence on men (see also Washington 2004, 210–11; Willis 2001, 225; Ellens 2008, 4–5, 13).

106. Compare Stulman 1992, 56; Rofé 2002, 173.

107. Hatred is connected with divorce in Deut. 24:1–4 (see Ellens 2008, 224). Note also the law protecting the rights of a hated wife and her son in Deut. 21:15–17.

108. Matthews and Benjamin 1991, 222–23.

109. So also Pressler 1993, 29; Frymer-Kensky 2004, 93.

110. Compare Philo, *Spec. Laws* 3.80–81; also Epstein 1967, 165; Benjamin 1983, 234; Tigay 1996, 206; and Fleishman 2008, 197.

111. Compare Matthews 2004, 109.

is not identified, and it is unclear if his accusation is official or gossip. The parents' appearance before the elders and the father's retelling of the girl's story, which turns out to be his story ("I gave my daughter . . ."), definitively brings the case to public notice. The parents' defense lies in their presentation of the evidence of their daughter's virginity (בְּתוּלִים, bĕtûlîm, v. 15). The word used here can simply mean virginity, as in verse 14.[112] In verse 17, the virginity of the girl is represented by a garment or cloth (שִׂמְלָה, śimlâ) spread before the elders. It is likely that this cloth, though not referred to elsewhere in the Hebrew Bible, is a bloodstained sheet or garment from the wedding night, publicly displayed as proof of the bride's prenuptial virginity (as is still the case in many parts of the world today).[113]

If the parents disprove the husband's slander, he is disciplined (יָסַר, yāsar) by the elders. It is possible that this discipline is a beating, as is the case in comparable laws from the ancient Near East.[114] In addition, as in Deut. 22:29, the husband is prohibited from ever divorcing his wife. The husband must also pay the girl's father one hundred pieces of silver, double the bride-price mentioned in Deut. 22:29. Because the false accusation dishonors the slandered bride's family, this particular punishment makes reparations to the entire household.[115]

While the father is repaid for the wrong done to him, his daughter only receives the assurance of a permanent household with a man who hates her.[116] Unlike the case of the rebellious son, though, there is at least opportunity in Deut. 22:13–19 for the evil laid on the woman's name to be cleared.[117] The parents are not accusing their daughter but defending her, and the woman in the end does not shame her father's house. In presuming on the husband's slander and the woman's innocence, this law protects the good names of the virgins of Israel, even if it is incidental to the protection of the names of their fathers.

The justice for the slandered woman in Deut. 22:13–19 (and for victims of rape in vv. 25–27) provides an important balance to the last two verses of the

---

112. Compare Lev. 21:13; Judg. 11:37–39. G. Wenham (1972, 326) suggests that the Hebrew word בְּתוּלָה (bĕtûlâ), from which "virginity," בְּתוּלִים (bĕtûlîm), in this text is derived, does not mean virgin but "a girl of marriageable age" who may or may not be a virgin. However, at least in Deut. 22:13–29 (as in Lev. 21:13–14 and Judg. 11:37–39), בְּתוּלָה and בְּתוּלִים clearly refer to a girl who is both a virgin and of marriageable age; cf. Pressler 1993, 26–27; Frymer-Kensky 2004, 79–80.

113. So too Pressler 1993, 26–27; but see also G. Wenham 1972, 334–35; Matthews 2004, 109.

114. See law 127 in the Code of Hammurabi (COS 2.131:335–53) and Middle Assyrian law 18 (COS 2.132:353–60); also Rofé 2002, 173.

115. On the basis of the punishment of the husband in Deut. 22:18–19, Benjamin (1983, 229–30) concludes that the law of false witness of Deut. 19:18–21 does not apply in situations where a man accuses a woman; Pressler (1993, 24) argues that 19:18–21 does not apply since the husband does not make an official accusation. Wells (2005, 56–70), on the other hand, suggests that the law of false witness is applied in Deut. 22:18–19: the husband seeks the refund of the bride-price and the humiliation of the bride's father, which is returned on his own head.

116. Though this situation may seem remarkably undesirable, Matthews (2004, 110) points out that the girl at least gets economic security.

117. As emphasized by Locher 1986, 382.

law, which consider the possibility that the woman is guilty: instead of "deeds of words" (v. 14), the "word" is true (v. 20). The woman can be condemned on the basis of the lack of positive evidence of her virginity. If evidence of her virginity is not "found," she is presumed guilty and executed.[118] Modern readers have wondered how the law could ever be instituted; surely the parents would simply fake the evidence if it was not available.[119] It seems that ancient readers had the same question. The rabbinic discussion of the slandered bride in *Sipre Deut.* 235–37 demands witnesses for both sides, and marriage regulations established in the *Damascus Document* require a father to tell a prospective suitor his daughter's defects (מום, *mûm*) in advance. In the case of a girl with a questionable reputation, trustworthy, experienced women should examine her before marriage.[120] This prenuptial examination presumably prevents the marriage of a nonvirgin as a virgin and thus preempts the accusation of Deut. 22:13–21. However, in Deuteronomy itself, since the local community's knowledge of the girl could provide some protection (as it could also stand in the way of faked evidence), the girl's condemnation depends on her husband's words and her parents' failure to produce evidence of her virginity rather than on positive proof of wrongdoing or on established behavioral patterns like those present in the case of the disobedient son.

In response to the charge, an unspecified group brings the girl to be stoned. This responsibility may rest on the elders, the men of the city involved in the execution, or as in the law of the disobedient son, one of the households wronged by the girl's action, either her father's or her husband's. The girl is executed at the door of her father's house. The disobedient son is stoned at the gate of the city; the public place of execution indicates the public nature of the problem. For the daughter to be stoned at the door of her father's house to some degree restricts the problem to her family. She has committed the shameful act while living in her father's house, and her father's house bears her shame.[121]

---

118. The punishment of the accused bride in Deuteronomy is significantly harsher than in equivalent ancient laws, including law 130 in the Code of Hammurabi (*COS* 2.131:335–53) and Ur-Nammu, law 6 (*COS* 2.153:408–10); cf. Middle Assyrian laws 12 and 55–56 (*COS* 2.132:353–60), and the extensive discussion of the comparative Near Eastern material in Locher 1986, helpfully summarized on 373–80, 385. In Deut. 22:20–21, the girl dies for lack of evidence, though there are no witnesses of the alleged crime (contra Otto 2004, 136). There is no wiggle room even for (e.g.) a girl who was a virgin but did not bleed on her wedding night or a girl who was raped (cf. Tigay 1996, 476; Rofé 2002, 174). See further Ellens 2008, 231–32.

119. See, e.g., Frymer-Kensky 1989, 93; 2004, 95; Tigay 1996, 476.

120. The text is preserved in 4Q271 3.7b–15; 4Q270 5.14–21; and 4Q269 9.1–7. See also 4Q159 2–4.8–10; Shemesh 1998, 253–54; Rofé 2002, 191; and Wassén 2005, 73–87.

121. So also Willis 2001, 226; Matthews 2004, 112. Alternatively, Fleishman (2008, 203–5) thinks the stoning of the girl "outside" her father's house indicates the separation of the girl from her family: she is "uprooted" from her people. Other references to the door of a house in the Hebrew Bible, though, suggest the identification of people located at the door with the household (cf. Gen. 43:19; 2 Sam. 11:9; Prov. 9:14).

The girl is executed because she has done a "foolish thing" (נְבָלָה, něbālâ).[122] Foolishness describes serious transgressions like taking something under ban (Josh. 7:15). It is often associated more specifically with sexual crimes like rape and adultery that bring dishonor and shame onto the victims and perpetrators (Gen. 34:7; Judg. 19:22–23; 20:6; 2 Sam. 13:12–13; Jer. 29:23). The foolishness (or shamefulness) of the girl in Deut. 22:20–21 is defined as prostituting (or harloting) the house of her father (לִזְנוֹת בֵּית אָבִיהָ, liznôt bêt 'ābîhā).[123] The shame is not perpetrated upon her, as in the case of rape; according to Deut. 22:21, *she* is the agent who brings shame on her father's house by engaging in sexual activity with a man who is not her betrothed husband.[124] The same charge of harlotry is brought on Tamar in Gen. 38 when she is found to be pregnant while living as a widow in her father's house. Her father-in-law orders that she be burned (v. 24). The daughter of a priest who acts as a prostitute, thus defiling her father, is also condemned to burn (Lev. 21:9). In each case, the shame of the woman extends to the men who should be in charge of her. The use of harlotry in Deut. 22:21 emphasizes again the dishonor the girl brings on her father's house.

The effect of the girl's execution on her father's household is not elaborated. The death of the girl might expiate the shame on the household (as Joseph Fleishman thinks),[125] but as a visible, audible sign of the father's lack of control over his household, it might also increase the shame. As in the case of the disobedient son, the girl's death purges evil from Israel (v. 21), a refrain echoed throughout the following laws concerning rape and adultery (vv. 22–24). The evil in these laws is not sex itself. In fact, Deuteronomy indirectly celebrates sex by identifying a wife's fertility (and the fertility of all female animals) as a blessing (7:12–16). It is important for a man to consummate his marriage and to give his wife joy (20:7; 24:5; 28:30). The problem in Deut. 22:20–24 lies in the timing and the identity of the partners. An unmarried girl living in

122. Alter (2004, 989) translates "foolishness" as "a scurrilous thing." Phillips (1975, 237–41) particularly focuses on foolishness as a form of social disruption.

123. "To prostitute" (זָנָה, zānâ) indicates illicit sex (see Bird 1993, 298–300). Fleishman (2008, 201) interprets "to prostitute" as a synonym of "to rebel" (סָרַר, sārar, Deut. 21:18); the daughter and the son commit the same wrong of challenging parental authority (cf. Kulp 2006, 35; Ellens 2008, 213).

124. Epstein (1967, 206) questions whether the sin is adultery (of a betrothed woman against her husband; cf. Deut. 22:23–24) or harlotry (of an unbetrothed girl against the father; cf. vv. 28–29). Willis (2001, 207–9) is likely right to see both issues in Deut. 22:13–21. More recently Fleishman (2008, 192–95) has argued that the unbetrothed girl who engages in sexual intercourse has not done wrong (though see also 207); I assume that even an unbetrothed girl owes sexual fidelity to her potential future mate to protect his name, inheritance, and honor, as well as owing obedience to the father in authority over her. See also the compelling argument of Ellens (2008, 189–234) that in Deut. 22:13–30 (22:13–23:1 MT), a woman's sexuality is the property of her patriarch, whether that is her father or husband (cf. Bird 1993, 298; Fuchs 2000, 116). Keefe (2008, 118–19) also draws attention to the communal significance of sex in ancient Israel.

125. Fleishman 2008, 205.

her father's house should not be sexually active. If she is, she dishonors her father and mother by challenging their authority over her body. If betrothed, she is also guilty of marital infidelity. The foolishness in Deut. 22:20–21 is the breaking of both the seventh commandment, the prohibition of adultery, and the fifth commandment, honor of parents. Comparable with 21:18–21, the evil in Israel arises from the girl's disregard for authority in the household and wider community.[126]

Tikva Frymer-Kensky argues that control over the sexuality of women is the only factor at stake in laws like Deut. 22:13–21.[127] This is a key to understanding the text. But in Deuteronomy, another factor does come into play. Israelite identity, membership in the covenant people of Yahweh, is a birthright, and controlling the sexuality of an unmarried girl, whether betrothed or not, relates directly to women's responsibility for reproduction.[128] A woman's fidelity to her husband before and after marriage ensures the paternity of any children, an understanding reinforced by the (divine) punishment of a wife suspected by a jealous husband of adultery in Num. 5:11–31.[129] According to this law, which bears some resemblance to Deut. 22:13–21, a woman guilty of adultery will be cursed with infertility, unable to bear either a legitimate heir or an illegitimate child. The bride executed for foolishness in Deut. 22:21 is likewise prevented from bearing another man's child, and thus also from corrupting her husband's family lineage.

Inheritance is a significant factor in Deuteronomy. Moses repeatedly reminds his audience within the story that the land about to be given to them by God was promised to their ancestors Abraham, Isaac, and Jacob (1:21; 4:1; 6:10, 18; etc.). The promise was handed down through the generations to reach the people in Moses's audience, those who will finally take possession of the land. There is a sense in which God is also inherited through the generations: the God of the ancestors has become the God of the current generation as well (1:10; 4:31; 7:8; etc.). Covenant identity and all that goes with it passes from parent to child by both instruction and inheritance. It is important for each

126. So also Stulman 1990, 622–23; Pressler 1993, 30–31; Frymer-Kensky 2004, 95. Cf. Fleishman 2008, 196–97, 199.

127. Frymer-Kensky 2004, 80–81, 84–85. See also Washington 2004, 210–11; Ellens 2008, 190, 207, 299. Frymer-Kensky specifically argues against the assumption that paternity is an issue in Deut. 22:13–21, suggesting that a baby born too soon to be of the husband's begetting could simply be raised by the daughter's family; although an eminently practical solution, there is no evidence for this in any text, and at least in Deuteronomy's ideal Israel (if not in the practices of actual ancient Israelites), paternity is too theologically significant to be discarded.

128. Compare Phillips 1975, 239; Matthews 1994, 8; 2004, 108; C. Anderson 2004, 80; Ellens 2008, 324.

129. On the similarities between Deut. 22:20–21 and Num. 5:11–31, see Willis 2001, 209. The distinction between the two lies in the motivation for punishment: in Deuteronomy it is the husband's accusation that has been "proved" by the absence of contrary evidence, but in Numbers it is his unconfirmable jealousy.

ancestral house to retain their land as the tangible sign of their share in the covenant. This desire undergirds property laws and the practice of levirate marriage (5:21; 19:14; 25:5–10), and it is likely that the law of 22:13–21 is also motivated in part by the need to protect the family's inheritance.[130] Therefore, in addition to challenging community authority, the evil in Deut. 22:13–21 also threatens the covenant as it passes from one generation to the next.

Finally, as with the disobedient son, the danger posed by the daughter's wrongdoing is strengthened by the language used of the people's relationship to Yahweh and to other gods. Like the foolish daughter, Israel foolishly rebels against their loving father in Deut. 32:6, 15. Israel's foolishness, of course, lies in turning from Yahweh to foreign gods, an act identified as harlotry (זָנָה, zānâ) in 31:16. Throughout the Torah, Israel is warned against and prohibited from prostituting themselves by worshiping gods other than Yahweh (Exod. 34:15–16; Lev. 17:7; 20:5–6; etc.).[131] This metaphor is extended to identify Israel as God's wife, unfaithful to her husband by taking other gods and foreign nations as lovers.[132] The broader context of Deut. 22:20–21 in the book and the canon as a whole allows for the foolish bride and daughter, like the disobedient son, to be seen as a symbol of Israel. The girl's infidelity is evil because it represents Israel's faithlessness to God. As Israel will suffer punishment for her foolishness, so also the girl is executed for her crime against family, society, and God.

Parents and Children in Deuteronomy and Beyond

Many interpreters have identified the community's involvement in disciplining wives and children in Deut. 21:18–21 and 22:13–21 as a limitation of the power of the patriarch and the local community in favor of a centralized state. The argument is that originally in the ancient societies that produced these texts, a patriarch would have had the right of life over his household, being able to put to death a member of the household who had disobeyed or shamed him without consulting anyone else. In Deuteronomy, the state attempts to take control of the household by giving patriarchal power to other, extrahousehold authorities like the elders, who act as representatives of the state. The move toward the centralized state is identified as one of the key purposes of Deuteronomy overall, extended in 21:18–21 and 22:13–21 into the household itself.[133]

130. Compare Phillips 1975, 239; C. Anderson 2004, 80.

131. Idolatrous worship can include literal adultery: the story of the golden calf in Exod. 32 may connect idolatry with sex (cf. "playing," צָחַק, ṣḥq, in v. 6), and in Num. 25, the Israelites' participation in the cult of Baal includes sexual relationships with foreign women.

132. Compare Judg. 2:17; Jer. 2:20; Ezek. 6:9; Hosea 1:2; etc. See esp. Bird (1993, 300–308) and Keefe (2008, 120–25) on Hosea; and Fishbane (1999, 495–97) and Milgrom (1999, 479) on prophetic imagery relating to adultery in Num. 5:11–31.

133. So Clements 1989, 65; Steinberg 1991, 163–65; Stulman 1992, 55, 57, 60–61; Dion 1993, 81.

Some fundamental questions can be raised about this assumption with regard to the laws of the rebellious son and foolish daughter. First, as Timothy Willis points out, the elders who witness the cases are themselves patriarchs.[134] Their involvement in judging other men's disobedient sons, daughters, and wives does not limit patriarchal power, but rather enforces the rights of the fathers in the community to determine issues of local concern. Second, the laws of Deut. 21:18–21 and 22:13–21 could be broken by fathers' executions of their own children, or the husband's execution of his wife, without official communal acquiescence. The laws would also be broken, however, if the father did not take his disobedient son to the elders for judgment, or if the husband who felt himself wronged by an unchaste bride did not make an accusation in the first place. Deuteronomy may legislate these two situations not to control patriarchs but to ensure that they do exercise their power.[135]

There is no reason to assume that these laws were more easily accepted by ancient Israelites than they are by modern readers. The history of interpretation of these laws indicates over and over again that ancient readers also struggled with these texts. Fathers in the old days loved their children and would not have wanted to initiate their execution; in this regard, it is notable that, unlike Deut. 13:6–11, the Hebrew Bible preserves no narratives in which a rebellious son or foolish daughter is punished to death by their parents. Rather, there are stories like Gen. 38, in which an apparently foolish daughter is justified and saved from execution, or 2 Sam. 13–19, in which David fails to punish his sons even when they rebel to the extent of instigating political coups against him. Patriarchs would also have wanted to avoid the shame of a public admission of their inability to control their households.[136] The interpretation of Deut. 21:18–21 in *Targum Pseudo-Jonathan* makes this shame readily apparent: the parents confess to the elders that they themselves have broken the law in their son's disobedience (v. 20). They are as guilty as their son, and perhaps more so, because they have not taught him to keep the law.

The presence of the laws of the stubborn, rebellious son and the unchaste daughter in the Torah provides incentive to children and parents, wives and husbands, to live in such a way that the laws need not be implemented.[137] These laws would encourage parents in particular to use their power from the beginning to teach and discipline their children to be faithful members of the community. Likewise, children would be encouraged to obey their parents, learning the traditions of Israel so that they could take their proper places as the fathers and mothers of a new generation. In the end, however, families

---

134. Willis 2001, 176.

135. Compare Pressler 1993, 17, tentatively; also note Frymer-Kensky 1996, 55, 69–70.

136. See also Hagedorn 2000, 113–15; Willis 2001, 178.

137. For Frymer-Kensky (1989, 93), Tigay (1996, 477), and Hagedorn (2000, 115), these laws were never intended to be used; their purpose was only to deter the behaviors they condemn.

that fail to heed the warning implicit in Deut. 21:18–21 and 22:13–21 are faced with the destructive violence of killing their sons and daughters.

Israel's Wisdom Tradition

The wisdom traditions preserved in Proverbs implicitly support an admonitory use of Deut. 21:18–21. In Proverbs, parents are instructed to teach and discipline their sons to save their lives and the family's honor. While Proverbs does not explicitly, unambiguously refer to Deut. 21:18–21, the language, theology, and social construction of family life in the book reflect elements of Deuteronomy's ideal Israel.[138] In fact, the law codes and wisdom literature are not as different as might be thought, concerned as they are with directing behavior.[139] Of particular importance for Deut. 21:18–21 is the ideal family life set forth in Proverbs: parents teach their sons to live wisely, and in response sons respect, honor, and obey their parents, so embodying the life of wisdom.[140] Wisdom is attained precisely through the instruction and discipline given by the parents.

The understanding of wisdom presented in Proverbs, especially in chapters 1–9, is comparable with the law and covenant in Deuteronomy.[141] For Deuteronomy, a long, prosperous life in the promised land rewards obedience to the covenant in general and to parents in specific (4:40; 5:16, 29; 6:3; etc.). In Proverbs, a long, prosperous life is the outcome of the search for wisdom (9:10–11), and thus also of honoring, respecting, and obeying parents (3:1–2; 4:10; 23:22–25). Just as Deuteronomy's Israelites should continually recite the law, wear it on their bodies, and write it on their houses (Deut. 6:6–9), so in Prov. 6:20–23; 7:1–5, a wise son will adorn himself with, converse with, walk with, and befriend the instructions of the parents (cf. 1:8–9; 3:3). Keeping the covenant provides the foundation for good community life in Deuteronomy; in Proverbs, seeking and living by wisdom lead to an orderly household, personal success, and communal harmony.

138. Compare Kidner 1964, 52; Malfroy 1965, 59; W. Brown 2005, 274–78.
139. See esp. Weinfeld 1983, 161–64, 244–68; Callaway 1984, 348–52; Jungbauer 2002, 57–58; W. Brown 2005, 253–54. The earliest traditions in Proverbs may come from the eighth century or even as early as Solomon; the final redaction of Proverbs was completed at the latest in the third century, prior to the writing of Sirach. See further Clifford 1999, 3–6; Fox 2000, 6–11; Perdue 2000, 1–3.
140. Proverbs is presented as a book of wisdom taught by a father to his son (note esp. chaps. 1–9; 19:27; 23:15; 24:13; 27:11), and in the last chapter a mother teaches her son. On the reality of this language, see Malfroy 1965, 59; Whybray 1994, 8; Estes 1997, 47–48, 94–95; Yoder 2005, 170. The "son" is clearly a son, not a gender-neutral child.
141. So also Fishbane 1977, 284; Overland 2000, 434–35; W. Brown 2005, 274–78. Proverbs frequently refers to law or instruction, torah (תּוֹרָה, tôrâ), which most interpreters understand to be teaching or advice (so, e.g., Toy 1904, xv; Kidner 1964, 51; Clifford 1999, 5), though W. Brown (2005, 278–80) argues that the Mosaic law is presupposed in Proverbs (cf. Brooks 2007, 20–23).

If the wise son in Proverbs resembles the ideal, obedient Israelite of Deuteronomy, the foolish son of Proverbs can be compared with the rebellious, stubborn son of Deut. 21:18–21. This son's foolishness lies in ignoring his parents' instruction and rejecting their discipline (Prov. 5:12–13; 13:1; 15:5). He dishonors, shames, and grieves his parents (10:1, 5; 17:2, 21, 25; 19:13; and also 28:7, where the shame relates to gluttony). He may even harm his parents by cursing, mistreating, or robbing them (19:26; 20:20; 28:24; 30:11, 17). This son's end is his own destruction, vividly depicted as careening through the inviting home (or body) of the adulteress, folly personified, into Sheol (2:16–19; 5:1–14; 7:10–27; 29:3; etc.).[142] Over and over again, the foolish son provides the counterpoint to the wise child. The resulting picture of the two sons acts as a rhetorical spur to the reader to be wise, thus avoiding the shame and pain that the fool experiences. It also motivates parents to raise wise sons, in whom they can rejoice and by whom they will be honored.

To aid in this process, parents are encouraged to discipline their children physically with a rod (שֵׁבֶט, šēbeṭ) in order to teach them obedience in Prov. 13:24; 22:15; 23:13–14.[143] The rod of discipline bears some affinity with the rod used to punish wrongdoing in Ps. 89:32 (33 MT) and Isa. 11:4, but it is more reflective of 2 Sam. 7:14: God promises to be a father to David's heir, specifically by correcting his wrongs with a rod and with blows. In Proverbs, this rod is the physical companion to the parents' instruction, intended to train a child.[144] As such, the use of the rod is motivated by the search for wisdom. The purpose of the parents' physical discipline is made explicit in Prov. 22:15: the rod drives out the folly bound in the child's heart, presumably leaving space for the binding of the parents' teachings in folly's place (cf. 6:20–22). Like the instruction of a child, physical discipline occurs within the context of, and even is an expression of, parental love. "The one who holds back his rod hates his son, but the one who loves him is diligent in disciplining him" (Prov. 13:24).[145]

Training a son through verbal instruction and physical discipline moves the child from folly to wisdom (29:15). Since folly ends with destruction and wisdom is rewarded with a prosperous life, discipline itself can be associated

---

142. Folly, the most problematic woman of Proverbs, is not condemned as is the new bride of Deut. 22:20–21, despite the common denominator of foolish faithlessness (note that Deuteronomy's word for the bride's folly, נְבָלָה [nĕbālâ], does not appear in Proverbs, which uses כְּסִילוּת [kĕsîlût] and אִוֶּלֶת ['iwwelet]); while the strange woman does end up in Sheol in Prov. 5:5, how she gets there is not explained. Proverbs remains focused on the son (e.g., 6:32–35; 7:22–27), mentioning daughters and wives only in passing (12:4; 18:22; 19:13–14; 30:15; 31:29). On the women of Proverbs, see further Camp 1997b, 93–94; Clifford 1993, 61, 69–72, etc.

143. "Discipline" (מוּסָר, mûsār), includes both teaching (as in Prov. 1:2–3) and chastisement or rebuking (13:24; 15:10). Sometimes it is difficult to determine which meaning is intended (as in 5:12; 10:17; 19:18). See Shupak 1987, 107–11; W. Brown 2008, 69–70.

144. Cf. Whybray 1994, 64; E. Davis 2000, 88; Heskett 2001, 182–83; W. Brown 2008, 71–72.

145. Alternatively, the second half of the verse may refer to disciplining the child from a young age. See further Whybray 1994, 210; Heim 2001, 169.

with life, and a lack of discipline with death. Exactly this is claimed in Prov. 5:23; 10:17; and 15:10. The connection carries over into the parental disciplining of sons so that, somewhat paradoxically, beating a child gives life in place of death. Parents are instructed to discipline sons instead of desiring or seeking their deaths (19:18). Furthermore, striking a son with the rod will not kill him but save him from Sheol (23:13–14).[146] The language of these two texts bears some resemblance to Deut. 21:18–21, which raises interesting questions for their interpretation. Is the death the parents are not to seek in Prov. 19:18 the execution of the son in Deut. 21:21? It is possible that this is the case. Parents should discipline their sons from a young age (while there is hope) precisely so that they need not make use of the law of the stubborn, rebellious son.[147]

On a literal level, the assertion in Prov. 23:13–14 that disciplining and striking a child will give life, not death, is questionable. A beaten slave does die in Exod. 21:20, and the imagery of striking with a rod in Isa. 11:4 is paralleled with killing the wicked. Beating a child with a rod could likewise lead to physical death. In the theological framework of Proverbs, though, beating a child to death would be preferable to allowing their folly to lead them straight to Sheol. Beating a son destroys the folly that would be his death: the beating saves the child's life.[148]

Proverbs bears consistent witness to the effectiveness of discipline, be it parental, divine, or personal, in the form of instruction and beating. It is through discipline that the son is trained to live rightly before God. Thus it is through discipline that the son truly lives. The purpose of discipline in Proverbs reflects the values undergirding Deut. 21:18–21. A disciplined son will show his discipline by honoring and obeying his parents, thereby fulfilling his social and theological responsibilities in the covenant community. In contrast, an undisciplined son is a disruptive force, and the community's salvation comes through his death.

Parents and Children, Husbands and Wives

The laws of Deut. 21:18–21 and 22:20–21 are not pleasant. They detail punishments that are abhorrent to natural instincts of familial care. Husbands

---

146. This proverb closely resembles *Ahiqar* 6:80–82. Direct borrowing from this sixth- to fifth-century BCE Aramaic source is possible, but the similarity may also reflect common Near Eastern values and expectations of the relationship between parents and children.

147. So Murphy 1998, 145; P. Wegner 2005, 724–28. On the other hand, McKane (1970, 534) and Heim (2001, 264) suggest that the son in Proverbs dies because of his own foolishness, a state that would have been rectified by parental discipline.

148. See also Kidner 1964, 51; E. Davis 2000, 125; P. Wegner 2005, 723–25. In this regard, Waltke (2005, 23) suggests that the death in mind in Prov. 23:13–14 is the metaphorical death of separation from God. Though this line of interpretation is often carried out in order to defend Proverbs against accusations of child abuse (as in P. Wegner 2005), it is possible that Proverbs' presentation of discipline is motivated by the desire to save the son from spiritual death.

should not slander their wives, particularly when the slander may lead to a wrongful death. Parents should not allow their daughters to be executed; they should not actively hand their sons over to the community to be stoned. The expansive explanations of disciplining sons in Proverbs are little better: the discipline could too quickly become abuse. It is easy to label these laws and wisdom texts as examples of the tyranny of an authoritarian, patriarchal society, created by the men in charge to protect their own privileged position within society at the expense of family and of the lives of the underlings in their household. It is natural to fear the abuse of these laws and to question the fairness of laws that demand the death penalty without giving the condemned (the victim, we might say) a chance to defend herself or himself. By modern standards, or at least by modern Western standards, the laws and wisdom texts examined here are morally suspect.

The challenge for us, as is also the case with Deut. 13:6–11, is to understand and appreciate the value of the community in Deuteronomy. Deuteronomy and indeed the whole of the Hebrew Bible do display a regard for good, close, caring relationships within a household. The laws in Deuteronomy that protect unloved sons and the honor of women reflect this concern (21:10–17; 22:13–19, 25–27). These relationships, however, take second place to the life of the community. Deuteronomy projects a vision of the ideal community composed of Israelites who keep the covenant with Yahweh. The covenant is central and essential to Israel's identity as the people of God. The laws of Deuteronomy seek to protect the covenant, even at the expense of parental and marital responsibilities of love and care.

Understanding Constructive Family Violence in Deuteronomy

For Deuteronomy, the covenant determines identity: those who keep the covenant by obeying the law of Moses are Israelites. Since the covenant is passed on by inheritance and teaching, Israelite identity is also inherited and taught in each new generation. This identity is communal. The covenant is lived by the community, kept in community, and passed on through communal relationships. Each Israelite is called to live in and for the community, and each Israelite's sin potentially endangers the entire community. The elevation of the community over the individual provides an important context for understanding the laws demanding the execution of family members in Deut. 13:6–11; 21:18–21; and 22:13–21.

Deuteronomy's construction of family life provides another key to understanding violence against family members. The family is the agent of the covenant. The covenant is inherited through families, and it is in the family that children learn the covenant. In daily life, celebrations, and worship, the family together keeps the covenant. The family embodies Israel in covenant with Yahweh. Because of the centrality of the family in the covenant, the laws of Deuteronomy protect the family from internal and external disruption. And precisely because of the importance of the family in the life cycle of the covenant, family members are instructed to deliver sons, daughters, wives, brothers, and other relatives who threaten the covenant over for judgment and execution.

The horror of these commands is balanced by several internal and external factors. Most obvious is the assumption of the daughter's innocence in Deut. 22:13–19. Context is also important. The law of the foolish daughter is followed by a law protecting (some) victims of rape, and the law of the rebellious son immediately follows a law protecting a son's rights against patriarchal abuse. Furthermore, Deuteronomy's positive expectations for family life appear, ironically enough, even within the very laws that demand the death of family members: the pity of 13:8 (9 MT), the parental instruction and discipline of 21:18, 20, and the defense of the daughter in 22:15–17. Finally, hope for the repentance, forgiveness, and restoration of the nation following their punishment for breaking the covenant runs through Deuteronomy. By virtue of the parallels and connections between individuals and the nation, this hope demands a measure of grace for the treasonous or rebellious family member. These factors provide an interpretive framework that balances the bleak commands to kill.

In the end, however, the laws of Deut. 13:6–11; 21:18–21; and 22:13–21 remain absolute. They demand the destruction of the family—the center of the covenant community—from within. But they can be understood within the book's construction of Israelite identity. The extreme punishment meted out to family tempters, disobedient sons, and promiscuous daughters and brides is an extension of Deuteronomy's subordination of the individual to the community. The condemned threaten the covenant community, and for Deuteronomy and its canonical echoes, loyalty to the entire community is more important than loyalty to an errant member of the household.

For Deuteronomy, the enemy within is not always an act of violence against a family member (but see 12:31; 18:9–12). The enemy within is a member of the household, someone who should be an Israelite, who instead rejects what Deuteronomy posits as the ideal for Israelite identity. This enemy endangers the family and the community as a whole by worshiping idols and attempting to spread idolatry in Israel, by refusing to learn to be an Israelite, and by bringing inheritance into question. For the good of the family and the covenant community, this enemy must be destroyed.

3

Constructive Family Violence
in Hellenistic Palestine

The process of defining Israelite identity and identifying insiders and outsiders remains a key concern in the Second Temple period. This period began in 515 BCE, when Judeans who returned from Babylonian exile under Cyrus of Persia finished rebuilding the temple in Jerusalem. For the next three and a half centuries, the Jews in Palestine lived first under Persian rule and then, after 332 BCE, under Greek rule represented by Alexander the Great and his successors, the Ptolemies of Egypt and Seleucids of Syria. Until the Hasmonean Revolt gained political independence for the Jews of Palestine in the mid-second century BCE, the returned exiles remained part of "foreign" empires.[1]

Living under foreign rule brings Judeans into contact with other cultures, a natural process intensified by Greek foreign policy.[2] Alexander the Great deliberately exported Hellenistic ways of life along with political control. Jews in Palestine in the fourth and third centuries BCE would have experienced increasing contact with Hellenistic culture through local government, trade, and simply living next door to Greeks. Evidence of the influence of Hellenism

1. There is a notable difficulty in nomenclature for the people of God in this era, in which "Jew" is being created and defined. I will use "Jew" and "Jewish" as a convenient shorthand for Judean people and traditions in this period, though recognizing that the terms may be anachronistic.

2. Extensive contact with foreign peoples began long before the Persian and Hellenistic eras (and indeed would never have been absent), but it was strengthened during this time by the presence of foreign rulers, armies, merchants, and others within Palestine itself.

in Palestine comes from the appearance of Greek-style houses, public build-
ings, and city designs in the archaeological record; translations of Hebrew
texts into Greek and the composition of legal documents and other writings
in Greek; and the presence of Greek values and customs in Second Temple
texts. At the least, Jews living under Greek rule would have adopted a Greek
social veneer to communicate, work, trade, and coexist in the new political
environment across the Near East.[3]

A range of responses to the integration of Hellenistic culture into Jewish
ways of life is evident in texts from this period. In Sirach, the wisdom tradition of Proverbs is adapted to instruct God's people in how to live in a Greek
world. While the book is not uncritically accepting of a Greek lifestyle (cf.
19:24), the influence of Greek culture is evident throughout, most obviously in
the overriding emphasis on honor and shame. Within Sirach's construction of
a wise, honorable lifestyle, discipline is used to control the natural proclivities
of sons and daughters to shame their father. Constructive family violence in
Sirach protects the honor of the patriarch.

Fierce rhetoric in other texts rejects "Hellenism" as an appropriate lifestyle
for God's people.[4] In 1 Maccabees and *Jubilees*, the situation in Second Temple
Palestine under the rule of Alexander and his successors embodies the most
feared danger of Deuteronomy: contact with other peoples and other ways of
life corrupts the identity of Israel as God's people. Jews who adopt foreign ways
thus become the enemy within. Biblical traditions of constructive family violence
are used in 1 Macc. 1–2 to justify violence against Israelites who collaborate
with foreigners. *Jubilees* likewise incorporates laws requiring constructive family violence against those who take on foreign ways, but within its narratives,
constructive violence fails to protect Israelite identity. For *Jubilees*, in the end
the enemy without is the appropriate object of violence, not the enemy within.

These three texts provide a witness to developments in the traditions of
constructive family violence in the Second Temple period rather than explicit
commentaries on Deut. 13:6–11; 21:18–21; or 22:13–21. In Sirach and 1 Maccabees, allusions to biblical constructive family violence, including the laws of
Deuteronomy, appear in the language, structure, and themes of certain texts.
These allusions primarily support the arguments and purposes of Sirach and
1 Maccabees, but they also reflect on and expand the tradition of constructive family violence.[5] *Jubilees*, an example of rewritten Torah, draws on the
thought, theology, and sometimes vocabulary of Deuteronomy, but rarely

3. On the influence of Hellenistic culture in Greek, Ptolemaic, and Seleucid Palestine, see
the classic work of Hengel 1974, esp. 32–57 and all chap. 2; Halpern-Zylberstein 1989, 13–30;
J. Collins 1997, 25–27.

4. Of course, the rejection of "Hellenism" is idealized. In reality, all Jews would have been
affected to a greater or lesser extent by Hellenistic culture; cf. Rajak 1990, 267–71; S. Schwartz
2001, 34–36; etc.

5. On the purpose of allusion, see Sommer 1998, 29–30.

echoes or alludes to 13:6–11; 21:18–21; or 22:13–21. The influence of biblical traditions of constructive family violence is nonetheless notable in the themes and concerns of several stories and laws in *Jubilees*, reinterpreted and at some points challenged as they become part of a new tradition.[6]

This chapter will first address Sirach, the earliest text and the only one written under unopposed foreign rule. Though it likely postdates *Jubilees*, 1 Maccabees comes next as an introduction to the use of violence in the Hasmonean era, followed by the alternative to this violence presented in *Jubilees*. These three texts stem from the same century, but they contain mixed messages about the use of constructive family violence. This contrast provides fruitful ground for the investigation of the development of the tradition.

Controlling the Family in Sirach

Sirach, also known as Ben Sira and Ecclesiasticus, was composed in Hebrew in Palestine around 180 BCE and translated into Greek in Egypt soon afterward.[7] The author of Sirach adapted the social constructs and theology of Proverbs to speak to the experience of the wealthy, educated Hellenistic-era Jewish man.[8] Included in the guidelines given to these patriarchs is ample instruction in how to control their households, including their wives, children, and slaves.

For Sirach, as for Proverbs, wisdom comes from knowing God and studying the Mosaic law (6:37; 24:23–29; 45:1–5).[9] Sirach's search for wisdom, however, is motivated by the acquisition of honor and avoidance of shame (cf. 10:19–31; 15:1–6). Honor and shame are values known in many ancient Mediterranean societies, including ancient Israel, but Sirach's explicit, emphatic interest in honor and shame exceeds biblical and other Second Temple texts, reflecting the stronger focus on honor and shame in Greek culture.[10] In addition to the search for wisdom, these cultural values also motivate the patriarch's strict authority over his household: the behavior of his wife, sons, and daughters reflects honor or shame onto him (cf. 16:1–4; 22:3–5, 7–8 [LXX]; 26:1–27; 42:9–14), and therefore the patriarch must control the members of his family.[11]

For Sirach, an ideal, honorable family maintains a proper hierarchy of authority within the household. In the extended meditation on the fifth

---

6. Compare Sommer 1998, 25–27, on textual influence as interpretation.

7. Sirach's textual history is confused, to say the least; see Skehan and DiLella 1987, 52–56; B. Wright 1989, 4–5; etc.

8. See esp. J. Collins 1997, 24–41; also Blenkinsopp 1995, 80; Horsley 2005, 125–28; B. Wright 2005, 106–11.

9. Compare Rogers 2004, 116–19.

10. See J. Collins 1997, 34, 77. Alternatively, DeSilva (1996, 435–38) identifies Sirach's focus on honor and shame as a reaction against Hellenistic culture.

11. For Camp (1997a, 173), control of self, household, and property is the essence of honor in Sirach.

commandment in 3:1–16, parents are identified as God's representatives in the household. As such, God demands that children honor and obey their parents throughout life. Between fathers and mothers, of course, the patriarch is the absolute authority. The insistence on the patriarch as the head and public face of the household differentiates the book from Proverbs and Deuteronomy, which also give a voice and public presence to the patriarch's wife.[12] This difference may correlate with the shift to a wealthy, urbanized, hellenized society.[13] In Sirach's social milieu, the male head of house is its representative and primary means of support. Women can therefore be presented as sequestered, ornamental ideals rather than contributors to the life of the household.

The patriarch's privileged position in the household does not give him the right to do as he pleases. Sirach warns that his treatment of the members of his household will reflect on him (7:18–28). Therefore, (elderly) parents should be honored; good and faithful friends, brothers, wives, slaves, and livestock should be cared for and nurtured. They will bring the patriarch honor and wealth. Children, however, should be controlled and disciplined from an early age (v. 23). Daughters are particularly singled out for the patriarch's notice. He must guard their bodies, a theme to which the book returns repeatedly, and he should not favor them (vv. 24–25). In contrast to the other close associates of the patriarch, including his livestock, it is notable that this text does not require the patriarch's respect or care for his children, but only his watchful control. Sons and daughters are peculiarly important in Sirach as sources of potential honor or shame, and in response fathers are exhorted to strictly discipline their children.[14]

Controlling Daughters and Sons in Sirach

According to Sir. 7:24–25, daughters must be physically guarded, controlled, and restricted lest they shame their fathers with their bodies through unsanctioned sexual activity.[15] This possibility is presented as a virtual certainty in the vivid metaphors of 26:10–12: a headstrong daughter will sin against her father by seducing any man who passes by. Again in 42:9–14, the worries a man will

12. In Sirach, mothers do not support the family financially, teach their sons, or appear outside their households. Even Lady Wisdom is restricted to the house or temple. In his study of women in Sirach, Trenchard (1982, e.g., 2) concludes that the author was a misogynist. Though his study could be more nuanced by contextualizing Sirach's comments on women within the presentation of other household underlings (sons and slaves), Trenchard is surely right to see an overall negative trend in Sirach's view of women (contra Gilbert 1976, 440–42).

13. See Camp 1991, 21; Snaith 1995, 171.

14. This control is violent, but not to the point of execution; whether or not Jews in Sirach's day had the legal right to carry out an execution is debated (see Trenchard 1982, 106–7; J. Collins 1997, 70–72).

15. Camp (1997a, 182) suggests that the strange woman of Prov. 1–9 moves inside the home in Sirach. The place of female sexuality in an honor-and-shame culture is explored in Skehan and DiLella 1987, 312; Camp 1997a, 175–76; Fontaine 2002, 25–26.

have over his daughter concern her sexuality. She may not get married; if she does, her husband might hate her or she might turn out to be barren. Even more troubling, she could offer proof of her fertility while still living in her father's house or commit adultery while in her husband's. And if she is known to be promiscuous, her father will be shamed by his daughter's dishonor and his own disgraceful inability to control her.

The list of concerns in Sir. 42:9–10 repeatedly alludes to Deut. 22:13–21.[16] First, the father fears that his daughter's husband might hate her. Omitting the possibility that the husband's hatred is baseless, Sirach then warns that the daughter may be found not to be a virgin by the very obvious sign of pregnancy while still living under her father's roof. In 42:13, the daughter's promiscuity is identified as an example of the evil of women, perhaps the same evil ascribed to the daughter in Deut. 22:21. Finally, the shame the daughter implicitly casts on her father's house in Deuteronomy is made explicit in Sir. 42:11, 14 (cf. 22:5).[17]

These similarities draw the instructions guiding fathers' treatment of their daughters in Sir. 42:11–12 into conversation with Deut. 22:13–21. Instead of violent punishment in response to wrongdoing, though, Sirach focuses on preventive discipline: fathers should physically restrict their daughters, guarding them and limiting their experience of society outside and even inside the home so that they do not learn the "evil of woman" (πονηρία γυναικός, *ponēria gynaikos*, Sir. 42:13).[18] In this way, daughters can be kept from dishonoring their fathers. Since the shame of the daughter is embodied, so should her discipline be.

The son of Deut. 21:18–21 makes an appearance in Sirach's descriptions of an undisciplined son, but fewer words or themes from Deuteronomy are used in Sir. 30:1–13 than in 42:9–14. The instructions for disciplining sons rather add to the general tradition of constructive violence, emphasizing in particular the need for preventive physical discipline even for very young sons. In Sir. 30:1–13, fathers are told to teach and beat their sons into obedient, honorable mirror images of themselves. The father of such a son will rejoice and glory in him. If the father does his job well, he will live on after death in the person of his son (vv. 1–6).[19] Physical discipline here is motivated by the father's desire to re-create

---

16. Note the linguistic echoes of father and daughter, living with (συνοικέω, *synoikeō*), hating (μισέω, *miseō*), virginity (παρθενία, *parthenia*), girl (νεᾶνις, *neanis*), and father's house (οἶκος πατρός, *oikos patros*), from Deut. 22:13–21 (LXX) in Sir. 42:9–10a: "A daughter is a secret anxiety to her father, and worry over her robs him of sleep; when she is young [νεότης, *neotēs*], for fear she may not marry, or if married [συνοικέω], for fear she may be disliked [μισέω]; while a virgin [παρθενία], for fear she may be seduced and become pregnant in her father's house [πατρικός, *patrikos*]; or having a husband, for fear she may go astray" (NRSV).

17. Compare also the evil name (ὄνομα πονηρόν, *onoma ponēron*) and empty deeds (προφασιστικοὶ λόγοι, *prophasistikoi logoi*) given to the bride in Deut. 22:14 LXX, with the father made a "laughingstock" (ἐπίχαρμα, *epicharma*), "byword" (λαλιά, *lalia*), and object of shame by the daughter's behavior in Sir. 42:11 NRSV.

18. Cf. Gilbert 1976, 439–40.

19. Cf. Skehan and DiLella 1987, 376.

his own identity and name in the person of his son. In addition to the avoidance of the shame and grief consequent upon a lack of discipline (vv. 7–13), these positive inducements should encourage fathers to strictly control—or, modern readers might say, physically and emotionally abuse—their sons.

Sirach 30 begins by attributing a father's joy in his son to constant whipping (v. 1). As in Prov. 13:24, this ongoing physical discipline is motivated by the father's love for his child, as well as by the hope of eventual gain from the son. The parameters of the discipline are laid out more clearly in Sir. 30:7–13. First, fathers are warned against indulging their sons (vv. 7–11): a son unchecked will end up stubborn (v. 8). A father's every interaction with his son should be guided by severity; the dangers of raising an undisciplined son are too great to allow for superficial kindness.

Instead of giving comfort, freedom, and fun, the father should, according to one version of Sir. 30:12 (the shortest Greek text, Greek I), beat his son in his youth lest the son grow up hard of heart and disobedient (ἀπειθέω, *apeitheō*, as in Deut. 21:20 LXX). The Latin version reads, "Bow down his neck in his youth, and beat his sides while he is a child, lest he be stubborn and disobey you and grieve you" (cf. the longer Greek text, Greek II). Finally, the longest and most violent text, the twelfth-century CE Hebrew manuscript B from the Cairo Genizah, could be translated as, "Like a cobra against [his?] life strike. Hit his loins while he is still a youth. Bow down his head in his youth and tear his loins while he is small. Why should he be cruel and rebel against you? Should the one born to you be death?"[20] The common denominator across these three versions is physical violence enacted against a young son (νήπιος, *nēpios*, in the LXX). This is preventive violence, not punishment. Strict physical discipline inflicted during childhood is intended to forestall the sort of stubborn disobedience exhibited by the rebellious son of Deut. 21:18–21.

Finally, in Sir. 30:13, the father is instructed to discipline the son and make him work (LXX, Vulgate; cf. 33:26) or, in the Hebrew, to discipline him and make his yoke heavy.[21] In 30:13 the father's control over the son is again attributed to the desire to avoid either the shame associated with an undisciplined son (LXX) or the rebellion of a foolish son (Hebrew). From verse 1 to 13, the focus remains on the significance of the son's character for the father. In Deuteronomy, the rebellious son is killed for the sake of the community. In Proverbs, parents instruct and discipline so that their sons will become wise. In Sirach, discipline is carried out for the sake of the father's honor.[22]

20. The versions of this passage and esp. this verse are confused. Skehan (1974, 541) laboriously reconstructs the original text of verse 12 thus: "In accord with his lack of discipline, belabor his ribs; and whack his backside while he is still a boy."
21. The yoke could be indicative of physical labor, as in the Greek version and also Sir. 40:1, or it could represent punishment (33:27) or disciplined wisdom (6:30; 51:26).
22. Cf. Trenchard 1982, 12–14; J. Collins 1997, 73; Horsley 2005, 134; and Fontaine 2002, 26.

The very low view of human character in Sir. 30:1–13 assumes that a son who has not been regularly beaten and indoctrinated with his father's values will rebel against that father.[23] Fear of the misbehavior and rebellion of a patriarch's subordinates is pervasive in Sirach. Wives, sons, daughters, and slaves can benefit a man's life, but they can also detract from his joy, wealth, and honor. Wives in Sirach are mostly beyond a man's control (cf. chaps. 25–26); men are warned against entering a marriage lightly because the husband of a bad wife can only lament and await her eventual punishment (25:18–19). But in the case of slaves and children, a man can exert his patriarchal power through harsh discipline (7:23–25; 26:10–11; 30:1–13; 33:25–30; 42:9–14). Sirach's instructions to the patriarch regarding his children are neatly summarized in 22:3, 6: "It is a disgrace to be the father of an undisciplined son, and the birth of a daughter is a loss. . . . Like music in time of mourning is ill-timed conversation, but a thrashing and discipline are at all times wisdom" (NRSV).

Honor and Shame in Sirach

In Proverbs, the instruction and disciplining of sons has the potential to prevent the death of a stubborn, rebellious son. In Sirach, this message is extended to the disciplining of daughters and made explicit through verbal allusions to Deuteronomy. The patriarch's control over his sons and daughters avoids the public shame consequent upon the admission of their lack of discipline. The elevation of honor and shame as key cultural values in Sirach leads to the severe disciplining of household dependents, demanding violence far beyond the ambiguities and the hope for the life of the son in Proverbs.

By no means does Sirach preach the full acceptance of Hellenistic culture at the expense of Israel's identity as the people of God. Rather, the book teaches Jews how to accommodate to Greek ways of life while remaining centered on Jewish tradition. For Sirach, it is possible and perhaps necessary to be a good Jew, even an honorable Jew like Phinehas (45:23–24), without rejecting Hellenism. First Maccabees presents a very different response to the presence of Hellenistic culture in Palestine. Instead of cultural accommodation, violent rejection of the sort modeled by Phinehas in Num. 25 is the order of the day.

Holy War in 1 Maccabees 1–2

Written near the end of the second century BCE, 1 Maccabees tells the story of the Hasmonean dynasty from the early days of its rebellion against the

23. See further Pilch 1993, 102–3.

Seleucids until the death of Simon, the last living son of Mattathias.[24] The years preceding the emergence of the Hasmoneans as a political power were marked by nearly continuous upheaval as the Ptolemies of Egypt and the Seleucids of Syria played tug-of-war over Palestine.[25] Antiochus IV Epiphanes, king of the Seleucid Empire from 175–164 BCE, was the last Greek to hold complete control of Palestine. His rule was challenged by the Hasmonean (or Maccabean) Revolt, which began in 167–166. The revolt succeeded in overthrowing the Seleucid government in Jerusalem in 152, and the Hasmoneans eventually (by 142) gained control of Judea and parts of Galilee (1 Macc. 13:41). The dynasty remained in power until, in 63 BCE, Pompey conquered Jerusalem for Rome.

First Maccabees 1–2 ascribes the Hasmonean revolt to a crisis of identity for God's people created by voluntary and forced apostasy under Antiochus IV, a crisis resolved when faithful, tradition-keeping Jews under the guidance of a priest named Mattathias took up arms against the Seleucids and their Jewish collaborators. This communal violence is narrated in language drawn from the tradition of constructive family violence against idolaters and tempters to idolatry, including Deut. 13; Exod. 32; and Num. 25. The reuse of the tradition in 1 Maccabees operates primarily to explain and justify the Hasmoneans' actions, but in so doing 1 Maccabees also provides a new interpretation of the tradition.

A key innovation in the use of constructive family violence in 1 Maccabees is that the enemy within is never identified as family. Violence against apostate Jews is surrounded by references to families and the family of Israel (e.g., 1:38, 60–61; 2:29–30, 40–41), and the story of Mattathias and his sons rests on the assumption that families should be unified in worship (cf. 1 Macc. 2:20; Josh. 24:15). In contrast, the people called "renegades" in 1 Macc. 1:11 NRSV are, literally, "children of lawlessness" who "go out from Israel." Because they dissociate themselves from the ancestral laws to keep the traditions of the gentiles, they are no relation to the faithful like Mattathias. This redefinition of family emphasizes the importance of identity to the traditions of constructive family violence. It also counteracts the morally disturbing or questionable nature of violence in the family. In 1 Maccabees, violence against the enemy within becomes wholly praiseworthy.

First Maccabees can rightly be called Hasmonean propaganda.[26] The Hasmoneans are glorified as heroes of the faith, fighting to preserve and restore God's honor, the purity of the temple, and the identity of the people of Israel. This version of Hasmonean history is sustained by the integration of references to the biblical story, God's honor and praise, and particular signs

24. Along with most scholars, Dancy (1954, 3) suggests that 1 Maccabees was written between 125 and 90 BCE, but see also S. Schwartz 1991, 17, 36–37.

25. See Hengel 1989a, 45–52, 63–72.

26. So Goldstein 1976, 64; Nongbri 2005, 86–88, 97–108. On the questionable historical value of 1 Maccabees, see also S. Schwartz 1991, 33–35, among others.

of identity like the Sabbath, circumcision, temple, and law.[27] Though these references sometimes seem superfluous (e.g., 4:30–33), their presence indicates the importance of providing a theological interpretation of the events of the second century BCE for 1 Maccabees. In this way, the story of the Hasmoneans becomes a new chapter in the ongoing story of the people of God. The language and imagery of the laws and narratives of constructive family violence support this presentation of the Hasmonean revolt. The following discussion considers first the use of constructive family violence to interpret the crisis faced by the Hasmoneans and their response before drawing some conclusions on the reinterpretation of the tradition in 1 Maccabees.

Enemies Within and Without

For Deuteronomy, the preservation of pure Israelite identity depends on separation from foreign peoples. In 1 Macc. 1:11–15, this separation is deliberately reversed as Israelites go out to the nations to learn their ways.[28] "In those days, children of lawlessness went out from Israel and persuaded many, saying, 'Let us go and make a covenant with the nations around us'": this language in 1 Macc. 1:11 echoes Deut. 13:6, 13 (8, 14 LXX). The scene described in 1 Macc. 1:11–15, moreover, is exactly the sort of situation against which Deut. 13 legislates.[29] Lawless Israelites encourage their fellow citizens to abandon the covenant with Yahweh, and those who accept their message become like the surrounding nations.[30] These reformers are in effect changing their identity, replacing their uniquely Israelite traits with the traditions of non-Israelite peoples (vv. 14–15). Accordingly, their behavior is identified in 1 Macc. 1:15 as apostasy from the ancestral covenant (cf. Deut. 13:10, 13 [11, 14]).

The children of lawlessness and their followers deserve death according to the laws of Deut. 13.[31] Instead, they succeed in yoking themselves with the nations (1 Macc. 1:15).[32] Despite royal (Seleucid) approval (v. 13), however, the reader knows that the reformers are heading for a sticky end. They have "sold themselves to do evil" (v. 15 NRSV)—evil of the sort that their reform aims at mitigating (v. 11), evil like that initially brought about by Alexander

27. S. Schwartz (1991, 30) argues that the language and "conceptual world" of 1 Maccabees is Deuteronomic (see also Goldstein 1976, 5–12). Alternatively, D. Schwartz (1998a, 223–24) dissociates 1 Maccabees from biblical narrative because God disappears after chap. 5. See further Rappaport 1998, 175–77.

28. Cf. VanderKam 1994, 319–21; also Bartlett 1973, 22. Mørkholm (1989, 279–83) and Nongbri (2005, 93–105) address the history behind 1 Macc. 1:11–15.

29. So also Dancy 1954, 58; Goldstein 1976, 200; Williams 2001, 140.

30. In Deut. 31:17 LXX, "many bad things" come on Israel when they join with the nations; 1 Macc. 1:11 reverses the argument, suggesting "many bad things" have come on Israel since separating from the nations.

31. Cf. Goldstein 1976, 122.

32. Compare Num. 25:3, 5 (MT); Fairweather and Black 1936, 60.

the Great's successors (v. 9).[33] The danger is strengthened when Antiochus IV Epiphanes establishes a military garrison in Jerusalem, staffed by apostate Israelites, which is accused of decimating Jerusalem and defiling the temple (vv. 33–40).[34] These apostates are truly enemies within.

The next event in the story is an imperial proclamation of unity that entails individual ethnic groups giving up their own traditions in favor of a common way of life (1:41–42). For the Jews, this decree replaces circumcision, the Sabbath, temple worship, and other covenant traditions with "foreign customs," including idolatry, sacrificing unclean animals, and the installation of the "abomination of desolation" in the temple (vv. 43–49, 54). Whatever reality may stand behind this passage (and many options have been proposed),[35] according to 1 Maccabees the imperial decree and the evil deeds of the apostate Jews threaten Israel's identity. The people of God stand on the edge of complete assimilation, facing the loss of the covenantal traditions in favor of the traditions of the gentiles.[36]

In biblical perspective, Antiochus's decree would dissolve Israel's relationship with its one God, replacing the daily signs and reminders of the covenant with abominations and evils (1 Macc. 1:51–59). The danger is underscored in verse 53 by the use of "Israel" to refer only to the faithful remnant who refuse to obey the king and are killed as a result (cf. vv. 57, 60–63). By the end of the chapter, the reader is left wondering if the covenant and the people of God can survive. Assimilation to the ways of the nations in 1 Macc. 1 presents as dangerous a situation as Deuteronomy's Moses, standing on the edge of the promised land, foresees in the meeting of his people with the Canaanites. The conclusion of this section in 1 Macc. 1:64 direly (and surely ironically) comments that great wrath arose in Israel.

Enter Mattathias and Sons

With the introduction of Mattathias and his five sons in 1 Macc. 2, the dying embers of hope from chapter 1 flame into a blazing bonfire. When the Seleucid

33. See also 1 Kings 21:20, 25; 2 Kings 17:17.
34. The "sinful nation" and "lawless people" in 1 Macc. 1:34 could represent foreigners and apostate Jews (so Dancy 1954, 72), but the grammatical construction is better interpreted as indicating only one group (the apostates; so Zeitlin 1950, 75; Goldstein 1976, 124).
35. E.g., Dancy (1954, 47, 76) reads this story as a historical account of attempted syncretism; Goldstein (1976, 104–60) thinks Antiochus IV was establishing his own Roman Empire; and Nongbri (2005, 97) identifies 1 Macc. 1:41–49 as purely Hasmonean invention.
36. The interpretation of 1 Maccabees as a fight for "Judaism" against "Hellenism" has rightly been critiqued. Gruen (1998, 3–6) even suggests that the Hasmonean rebellion is only against collaboration with a (merely) political enemy, but this reading risks underemphasizing the focus on losing the ways of the ancestors to follow the ways of the nations in 1 Macc. 1–2 (see also S. Schwartz 2001, 34–36, and on 2 Maccabees, Rajak 1990, 262). It is perhaps most helpful to read 1 Maccabees as part of the ongoing process of defining community boundaries. See further Rajak 1990, 261, 267–71; S. Schwartz 1991, 21–35; Gruen 1998, 1–9, 39–40.

officials responsible for enforcing the imperial decree reach Mattathias's hometown, they ask him (as a priest and thus a local leader) to be the first to offer an illicit sacrifice (2:15–18).[37] He refuses the officials' invitation: "I and my sons and my brothers will walk in the covenant of our fathers" (vv. 19–22). The echoes of Deut. 13 in this scene connect it with 1 Macc. 1:11–15.[38] Unlike the apostates in the earlier text, though, Mattathias withstands the seduction of apostasy, instead fulfilling the injunctions of Deut. 13 by executing the seducers and apostates.

When another Jew obeys the royal decree and offers sacrifices on the altar, Mattathias is overcome with zeal like Phinehas and kills him along with the royal official (1 Macc. 2:23–24; cf. Num. 25:11, 13; Sir. 45:23).[39] As in Exod. 32:29 and Num. 25:13, Mattathias's action is narrated in cultic terms. He "brings near" or offers his wrath and slaughters the man on the altar like a sacrifice (1 Macc. 2:24; cf. Exod. 24:5; 29:11; Lev. 1:5; 2:16; etc.).[40] He also destroys the altar (1 Macc. 2:25), an act that fulfills the command to tear down foreign cultic sites in Exod. 34:13 and Deut. 7:5. The particular lexical conglomeration in 1 Macc. 2:24–26 places Mattathias's actions firmly within the established tradition of protecting God's covenant with Israel by means of violence.[41]

Following his cultic coup, Mattathias rallies together those who are, like himself, zealous for the law and covenant, and they flee to the hills (1 Macc. 2:27–28).[42] There this fighting group, joined by Hasidic warriors and other refugees, begins an offensive against the apostates (vv. 42–48). They go around destroying Antiochus IV's altars and circumcising the uncircumcised boys, a scene comparable with the Levites, called forth by Moses, going back and forth in the camp and killing the Israelites (Exod. 32:26–28). According to 1 Macc. 2:47–48, the work succeeds. Mattathias's band of refugees saves the law from apostasy, leaving the "sinner" powerless. Mattathias's final words to his sons charge them to continue the fight, imitating the faithfulness of their ancestors,

37. Goldstein (1976, 232) notes that, while most of the assembly goes actively (προσῆλθον, *proselthon*), Mattathias and sons are taken passively (συνήχθησαν, *synechthesan*).

38. Thematically, cf. going to a city (Deut. 13:12–13 [13–14]; 1 Macc. 2:15) and going to worship (πορεύομαι [*poreuomai*] in Deut. 13:13 [14]; 1 Macc. 2:20). Verbal links include listening (εἰσακούω [*eisakouo*] in Deut. 13:9; ἀκούω [*akouo*] in 1 Macc. 2:19, 22), worship (λατρεύω [*latreuo*] in Deut. 13:3, 7, 14; λατρεία [*latreia*] in 1 Macc. 2:19, 22), and apostasy (ἀφίστημι [*aphistemi*] and ἀποστασία [*apostasia*] in Deut. 13:11 and 1 Macc. 2:15, 19); cf. Fairweather and Black 1936, 78; Goldstein 1976, 232.

39. On the connections between Phinehas and Mattathias, see Dobschütz 1968, 9; Goldstein 1976, 6, 232; Seland 1995, 50–53.

40. Compare Dancy 1954, 85. Martola (1984, 218) thinks the murder is a real cultic act, thus reinforcing the connection with Phinehas (who atoned for Israel in Num. 25:8, 13 by killing Zimri and Cozbi).

41. See also Bartlett 1973, 37; Goldstein 1976, 5.

42. In 1 Macc. 2:29–38, another group of refugees in the wilderness is slaughtered when they refuse to defend themselves on the Sabbath. Rather ironically in light of 1:43, 45, after mourning their siblings (ἀδελφός, *adelphos*), Mattathias's group decides to fight even on the Sabbath (2:39–41).

including their father Phinehas (2:49–68). Israelite identity as it is interpreted and constructed in 1 Maccabees is thus preserved for future generations.

Interpreting Constructive Family Violence

The integration of traditions of constructive violence into the Hasmonean story in 1 Macc. 1–2 provides an interpretation of that story. The wording, imagery, and explicit references to the heroes of Israel's past woven into the story of Mattathias and his sons forcefully identify them with the Levites of Exod. 32, Phinehas, and the executioners of Deut. 13—faithful Israelites who protect the covenant from internal corruption. This connection explains and justifies the Hasmoneans' violence against other Israelites.[43] At the same time, the reuse of the earlier traditions in a new context reinterprets their message, expanding their focus on idolatry to indicate the complete disruption of covenant identity and removing the implicit moral questionability of constructive family violence.

In 1 Macc. 1–2, true Israelites are distinguished from false based on allegiance to the covenant way of life. Significantly, family language marks identity. The Jews who remain faithful to the covenant appear in the story with their families (e.g., 1:60–61; 2:1–6, 28–30). They are identified with their ancestors in the covenant (2:19–20, 50–60), and they identify each other as kin (2:39–41). The apostates, on the other hand, are never explicitly identified as the family of the faithful despite their connection through the covenant of their ancestors (2:19–20, 50). In light of the use of the traditions of constructive family violence to interpret the actions of Mattathias and his followers in 1 Macc. 1–2, the absence of family language in the description of the apostates is unexpected. It is understandable, though, as a necessary corollary of the definition of family in 1 Maccabees. If family members are those who are faithful and loyal to the covenant, apostate Jews cannot be family (though they may be family to each other; cf. 2:17–18). Their association with Israel's political enemies, the Seleucids, instead identifies them as traitors to their people. The apostates' response to the offensive of Mattathias and company, flight to the gentiles, moves them further from Israel: those who chose to become outsiders in lifestyle physically leave their people.[44] The enemy within becomes the enemy without.

After the death of Mattathias, the focus of 1 Maccabees shifts to political fights and alliances (a move foreshadowed in 2:67–68). Except for brief notices in 3:5–8; 10:14; and 15:21, the apostates almost completely disappear from the story. The initial introduction of the Hasmoneans as holy warriors, zealous for the law, however, highlights the importance of the tradition of constructive violence for the book's interpretation of the story of the Hasmonean

43. Cf. Seland 1995, 50–53.
44. Whether the renegades are still "Jews" in 1 Maccabees is debatable; see D. Schwartz 1998b, 33–35.

dynasty. Mattathias and his sons, even when they seem to be fighting solely for political purposes, are first and foremost defined by zeal for the covenant. They are protectors of Israelite identity.

In 1 Maccabees, violence is presented as the most secure means of ensuring the survival of the covenant community. Violence against foreigners certainly fits this mold; violence against apostate Israelites is also firmly established as the way to protect the covenant. There is no sense in 1 Macc. 2 that violence against Israelites is shocking or painful for the community. In fact, the description of Mattathias's initial act of violence as a sacrifice is even (darkly) humorous. The absence of tension concerning the deaths of apostates at the hands of the faithful is possible because 1 Maccabees characterizes the apostates and their foreign associates as wholly wicked.[45] They are bent on evil, and they bring evil upon themselves. First Maccabees can therefore present the Hasmoneans as saints, God's holy warriors, who purify the nation and gain its political independence. The moral problem of violence against family and community members notable in biblical traditions is rendered unnecessary.

The story of the Hasmoneans in 2 Maccabees is very different. God disciplines the Israelites (6:12–17; etc.), leaving Judas the Maccabee to fight only against foreign forces. At the same time, martyrdom is idealized as salvific violence. One man refuses even to pretend to eat pork lest he lead any of his people astray, and so he dies (6:18–31); a mother and her seven sons die rather than succumbing to idolatry (chap. 7). For 2 Maccabees, instead of violence against apostates, submission to violence from foreigners is the way to remain true to the covenant and save Israel (cf. 7:37–38).[46] This very different version of the Hasmonean revolt is comparable to the absence of intra-Israelite or family violence in the renarration of Exod. 32 and Num. 25 in Deut. 4 and 9; Ps. 106:19–31; and Sir. 45:23–24. In contrast to the tradition of constructive violence, in these texts violence as an appropriate protective measure is markedly absent. This alternate tradition is also discernable in *Jubilees*.

Jubilees: Rewriting Family Violence

Jubilees most likely dates to the mid-second century BCE, the era of Antiochus IV Epiphanes, the Maccabean Revolt, and the early Hasmonean dynasty. Historically, then, this book developed under the same sorts of cultural, political, and religious pressures that lie behind Sirach and 1 Maccabees.[47] As rewritten Torah, *Jubilees* adds a distinctive voice to the mix. The book is

45. See S. Schwartz 1991, 21–22; D. Schwartz 1998b, 33.
46. Compare esp. 1 Macc. 2:18–26 with 2 Macc. 7:24–40; see further Goldstein 1976, 4–5.
47. On the date of *Jubilees*, see VanderKam 1977, 283; Nickelsburg 1984, 102–3; Crawford 2008, 62. Because numerous fragments of *Jubilees* were found among the Dead Sea Scrolls, Brooke (1988, 42) and Knibb (1989, 16–17) identify it as a proto-Essene composition.

presented as the divine revelation given to Moses on Mount Sinai. The revelation consists of the narrative of Gen. 1 through Exod. 20, with select stories
and laws from the rest of Exodus, Leviticus, Numbers, and Deuteronomy
woven in; it introduces a new vision of what it is to be Israel.[48]

For *Jubilees*, Israelite identity centers on keeping the law in order to preserve Israel's relationship with God. Protecting this identity from lawbreaking
is thus also important, and the book outlines severe and even excessively
violent punishments for wrongdoing, including expulsion from the community, death, and absolute, eternal destruction. These punishments, however,
are not put into practice in the narratives of *Jubilees*, even when they should
be. The resulting tension over the place of violence in community life is also
present in three narratives of constructive family violence, which make use
of the vocabulary and themes of the traditions represented in the Torah.[49]
The failure to punish errant family members in these stories, despite the
requirements that *Jubilees* dictates in its own laws, raises critical questions
concerning the practice of constructive family violence. In the same era that,
according to 1 Macc. 2, the violence of Deut. 13 is the very thing protecting
Israelite identity, *Jubilees* challenges the effectiveness of constructive family violence, replacing it with a strong commendation of familial love and
unity.

This exploration of *Jubilees* begins with a survey of the book's definition
of Israelite identity before focusing on the three passages concerned with
constructive family violence. The story of Judah and Tamar and the story
of Dinah and Shechem incorporate laws requiring punitive violence. The
absence of punishment in these two stories is therefore unexpected and
undermines the apparent support of constructive family violence. This argument is supported by the failure of constructive family violence to protect
Israelite identity in *Jub.* 23.[50] In place of violence, for *Jubilees* the pursuit of
the law, communal peace, and familial unity is the way to preserve Israel's
identity.

48. VanderKam (1977, 94–95; 1989a, ix–xvi) traces the textual history of *Jubilees*, which
is fully extant only in Ethiopic translation. A third of the text is also preserved in Latin (both
versions were translated from the Greek). There are a variety of Greek and Syriac quotations of
the book, and the original Hebrew survives in the fragments of at least fifteen copies of *Jubilees*
found at Qumran (including 1Q17, 2Q19, 4Q216, 4Q219, 11Q12, etc.). As noted throughout,
the ET of the Ethiopic text of *Jubilees* is from Wintermute (1985) and VanderKam (1989b),
identified by last name only for in-text citations.

49. Though the three laws of Deuteronomy are not part of *Jubilees*, there are verbal allusions
to Exod. 32; Num. 25; Deut. 21:18–21; 22:13–30. *Jubilees* as a whole is heavily dependent on
the Torah (as well as several other biblical and Second Temple texts) for its content, language,
and theology (cf. Crawford 2008, 62–65).

50. This exploration of constructive family violence in *Jubilees* depends on an accumulation
of evidence across the book. See further Lambert (2004, 83–84) on the need to seek out tendencies and recurring motifs in interpreting the aims of books of rewritten tradition like *Jubilees*.

Jubilees *and the Torah*

Although *Jubilees* is dependent on the Torah for form and content, its use of the Mosaic traditions revises them.[51] As in Exod. 19–20, in *Jubilees* Moses receives divine instruction on Mount Sinai in how Israel should live as God's own people. Like Deuteronomy, *Jubilees* is almost entirely composed of one long speech, a literary whole in and of itself. This speech is not Moses's speech, however: it represents God's words. Moses becomes the amanuensis of divine revelation, writing only what he hears the angel of the presence read from the heavenly tablets (1:29–2:1).[52] The book's self-identification as revelation straight from heaven increases its own authority even as it potentially undermines the authority of other presentations of Israel's story (including the books of the Torah, on which it depends).[53]

Jubilees follows Genesis and Exod. 1–20 in telling the story of the world and Israel from creation until Moses's ascent of Mount Sinai to receive the law. The remainder of the Torah is collapsed into this narrative so that select laws of Exodus, Leviticus, Numbers, and Deuteronomy become part of the story of the ancients and the patriarchs rather than a later revelation.[54] This grandfathering of certain Mosaic laws makes them integral to Israel's life from the beginning, establishing the law as authoritative and eternal (see *Jub.* 1:7–14; 2:27; etc.). It allows the patriarchs themselves to keep the laws, so giving their descendants good models to follow.[55] Finally, integrating the law into the stories of Genesis unifies the multiple covenants of the Torah. For *Jubilees*, there is one single covenant with God, renewed many times by different figures.[56]

This covenant defines Israelite identity.[57] According to *Jubilees*, each "kind" of creature has been given their own "way" to live, and it is not permissible to follow another way (5:12–16 [Wintermute]). Identity consists of difference.[58] Corresponding to this understanding of identity, the laws and customs that visibly mark God's people as different from all others are central to the Israelite

51. While there was no canon in the second century BCE, it is likely that the books of the Torah were considered authoritative; cf. 1 Macc. 1:56–57; Crawford 2000, 177, 184; Najman 2003, 44; etc.

52. In VanderKam's translation of *Jub.* 1:27, God orders the angel of the presence to "dictate" the revelation to Moses (הכתיב, *hktyb*, in 4Q216 4.6). The angel then speaks "on the Lord's orders" (*Jub.* 2:1); cf. Noack 1958, 206; Najman 2003, 50.

53. Compare Dimant 1994, 155–57; Najman 1999, 379–80; 2000, 316–17; Crawford 2000, 184. Knibb (1989, 12), Najman (1999, 379, 408; 2003, 48–50), and Kvanvig (2004, 254–56) argue persuasively that *Jubilees* is presented as the correct interpretation of Torah.

54. Compare Gen. 9:4–6; 17:10–14; etc.

55. See Charles 1902, xiv, li; Endres 1987, 49; Nickelsburg 1999, 103.

56. So Endres 1987, 6; VanderKam 2000, 98–99; Huizenga 2002, 52.

57. See esp. Schwarz 1982, 21–23, 99–100; also Endres 1987, 15; Nicklesburg 1999, 91.

58. See Schwarz 1982, 21; and, briefly, Horbury 1998, 59–60.

way. Obeying these laws separates a true Israelite, figuratively and literally: Israelites should avoid any sort of contact with the inherently impure gentiles (22:16–22; 25:4–5; 30:7–17). The gentiles do not have, and can never gain, the privilege of keeping the laws of Israel, a special gift given to Israel alone (2:26–31; 15:25–34).

Living according to the law of Israel as it is interpreted and set forth in *Jubilees* is the key to a blessed, peaceful life, and abandoning this way leads to destruction and suffering (cf. 30:21–22). In 1:7–18, God warns Moses of the people's future idolatry, apostasy, and following the ways of the nations rather than the ways of the ancestors. The language and imagery of this warning are strongly Deuteronomic. Verse 7 is particularly notable: the people will be stubborn and rebellious (in Wintermute's translation), like the nation in Deut. 31:27 and the son in 21:18–21. The placement of this divine warning at the beginning of *Jubilees* and its singular claim to contain the direct, unmediated speech of God attest to its importance. The danger of losing community identity through assimilation to the ways of the nations guides the focus of *Jubilees* on the distinctive laws that can be related to the traditional narratives of the ancestors of Israel.

The vision of the future reconciliation and restoration of God's people following their apostasy again emphasizes the law as the essence of Israelite identity (*Jub.* 1:23–25). This hope for restoration is set within family language. When the people return to God and law, God will be their Father, and they will be God's children (v. 25).[59] When the temple of God is established in the midst of the people, moreover, God will be recognized as the God of Israel, King of Mount Zion, and Father of the children of Jacob (1:27–28). This promise reappears in 2:19–20; 19:29. The hope of Israel lies in being the family of God.

The Ideal Family in Jubilees

The ideal family outlined in the narratives of *Jubilees* reflects ancient Israelite and Second Temple tradition.[60] The readers meet good fathers, who teach their sons wisely, and good sons, who respect their fathers' commands. Jacob, for instance, is taught by his parents to respect the family. He obeys his parents and cares for them in their old age (*Jub.* 25:4–10; 26:7–10; 27:6–12; 29:15–20). He considers it an honor to honor and love his family (35:1–4). Esau, on the other hand, steals from his parents and breaks his vow to live in peace with his brother (29:18; 35:22–24; 37). The rewards heaped on Jacob for his obedience and familial love encourage the reader to emulate him; Esau's bloody end ensures his commemoration as an example of how not to live.

59. This language is reminiscent of Mal. 4:6 (3:24 MT).
60. The omnipresence of the family in *Jubilees* is common in ancient texts (cf. the use of family life as a narrative tool in Genesis).

The traditional values of family life find significance in *Jubilees* (as in Deuteronomy) by the identification of the family as an agent for propagating the covenant. Fathers transmit the covenant to their sons through instruction and blessings, exemplified by the last testaments of the patriarchs. While all the sons in a family receive some degree of teaching and blessing, the chosen son is given the full treatment. For example, when Abraham is dying, he gathers all his sons and gives them a series of commandments encouraging righteous behavior, circumcision, and the avoidance of fornication (chap. 20). He then instructs Isaac alone in the proper way to make sacrifices (chap. 21), exhorts Jacob to separate from the gentiles, and blesses him as his successor in the covenant (22:10–30).

Mothers and daughters do not actively participate in teaching and learning the covenant, but they do become important when the time comes to select suitable brides for the chosen sons.[61] A consistent insistence on endogamy for Israelite men and women runs through *Jubilees*.[62] Marrying within the national family protects the seed line from contamination by nonchosen blood, thus ensuring the inheritance of the covenant in future generations.[63] The prohibition of intermarriage also prevents impurity.[64] Though impurity can arise simply by contact with the impure gentiles (22:16–18), sexual contact with gentiles increases the dangers of infection (cf. 25:1–10!). Moreover, impurity can come about as gentile wives and families gain control over the Israelite man and tempt him away from the covenant (35:14; 41:2, 7). Along with teaching and learning the ways of Israel, *Jubilees* emphasizes the importance of intrafamilial marriage as essential to the preservation of identity. The covenant is a family inheritance.

The issue of inheritance may correlate with the historical context of the book. *Jubilees* comes from a time when the people of God in the promised land were living among gentiles, perhaps being ruled by gentiles (the Seleucids). According to the evidence of 1 Maccabees and Sirach, in this period Jews were adopting cultural customs of the gentiles to a lesser or greater degree. The fear of assimilation and the consequent loss of traditional Israelite identity is a strong undercurrent in *Jubilees*. The book's insistence on the inheritance of the covenant, carried on through families who practice endogamy and teach their children the ways of the covenant, directly answers the threat of assimilation.

61. Rebekah is the only matriarch to teach her sons (*Jub.* 19:15–25; chap. 25). Apart from endogamy, daughters are not given a role in transmitting the covenant.

62. By prohibiting intermarriage for women, *Jubilees* exceeds the practice of endogamy in texts like Ezra, Nehemiah, and Tobit. Cf. esp. Werman 1997, 11–17; Zlotnick 2002, 68–72.

63. So also Hayes 1999, 16–21. In this respect, endogamy also allows the chosen people to evade the inheritance of the Canaanites: eradication from the promised land (*Jub.* 10:30–34; 20:4; 22:20).

64. On impurity and the gentiles in *Jubilees*, see Klawans 1998, 404–5; Hayes 1999, 16–24; Ravid 2002, 69–70.

Protecting the Family of God

Along with the threat of national punishment consequent upon breaking the law, the inheritance of the covenant is supported by strict regulations for protecting the community from sin and impurity. According to *Jubilees*, infractions of the covenant are to be punished with death, expulsion from the community, or "uprooting." The actual practice of punitive sanctions in the narratives of *Jubilees* presents a very different picture, however, as offenders within the community repeatedly go unpunished. The tension between the stated consequences of lawbreaking and the absence of punishment for lawbreakers creates a sense of ambiguity regarding the value and use of constructive violence.

The laws of *Jubilees* feature fierce rhetoric against offenders: an uncircumcised Israelite man is destroyed, annihilated, and uprooted from the earth (15:14, 26); rebellion against the special times that Israel alone keeps leads to the death of the offender (2:27; 49:9; 50:8, 12–13; cf. 6:32–38); incest, adultery, and intermarriage with gentiles are also punished by execution and uprooting (20:4; 30:7–9; 33:10–14). These punishments are absolute. An uprooted offender, for example, is left without even a memory on earth. The punished person and their descendants are "expelled and lost from the earth" (*exterminii et perditionis a terra* in 15:26; cf. 6:12–13). The "obliteration" of an offender in *Jub.* 7:27–29 (VanderKam) likewise pictures the absolute destruction of the offender and their descendants, all of whom enter Sheol by means of a violent death. Uprooting offenders and their entire family lines goes beyond the execution or excommunication of a sinner. This punishment for sins against God and the community entails complete annihilation, leaving no memory or offspring to preserve the sins of the parent.[65] The array of punishments listed in texts like *Jub.* 15:26 and 33:13 emphasizes the totality of the punishment.

The rhetoric of absolute punishment in *Jubilees* corresponds to the serious nature of not keeping to the ways of life given to each kind of being by God. Abandoning the ways of Israel, including the physical signs of the covenant and physical separation from the nations, results in a change of identity: such Israelites become impure, defiled foreigners, out of divine favor, apparently having no chance of return, as in *Jub.* 30:21–22 (though see also 5:17–18). Furthermore, by acting like the gentiles, they endanger the whole nation (2:27; 15:28–29, 34). The exile, being uprooted from the land, is divine punishment on Israel for following the ways of the nations (1:9, 13–14). In light of the vital importance of respecting and maintaining communal identity (keeping the "ways" of Israel), the only response to covenant breaking for *Jubilees* is absolute, complete annihilation. The boundaries of communal identity are protected by removing the source of impurity and danger.

---

65. Sivertsev (2005, 79–80) suggests that, for *Jubilees*, piety and impiety are inherited. To protect the life of the community now and in the future, the family of an offender must be utterly removed.

Despite the rhetoric of absolute punishment in *Jubilees*, however, the practice of punishment is muted. While laws, offenses, and their consequences
pervade the stories of *Jubilees*, the book lacks the detailed descriptions of
punishments provided in the Torah. The method of execution, extermination,
annihilation, or uprooting is rarely explained. Moreover, those who deserve
uprooting on the basis of the laws woven into their stories, including Dinah
and Tamar in *Jub.* 30 and 41, are not punished. In 23:11–32, constructive family violence is used, but it spectacularly fails to protect the community. While
each of these passages on its own would be inconclusive, taken together, they
present an important challenge to the efficacy of constructive family violence.
For *Jubilees*, violence protects the community against external threats, but the
use of violence within the family of God is problematic.

Tamar and Dinah: Foolish Daughters?

The stories of Dinah and Tamar in *Jub.* 30 and 41 incorporate laws against
intermarriage and incest. In both cases, the punishment decreed for offenders
is execution. According to these laws, Dinah should die with Shechem, and
Tamar and Judah both should be condemned to death. However, despite the
severity of the crimes (emphasized by the additions to the narratives of Genesis
and the space given to consideration of the laws in *Jubilees*), in neither story
are the guilty Israelites punished. This absence of punishment is demanded
by the story line of Genesis, but in light of *Jubilees*'s interest in reinforcing
the importance of the law for Israelite identity, the failure to keep the law is
remarkable.

Dinah

The story of Dinah in *Jub.* 30 exemplifies the tension between the stated
approval of and support for constructive family violence and the implicit
narrative disavowal of the practice. In the basic story told in Gen. 34 and *Jub.*
30, after Dinah becomes sexually involved with Shechem, son of a Canaanite
ruler, Levi and Simeon avenge their sister's honor by deceiving and killing
Shechem and the men of his city.[66] In Genesis, the telling of the story allows
and even encourages its readers to interpret the murder and pillaging of the
Shechemites by Levi and Simeon as a blot in Israel's history, as wrong as the
rape of Dinah by Shechem in the first place (note esp. Gen. 34:3, 13–17, 25, 30;
49:5–7). The tendency of *Jubilees* to smooth over the failings of the patriarchs
necessitates some editing of this account. Moreover, as the ancestor of the
priests, Levi takes on a priestly role in *Jubilees*. Such an exalted character cannot be associated with an act of dishonor nor cursed as a man of wrath and

---

66. Kugel (1997, chap. 13) compares *Jub.* 30 with other retellings of this story across Jewish
tradition. The version in the Aramaic *Testament of Levi* is most similar to *Jubilees*.

anger. Dinah's story is therefore revised to become a panegyric on Levi and Simeon, heroes who protect the covenant community from gentile impurity.

This reinterpretation influences the entire narrative. Instead of willingly visiting the people of the land (Gen. 34:1), Dinah is kidnapped by Shechem (*Jub.* 30:2), removing the guilt of initiating relations with gentiles from Dinah and her male relatives (cf. 22:16–22). Dinah's innocence is supported by reference to her youth (30:2). Shechem's love for Dinah in Gen. 34:3, 8, 19 is missing in *Jubilees*, which instead highlights his offense of defiling "an Israelite virgin" (v. 6 [Wintermute]; cf. Deut. 22:25–27). Though Dinah's family does deceive the Shechemites (*Jub.* 30:3), no mention is made of circumcising them. There is no option for conversion on the part of the Shechemites (cf. v. 12).[67]

The identification of the Shechemites as outsiders, non-Israelites who have no chance of becoming Israelites, connects the story with the ban on intermarriage. The reader has already been warned of the dangers of intermarriage (22:20–21; 25:1–10; 27:9–11), and now the law prohibiting intermarriage is detailed in a diatribe against Israelite men and women who intermarry with gentiles (30:7–17).[68] The context of Dinah's story draws particular attention to women: if an Israelite man arranges the marriage of his sister or daughter with a gentile, he should be stoned and the woman burned (vv. 7–8). The offenders are also (somewhat unnecessarily!) excommunicated from the cult and communal goodwill (v. 16).[69] The sinners and their potential offspring are annihilated from the community, thus protecting Israelite identity from corruption and the nation from judgment (vv. 13–15).

The intercalation of the prohibition of intermarriage within Dinah's story justifies Levi and Simeon as avengers of God's holy name and people, protecting their family from sin. Replacing the curse of Gen. 49:5–7, in *Jubilees* Levi and Simeon are blessed on account of the Shechem incident. Jacob is not completely at peace with his sons, to be sure (*Jub.* 30:25), but heaven rejoices over them (cf. v. 23). The angelic mediator of the revelation breaks into the narrative to tell Moses that the destruction of Shechem had been preordained in the heavenly tablets because of the way he shamed Israel, so actually God was punishing the Shechemites through Levi and Simeon (vv. 5–6). The violence of Levi and Simeon fulfills a divine plan. Murdering the entire population of Shechem can rightly be described as a "just act" (v. 17 [VanderKam]).

---

67. The circumcision of the Shechemites is also absent in *T. Levi* 6:3–6 and in Josephus, *Ant.* 1:338–40. For *Jubilees*, conversion is impossible because it would break the boundaries set up in creation (cf. 2:19–20); cf. Klawans 1995, 291, 294–95; Halpern-Amaru 1999a, 7.

68. As Loader (2007, 114) points out, in the middle of the story the angel of the presence addresses Moses directly ("You, Moses, command the children of Israel . . ." in *Jub.* 30:11 [Wintermute]), a break in the narrative that underscores the importance of the law.

69. Boccaccini (1998, 97) interprets relations with gentiles in the book of *Jubilees* as a mortal danger. Infractions must be attacked immediately and with every means possible.

The glorification of violence in this story extends beyond praise. In *Jub.* 30:18–20, Levi and his descendants receive the priesthood precisely because of his wrath and vengeance.[70] The connection of ordination with bloodshed echoes Exod. 32:26–29.[71] As in the story of the golden calf, sexual impurity figures in the sin threatening Israel, though idolatry is not explicitly at issue.[72] The readiness of Levi to avenge the sin against Israel in *Jub.* 30:18 recalls the Levitical volunteers of Exod. 32:26; the sword girded on by the Levites in Exod. 32:27 was used by Levi and Simeon to destroy Shechem (*Jub.* 30:6). The story of Phinehas in Num. 25 also lies behind *Jub.* 30.[73] Like Phinehas, Levi is zealous for God, and both receive the priesthood for all time on account of their zeal (cf. Num. 25:13 and *Jub.* 30:18). The allusions to these two stories take the association of the priesthood with punishing sin and retrovert it into the life of Levi himself.[74] The Levites of Exod. 32 and Phinehas in Num. 25 thus become echoes of their ancestor. From the earliest days of the Levitical priesthood, *Jubilees* suggests, the Levites have been judges in Israel, agents of God's vengeance, and warriors protecting the covenant community from defilement.

The major difference between the pentateuchal narratives and *Jub.* 30 lies in the identity of the ones defiling Israel. In Exodus and Numbers, Israel is its own worst enemy. The incident of the golden calf concerns only Israel, and the text specifies that the Levites are to kill their brothers, sons, friends, and neighbors (Exod. 32:27, 29). Phinehas was faced with a situation in which foreign idolaters had penetrated the Israelite camp, but again the Israelites involved freely adopted unlawful customs. The violence in that story places an Israelite against another Israelite (and his foreign lover), a situation emphasized in the Septuagint translation of the story (cf. Num. 25:5 LXX). In *Jub.* 30, however, only the foreigners, people who are not and can never be Israelites, are objects of violence. That Dinah is not punished underscores this distinction. To be sure, Dinah is a victim in the story (even more clearly than in Gen. 34). In *Jub.* 33:7–9 and 41:23–24, however, victimization does not keep Bilhah or Judah from facing the consequences of defiling sin, and the law of intermarriage in the middle of Dinah's story demands the death of a girl connected to a gentile—whether

---

70. This story is only one of the explanations *Jubilees* gives for the Levitical priesthood; see Kugel 1993, 5–7. Simeon does not receive a similar promise, perhaps because he himself marries a Canaanite (he eventually repents and marries a Mesopotamian woman as well; *Jub.* 34:20–21).

71. VanderKam (1999, 504) also connects Exod. 32:29 with Isaac's blessing of Levi in *Jub.* 31:13–14.

72. Note, though, that in *Jub.* 30:10 marrying a daughter to a gentile is described as sacrificing her to Molech, an intriguing internal connection of intermarriage with idolatry (*Jub.* 30:10; see also *Jub.* 22:16–22; Lev. 18:21; 20:4; Himmelfarb 1999, 29).

73. Compare Jonge and Tromp 1998, 231; Hayes 1999, 22.

74. See also Endres 1987, 149–50.

she wanted the connection or not.[75] According to the law of *Jub.* 30:7–17, Dinah should die, but instead violence and vengeance are laid only on those who are not Israelites.

To explain and glorify the violence of Levi and Simeon, the story told in *Jub.* 30 draws on the biblical tradition of the Levitical response to the worshipers of the golden calf and Phinehas's zeal for Yahweh. In alluding to these traditions within a story about violence against an external threat to Israelite identity, though, the story also questions the traditions. This reuse of tradition implicitly (perhaps inadvertently) critiques the ethics of constructive family violence. The emphatic otherness of the victims of Levi and Simeon marks foreigners, not Israelites and certainly not family members, as appropriate objects of the violence that aims to protect the community.

Of course, several questions can be raised about this reading of *Jub.* 30. First, the direction of the violence is in part determined by Gen. 34. To punish Dinah would fundamentally change the story. Perhaps the inclusion of the law against intermarriage is an attempt to encourage constructive family violence despite its absence from the tradition of Gen. 34 (cf. *Jub.* 33:15–17).[76] In light of other modifications made throughout *Jubilees*, however, punishing Dinah would not be as unfeasible as it might seem. It would also show the patriarchs keeping the law, something that *Jubilees* is concerned to do. Second, the links to Exod. 32 and Num. 25 may be incidental to the characterization of Levi and not intended as a commentary on the violence in those stories. Since *Jubilees* does not go beyond Moses's mountaintop experience in retelling the story of Israel, how the author would have dealt with the stories of the golden calf and Phinehas is unknown. Third, the determined identification of the Shechemites as outsiders may be motivated to some extent by the desire to present the patriarchs as good men who would not trick their neighbors into circumcision. However, the denial of the possibility of circumcision in *Jub.* 30:12 seems to be more significant than simply being a way to justify the brothers' action. After all, Simeon and Levi do deceive the Shechemites (v. 3): their characterization is not wholly positive even in *Jubilees*.

The legislation of violent action against Israelites, the identification of the Shechemites as outsiders, and the omission of the punishment of guilty insiders—these features result in an internally conflicted narrative. Taken as a whole, the book's presentation of the violence of Levi and Simeon questions the appropriateness of such violence within the family. The length to which *Jubilees* goes to identify the Shechemites as other stands in clear dichotomy to the defilement of Israel from within in Exod. 32 and Num. 25,

75. Cf. Endres 1987, 140; Loader 2007, 168.
76. See further G. Anderson 1994, 19–23.

and the relocation of violence in *Jubilees* goes beyond the apologetic for the patriarchs. The reading of *Jub.* 30 as an ethical challenge to the constructive violence of Exod. 32 and Num. 25 stands as a serious possibility, especially when reinforced by the story of Tamar in chapter 41.

Tamar

The story of Tamar in *Jub.* 41 contains a hodgepodge of sticky situations: intermarriage, adultery, and incest. *Jubilees* contains most of the elements of the story in Gen. 38 along with additions that further the book's interest in condemning intermarriage and whitewashing the patriarchs (an interest that means Tamar, despite her central role in the story, is nearly lost). Of particular concern here are the allusions to the laws against intermarriage, adultery, and incest in *Jub.* 41, all of which require death for offenders in *Jubilees*, and none of which are put into practice in this story.

The serious problem of intermarriage, an act that represents the height of disloyalty to Israel for *Jubilees*, is introduced in the first verses of chapter 41: Judah's son Er, born of a Canaanite woman, hates the Aramaean wife whom Judah has given him, wanting instead a Canaanite wife. In his hatred, Er refuses to have sex with Tamar (v. 2). This addition to Gen. 38:6–7 explains that Er's evil in Yahweh's sight lies in disrespecting his father and wickedly desiring to intermarry with a Canaanite. At the same time, the somewhat lengthy narration of Judah's own marriage with a Canaanite in the first verses of Gen. 38 is shortened to a brief mention of Judah's wife's origins in *Jub.* 41:2. Er's rebellion reminds the reader of the moral danger of intermarriage, but the problem of Judah's own intermarriage receives no other attention. And though Er is killed by God for his evil, Judah is not punished for his.

Judah's attempt to carry out the practice of levirate marriage by giving Tamar to his second son, Onan, is foiled as in Gen. 38 by Onan's refusal to comply and his subsequent death. In Gen. 38:11, Judah chooses not to give Tamar to his third son because he fears Shelah will also die. This part of the story is rewritten in *Jub.* 41:7 to put the guilt on Judah's Canaanite wife. Again, at the same time that the reader is implicitly reminded of Judah's sin of intermarriage, Judah's character is redeemed, removing the potential for judgment.

The next part of the story, in which Judah sleeps with Tamar, thinking she is a prostitute, is largely the same in Gen. 38:12–23 and *Jub.* 41:8–15. The discovery of Tamar's pregnancy and her subsequent condemnation for prostitution, however, have intriguing differences:

Gen. 38:24–26 (NRSV)	*Jub.* 41:16–20 (Wintermute)
About three months later	And when [Tamar] completed three months it was obvious that she was pregnant.

Gen. 38:24–26 (NRSV)	*Jub.* 41:16–20 (Wintermute)
Judah was told, "Your daughter-in-law Tamar has played the whore; moreover she is pregnant as a result of whoredom." And Judah said, "Bring her out, and let her be burned."	And they told Judah, saying, "Behold, Tamar, your daughter-in-law is pregnant through prostitution." And Judah went to her father's house and said to her father and her brothers, "Bring her out and let them burn her because she has caused a defilement in Israel."
As she was being brought out, she sent word to her father-in-law, "It was the owner of these who made me pregnant." And she said, "Take note, please, whose these are, the signet and the cord and the staff."	And it came to pass when they brought her out to burn her that she sent to her father-in-law the signet ring and the necklace and the staff. And she said, "Recognize whose these are because I am pregnant by him."
Then Judah acknowledged them and said, "She is more in the right than I, since I did not give her to my son Shelah."	And Judah recognized (them) and said, "Tamar was more righteous than I. And therefore let them not burn her."
And he did not lie with her again.	And on account of that she was not given to Selah. And therefore he did not approach her again.

The involvement of Tamar's two households and the nature of her crime are distinctly different in the two versions of the story. The shift from the passive verbs of Gen. 38 (Judah "was told," "let [Tamar] be burned," Tamar was "brought out") to the active voice in *Jubilees* highlights the change.[77] In Genesis, Judah apparently exercises his patriarchal power over Tamar from a distance, and the sentence is carried out anonymously. Neither Judah nor Tamar's father's household explicitly plays a part in her execution. For *Jubilees*, however, Judah, Tamar's father, and her brothers are directly involved in the physical realities of the sentence. Judah announces his condemnation and Tamar's fate to her family. He commands her father and brothers to bring her out for execution. Though the identity of the ones carrying out the sentence is not specified ("Let them burn her"), the responsibility for Tamar's execution unambiguously lies with her family.

Although Tamar is not a new bride nor an unmarried girl in her father's house, the development of Gen. 38 in *Jub.* 41 is reminiscent of the laws of Deut. 22:13–29 on several counts (and the prohibition of incest in *Jub.* 41:25–26 relates directly to Deut. 22:30 [23:1 MT]). In *Jub.* 41:2, Er hates Tamar, wanting to replace her with a Canaanite woman, just like the new husband's hatred motivates his attempt to get rid of his wife in Deut. 22:13–17. Tamar is accused of prostitution and "defilement" (*Jub.* 41:16–17 [Wintermute]),

---

77. The extant versions of *Jub.* 41 (Latin, Syriac, Ethiopic) differ as to the voice of the verbs in this passage. In verse 18, the Latin states that Tamar was brought out (cf. Gen. 38:25), but in the Ethiopic and Syriac, "they" (in context, Tamar's father and brothers) bring her out.

much as the foolish sexual indiscretion of the daughter in Deut. 22:21 and the acts of adultery and rape in verses 22–24 bring evil into Israel. Finally, the role played by the bride's husband and father in Deut. 22:13–21 is echoed in the explicit involvement of Tamar's two households in her condemnation in *Jub.* 41:17. The similarities are not complete. The father's household makes no attempt to defend Tamar (indeed, in the face of her obvious pregnancy, defense is impossible); Tamar is to be burned rather than stoned; and the elders of the city have no place in *Jubilees*. Nonetheless, the overall importance of Deuteronomy in *Jubilees* and the specific developments of Tamar's story in chapter 41 suggest that Deut. 22:13–29 has influenced *Jub.* 41.

As in Gen. 38, the sentence on Tamar is not carried out. She steps forward in her own defense, proving that her behavior is "more righteous" than Judah's (*Jub.* 41:19).[78] At this point in *Jub.* 41, the guilt in the story instead rests on Judah, who has broken the law against incest (as has Tamar, but her guilt in this matter is not detailed). The law given in verses 25 to 26 announces that an incestuous relationship between a man and his mother-in-law or daughter-in-law threatens Israel with evil, defilement, and divine "wrath and punishment" (Wintermute), and both parties should be executed by burning. As in 30:11, the significance of the law is emphasized by the angel's direct speech to Moses in 41:26.[79] And as in *Jub.* 30, the law is not put into practice. Although Judah admits his own guilt (he "condemned himself in his own sight," v. 23 [Wintermute]), no one else in the community does so (vv. 23–24). Judah and Tamar are not punished for their sin, and God forgives Judah despite the stark declaration in *Jub.* 33:13 that anyone who sleeps with an in-law can never be forgiven. This conclusion to the story, as the excursus on Judah's innocence in *Jub.* 41:23–28 recognizes (cf. 33:15–17), effectively undermines the power of the law by letting the guilty go unpunished.[80]

Ironically, or perhaps purposefully, the nonpunishment of Tamar in *Jub.* 41:17–19 is the book's only example of a sin committed by a member of the covenant community being punished by the community. The interruption of her execution for adultery is necessary to the story of the patriarchs, but it is nonetheless significant that, in spite of the fierce, strong rhetoric demanding the annihilation of sinners in *Jubilees*, the only attempt to carry out punitive violence against a community member fails. The subsequent reminder of the law against incest and the failure to punish this additional sin add to the ambiguity. As in the case of Dinah, Tamar's story leaves the reader wondering if wrongdoing should be punished or not. On their own, *Jub.* 30 and 41 do not constitute critiques of family violence. The implications of these stories, though, become explicit in *Jub.* 23:16–32, in which constructive family violence fails to return transgressors to the covenantal way of life or protect the community from destruction.

---

78. Wassén (1994, 360–62) insightfully comments that the additions to the Genesis story in *Jub.* 41 imply the exact opposite: Tamar retains her guilt while Judah is fully exonerated.

79. Compare Loader 2007, 200.

80. See further Loader 2007, 185–86.

Jubilees 23

The first chapter of *Jubilees* establishes the book as an apocalyptic-style revelation of world history from the divine viewpoint.[81] This framework is augmented by the more classically apocalyptic passage in chapter 23. In *Jub.* 23, Abraham's death at the youthful age of 175 years sparks an excursus on the trend toward increasingly short, troubled life spans from the days of the ancients. This trend will culminate in the "evil generation" in which social order and traditional authority will be undermined, and the sins of those who fall away from the covenant will create a situation of suffering and impurity in the land (vv. 11–19 [Wintermute]).[82] An attempt to force the sinners back into obedience by means of violence will fail, and the situation will deteriorate to the point that God will punish the people at the hands of the gentiles (vv. 20–25). In the midst of punishment, some will return to the law, eventually restoring right order to creation (vv. 26–31). The passage ends with a reiteration of the command to Moses to write the divine revelation as a testimony for future generations (v. 32).

This apocalyptic passage has been nearly unanimously read as a "prophecy" of the Maccabean Revolt written after the events had taken place.[83] The function of the chapter within the book should not be overlooked, however.[84] A parallel to 23:11–32 in chapter 1 can be a guide for interpretation. In *Jub.* 1:7–18, God reveals the cycle of sin, punishment, and restoration that will characterize Israel's history. As the recipient of divine revelation, Moses is instructed to transcribe this prediction of Israel's future as a witness for the people of God's faithfulness and their own wickedness (vv. 5–6, 8). The cycle of history in chapter 1, which draws on the language and imagery of Israel as God's rebellious son, reflects the pattern present in Deuteronomy and the prophets.[85] *Jubilees* 23 echoes the same Deuteronomic cycle.[86] For *Jubilees*, the apocalyptic narrative of chapter 23 makes the future of God's people part of their ongoing story of sin, judgment, and restoration.

81. So J. Collins 1979, 32–33; 1984, 65–66; Nickelsburg 1999, 102–5; Huizenga 2002, 51; cf. Davenport (1971, 2), who argues that the eschatological outlook of chap. 1 makes the entire book apocalyptic.

82. Cf. CD-A (*Damascus Document*) 10.8–10; and Kugel (1994, 325–26), who identifies the human condition in *Jub.* 23:11–15 as punishment for sin.

83. Support for this identification comes from *1 Enoch* 90:6–7, which describes smart little lambs bleating at their dim-witted elders. This scene has been correlated with the Maccabean Revolt, and the opposition of young to old bears obvious comparison with *Jub.* 23. Yet *Jub.* 23 is literarily distinct from *1 Enoch*'s animal apocalypse in focusing on a short period of time; if it is an *ex eventu* prophecy, it is much less transparent than *1 Enoch* 90 (cf. J. Collins 1999, 53). For a selection of theories on the symbolism of *Jub.* 23, see further Charles 1902, 146; Davenport 1971, 43–44; Nickelsburg 1972, 46–47; J. Collins 1979, 32; 1984, 67.

84. Compare Doran 1989, 7–10; Kugel 1994, 336–37.

85. Compare Lambert 2006, 638–40.

86. See also Endres 1987, 54; Nickelsburg 1999, 105.

According to *Jub.* 23:14–17, the evil generation sins and pollutes the land with uncleanness, sexual impurity, and abominations. Their lives are full of evil and empty of peace. Since peace and the absence of evil in *Jubilees* signify the unity of the covenant community with each other and their divine Father (as in 50:5), the abundance of evil and lack of peace in chapter 23 represent the complete negation of the ideal world order in *Jubilees*. Verses 16 to 17 confirm the extent of the problem: the evil generation has abandoned the covenant with God. Every word of their mouth and deed of their hands is evil, impure, and sinful. According to the Latin version of verse 17, their "way" is "uprooting" (*exterminium*). These people change their identity, choosing for themselves the ultimate punishment of *Jubilees*.

In *Jub.* 23:18, the degeneration of the covenant community causes destruction in nature, a disruption of the order of creation that reflects the disruption of the proper order of Israel. Several other passages recognize the possible effects of widespread sin on creation. In the era before the flood, people sinned greatly, committing injustice and corrupting their world beyond the point of healing (5:2–3). The age before the birth of Abraham is also notable for the sin, idolatry, and pollution that caused the disruption of the natural order (11:1–6, 11–13).[87] Abraham himself is righteous and just, but the world around him is full of wickedness and defilement (21:21; 23:9–10). The catalog of sin in *Jub.* 23 attributes the acts of the nonchosen peoples in these other passages to the covenant community. The fear in 1:9–10 that Israel would one day follow gentile ways is realized by the evil generation depicted in 23:14–18: "All of their ways (are) contamination and pollution and corruption" (v. 17 [Wintermute]).[88]

In response to the wickedness running rampant through the covenant community, families take on the responsibility of challenging the sinners within their households. The reference to parents and children in association with rebuking disobedience in *Jub.* 23:16 accesses the family's responsibility to the covenant. Particularly in light of the book's focus on fathers' instructions to their sons in the covenant, *Jub.* 23, like Deut. 21:18–21 and Proverbs, would be a natural place to recommend that the parents of the wicked sinners rebuke and discipline them. The text upsets the reader's expectations in verse 16 when the children reproach their sinful parents for their sin.[89] Here the text makes no mention of physical reproof; it rather seems that the approach taken is one of verbal disciplining. The parents in *Jub.* 23:16, like the stubborn and rebellious son of Deut. 21:18–21, refuse to accept discipline: the children's

87. Abraham's righteous rejection of sin and idolatry correspondingly gives him control over nature (*Jub.* 11:18–24).

88. Note the contrasted "ways" in *Jub.* 23:17 and 23:20–21.

89. Some scholars have tried to identify the children of *Jub.* 23:16 with specific (adult) groups in the Maccabean era (e.g., Charles 1902, 146; Davenport 1971, 41). In light of biblical and Second Temple tradition, though, the household context of the conflict is quite important (cf. Doran 1989, 7).

attempt to avert the threat of the punitive consequences of communal sin
fails (cf. *Jub*. 1:12–13), as emphasized when the description of impurity and
the disruption of nature resumes in 23:17–18. It may even be that, in revers-
ing traditional social order and authority, the children actually accelerate the
deterioration of society.[90]

Verbal reproof is only the first step. As in Deut. 21:18–21, the attempt to
preserve Israelite identity is liable to be the death of the rebellious and stubborn:

> Some of these will strive with others, youths with old men and old men with
> youths, the poor with the rich, the lowly with the great, and the beggar with
> the judge concerning the Law and the Covenant because they have forgotten
> the commandments and covenant and festivals and months and sabbaths and
> jubilees and all of the judgments. And they will stand up with bow and swords
> and war in order to return them to "the way," but they will not be returned until
> much blood is shed upon the earth by each (group). (*Jub*. 23:19–20 [Wintermute])

The abandonment of the way of Israel leads to increased social disruption. In
light of the upset of traditional order in verse 16, the most obvious reading of
verses 19–20 is that the socially inferior—the young, the poor, the lowly, and
the beggars—take up arms against their social superiors to force them back
into the covenant.[91] The weapons, war, and bloodshed in verse 20 provide a
measure of the extremity of the physical discipline envisioned. The parents
and children of verse 16 are not specifically mentioned in the list of dichoto-
mous relationships in verse 19 (though youths and elders are present), but it
is possible that they are still involved on opposite sides of the divide. In *Jub*.
23:16–20, along with the covenant community as a whole, families are broken
apart by violence.

The communal upheaval pictured in *Jub*. 23:16, 19–21 begs comparison
with other apocalyptic scenes of social disruption.[92] In Mic. 7:6, children rebel
against their parents as part of the general degeneration of society; in Isa.
3:5, youths dishonor their elders in the context of the divine punishment of
Jerusalem. This theme also appears in *1 Enoch* 100:1–3, a particularly bloody
depiction of family disruption, and in later texts like *4 Ezra* (= *2 Esd*.) 6:24;
2 Baruch 70:3–4; and *m. Soṭah* 9:9–15. An important distinction can be drawn
between these apocalyptic texts and *Jub*. 23. The social upheaval in the other
examples serves to indicate the extent of sin or signify judgment. In *Jubilees*,
however, the violence is intended to solve the problem of sin.[93] The familial

---

90. So Doran 1989, 9. Nickelsburg (1981, 78) identifies a strong sense of communal guilt in
Jub. 23; though the chapter superficially separates the righteous from the apostates, all are guilty.
91. Cf. Hengel 1974, 54; Nickelsburg 1999, 105; etc.
92. See esp. M. Stone 1990, 78–80.
93. Endres (1987, 54) reads the conflict in *Jub*. 23 as the result of sin. This is broadly true: if
the sinners were not sinning, the conflict would not be necessary. The immediate cause of the
conflict, though, is the desire to bring sinners back into the covenant.

and social inferiors in *Jub.* 23:16, 19 are attempting to physically force their society to obey God's law.

This violence on a large scale goes beyond the disciplining and execution of rebellious sons and daughters, calling to mind instead the three situations of Deut. 13.[94] The mention of the sword in *Jub.* 23:20 also connects with God's sword of punishment in 5:7–9; 9:15 and with the swords of Levi and Simeon in chapter 30, and thus also the narrative of the Levites in Exod. 32. The contrast with *Jub.* 30 sharpens the similarity with Exod. 32: in *Jub.* 23, the violence targets Israelites who follow the ways of the nations. The association of the sinners in verses 14 to 20 with impurity, wickedness, immorality, apostasy, and the corruption of sacred time indicates their repudiation of *Jubilees*'s covenant, a situation reflecting the internal threat to the covenant made by Israelite idolaters in Exod. 32; Num. 25; and Deut. 13. The sinners of *Jub.* 23 are identified as impure, like the gentiles. Their behavior reflects the very activities that the book repeatedly warns against, the kinds of activities that lead to catastrophic judgment like the flood and exile (1:8–14; 7:20–33; etc.). In comparing the sinners with the other nations in their behavior and in their abandonment of Israel's special laws, *Jub.* 23 identifies them with the idolatrous nations surrounding Israel (cf. Deut. 13:7 [8]). The war against the sinners, then, represents the attempt to save Israelite identity and protect the covenant community from the punishment promised for such wrongdoing.

Family and communal violence in *Jub.* 23 is meant to be constructive. The conflict against sinners in *Jub.* 23 is carried out in order to "turn them back to the way" (according to the Latin version of v. 20), to draw them back into the covenant and enforce obedience. According to the model provided in Deut. 13, destroying the idolaters and removing all signs of them from the land will purge the evil of their sin and abominations from among the people. God will relent from his wrath and be merciful to the faithful who remain (13:5, 11, 17–18). The effect of the punishment in Deuteronomy may be behind repeated commands in *Jubilees* to uproot sinners from the land, and chapter 23 provides an example of the attempt to carry out this process. The war in *Jub.* 23:19–20 should purify Israel and renew the righteousness of the covenant community.

The violence of *Jub.* 23:19–20, however, is not functional. It does not return the sinners to the covenant. Apparently no one heeds the message at all. The sinners fight back, a situation not foreseen in Deut. 13; Exod. 32; and Num. 25. Far from being purified by the deaths of the wicked, the land falls further into sin and corruption (*Jub.* 23:21). The failure of constructive violence in this chapter draws attention to the absence of laws like Deut. 13:6–11; 21:18–21; and 22:13–21 from *Jubilees*. There is a repetitive insistence that those who bring

---

94. Compare esp. the overthrow of an authority in Deut. 13:1–5 (2–6 MT). As with the reversal of the expectation of parents' disciplining of children in *Jub.* 23:16, so also 23:19–20 reverses the expectation of the patriarchal action against inferiors in Deut. 13:6–11 (7–12).

impurity on Israel should be uprooted and destroyed, but detailed instructions on how this should be carried out are lacking; in the present example the attempt to protect Israelite identity with violence fails. In the narratives of *Jubilees*, the community does not have the power of the specific physical threats found in Deuteronomy. The war begun by the righteous in *Jub.* 23 was doomed from the beginning; violence cannot return sinners to the covenant community.[95]

The reference to bloodshed in *Jub.* 23:20 supports this interpretation. Elsewhere in *Jubilees*, bloodshed signifies great wickedness (see, e.g., 4:3–4; 6:7–10). The major failing of the preflood generation, according to Noah, was their violence against each other. The flood poured its waters across the land because of the blood poured out on the earth (7:22–25). The consistent interpretation of violence brings the sinners and the rebukers of *Jub.* 23 into a closer relationship with the children of the fallen angels than with the faithful Israelites of Deut. 13. Like the punitive civil war of the wicked offspring of the angels in *Jub.* 5:9, the war that destroys sinners and rebukers in *Jub.* 23:20 may represent judgment on them.

The failure to return the sinners to the covenant leads to further sin and wickedness, defiles God's holy temple, and eventually brings about the end foreseen in *Jub.* 1:13: the people of the covenant community are handed over to the nations for destruction. God "plagues" them, allowing them to be killed, judged, taken captive, pillaged, and destroyed (23:22 [Wintermute]). The gentiles turn against them and treat them mercilessly, both young and old (that is, righteous and wicked), killing so many Israelites that there are not enough living left to bury the dead (v. 23). The situation outlined in verses 24–25 is grim indeed. For those who eventually cry to God for help, "there will be no one who rescues" (v. 24 [VanderKam]).[96]

In *Jub.* 1:15–18, 23–25, God promises to heal the people when they return to God. In chapter 23, restoration for the covenant community comes through a return to the law (v. 26). Children again take a lead role, but instead of trying to enforce the covenant with violence like their antecedents in verse 16, the children in verse 26 withdraw from the corruption and destruction of society in order to study God's law.[97] As in *Jub.* 1:15, these children seek God, and God reverses the deterioration of the natural world and brings peace and healing to Israel (23:27–31). The Deuteronomic cycle of sin, punishment, and restoration moves forward.

The children of *Jub.* 23:16 provide a literary foil for the children in verse 26, highlighting study of the law as a central concern for God's people. This

---

95. Compare J. Collins 1999, 53, hesitantly.

96. Wintermute translates this verse thus: "There will be none who will be saved."

97. Kister (1992, 571–72) suggests *Jub.* 23:26 represents the history of the early Qumran community. Though withdrawal from society to study the law has a striking similarity to the presumed beginnings of the Qumran community, it has more immediate relevance to the focus on the law throughout *Jubilees*.

focus correlates with the book's pervasive interest in the study and keeping of the law. But while this interest explains why the second set of children in chapter 23 turn to the study of the law in the face of the disasters overtaking Israel, a positive focus on the law does not explain why the earlier violence fails to heal and restore the community. Violence is not necessarily the opposite of studying the law (cf. 1:12), and the laws of *Jubilees* do require the violent punishment of those who break the covenant. That violence acts as a foil to the study of the law in chapter 23 suggests a disapproval of familial conflict. Withdrawal from iniquity and wickedness to live like people of the covenant is the proper answer to a society disrupted by sin. The covenant community is saved from enemies within not by destructive family violence but through separation from sin.

Violence in Jubilees: *Protecting or Destroying the Covenant Community?*

In *Jubilees*, fierce punishments are prescribed for infractions of divine law. Sinners are to be executed, cast out of the community, and uprooted from the earth. No part of them should be left to keep their memory alive in Israel; they are utterly lost from the world and from the people of God. The holistic destruction of sinners indicates an acceptance of violence, including violence against family members, as an appropriate means of maintaining internal communal boundaries. The three passages examined in more detail, however, present a different picture. In *Jubilees*, there is a tension (or even contradiction) between the strong rhetoric of punishment in the laws and the absence of deserved punishment in the narratives.

In the story of Dinah and the Shechemites, the failure to punish Dinah for her part in bringing impurity into Israel sits uneasily with the laws concerning intermarriage introduced within the narrative. According to the law, Dinah deserves death, but instead she lives on in her family (cf. *Jub.* 44:18; Gen. 46:8, 15). The end effect of the story is to uphold violence as a protective measure for the community only when the violence is directed against outsiders, who could in no way be considered Israel. In Tamar's story in *Jub.* 41, the condemnation and punishment of a wrongdoer is begun, and its location, even more emphatically than in Genesis, is within the family. The language of the story reflects Deut. 22:13–29 and thus makes the failure of punishment all the more apparent. In addition, the story explicitly raises the question of incest, which would require the condemnation of both Tamar and Judah. Instead, Judah is forgiven by God. In place of utter destruction is new life.

Finally, in *Jub.* 23 the disastrous effect of violence within the community suggests that constructive family violence is harmful and fundamentally misguided. The rebuking and punishment of the sinners who break the covenant should absolve Israel of impurity and restore the covenant community. Instead, the sinners fight back. Violence begets more violence. The disruption in the covenant community leads directly to divine punishment in oppression under the gentiles. The second plan for salvation presented in *Jub.* 23 is the better option: not violence but study of the law will save Israel.

For *Jubilees*, the rhetoric of the absolute destruction of offenders remains rhetoric. Instead of punitive violence, the narratives of *Jubilees* show members of the community protecting it by following the virtuous example set by the ancestors, studying the law, and embodying the covenant. As in *Jub.* 1:12, the witness of a faithful life directs the future of the community.[98] In a sense the book is an incarnation of its own theology, exemplifying the faithful keeping of the covenant for members of the community to follow. *Jubilees* is a study of the law. It clearly defines community boundaries and leaves no room for the Shechemites to sneak into Israel. It refuses intrafamilial violence as a tool of salvation, preaching instead a community formed by the law, living in unity and peace.

Peace and Unity in Jubilees

Family violence of a sort does protect the covenant community from the threat of destruction in the story of Esau and Jacob in *Jub.* 37–38. This narrative, an addition to the story line of Genesis, tells of the definitive separation of the chosen family line from the noncovenant family as Esau's half-Canaanite sons incite their father to war against his brother (37:1–13).[99] Esau's violence is of a piece with the wicked proclivities he has demonstrated since birth (cf. 19:13–14; 24:1–7; 26:35; 29:14–20): Jacob is the true Israelite, the covenant bearer, and Esau is no more than a beast (37:24). Although family, Esau turns out to be an external threat to the covenant. The family violence in this story is wickedness on Esau's account, and defensive, not constructive, from the point of view of Jacob.

Jacob's response to Esau's attack highlights his own filial obedience and desire for familial unity. Instead of immediately picking up the weapons of war, Jacob tries to reason his brother into peace (37:17, and also v. 19 in Syriac). He does eventually defend his family by killing Esau, but only as a last resort. Further emphasizing the difference between the families—though Esau and sons want to uproot Jacob and sons (37:5–6), Jacob's sons refuse to take arms against their father's brother (38:1), and Jacob prevents his sons from annihilating Esau's family (vv. 11–12). Jacob and his sons have reservations concerning the appropriateness of violence against family members even when they are so clearly the enemy, thus demonstrating the value of family unity for *Jubilees*.[100]

98. See also Noack 1958, 206.

99. The story in *Jub.* 37–38 has been associated with the wars of the Hasmoneans against the Idumeans (e.g., Charles 1902, xlii, 216, 221; VanderKam 1977, 233). The function of the conflict in the narrative of *Jubilees* is also important to note (cf. Goldstein 1983, 77; Doran 1989, 3–7).

100. See also Söding 1995, 604–6.

This value is reinforced by the limitation of family conflict to those who are not part of the chosen covenant community. Cain's murder of Abel (4:2–4), the conflict of Ham and his descendants with the rest of Noah's family (7:8–15, 26–27), and Esau's intrafamilial warfare are indicative of their position outside the covenant. Correspondingly, the conflict between heirs of the covenant in the traditional stories known from Genesis is minimized or absent in *Jubilees*.[101] Perhaps a situation of conflict in the nation when *Jubilees* was being written motivated its exaltation of family unity and love.[102] Particularly in light of the association of the book with the Hasmonean era, *Jubilees* would encourage the rejection of violence against renegade Israelites praised in 1 Maccabees in favor of unity and the study of the law among the faithful. The historical correlation is not, however, absolutely necessary (or necessarily causative). Genesis is known for its stories of conflict, and *Jubilees* could be responding to this narrative context rather than a sociohistorical situation.[103] What is certain is that *Jubilees* presents a vision of peaceful family life as the desired norm for the covenant community.

The general trend of *Jubilees* is toward the creation of a community dedicated to living out God's covenant, at peace with each other and with their divine Father.[104] Within the narrative, the violence and conflict that characterize Esau's sons accentuate the peace that exists among the sons of Jacob in the days of Joseph (chaps. 42–46). The juxtaposition of the two cycles of conflict—Esau against Jacob, and the sons of Jacob against Joseph—stresses unity as a key value for the covenant community.[105] This message is voiced in Isaac and Rebecca's extended exhortation to their sons in chapters 35–36 and realized in the peaceful, unified family life among Joseph and his brothers in Egypt (45:5–7; 46:1–2): the people love and help each other, and their number increases. They are held in honor by the Egyptians, and Satan and evil leave them alone.[106] This scene, the culmination of the contrast between the narrative cycles, encourages readers to avoid family conflict, which leads only to death and being uprooted from the earth. True Israelites should follow the example of Jacob's sons, honoring the family and living in peace.

The contextualization of divine revelation in *Jubilees* after the exodus from Egypt reinforces the lesson in unity. In the renarration of Moses's own story near the end of the book, the angel reminds Moses of the time he found two Israelites fighting, and one of them struck the other (47:11–12). This vignette indicates the change in Israel's fortunes from being unified and honored by

---

101. Compare, e.g., *Jub.* 34:10–11 with Gen. 37:2–28. See Halpern-Amaru 1999a, 92; 1999b, 62–63.

102. So Endres 1987, 203; Doran 1989, 11; Docherty 2002, 211.

103. Cf. Lambert 2004, 100–101.

104. See esp. Söding 1995, 610.

105. See further Endres 1987, 183; Doran 1989, 6–7; Söding 1995, 604–5.

106. Cf. Endres 1987, 192, 203.

the Egyptians in the days of Joseph to being their slaves. It also exemplifies the need (in the narrative days of Moses) to bring God's people back into peace with each other. This need drives the retelling of the biblical narratives within the book and also centers the eschatological vision of Israel's salvation, a vision that includes the peace of the nation, the absence of impurity of every kind, and the disappearance of demonic and human enemies (23:29; 50:5).[107] For *Jubilees*, unity and love are key values of family life. Violence, or indeed conflict in any form, has no place in the unified community of the covenant.

Constructive violence within the family holds an ambiguous place in a book focused on unity. While the unchosen members of a family instigate violence and conflict, those who carry God's covenant avoid violence and conflict within the family by any means possible, engaging in it to defend the covenant community only as a last resort. The use of violence as protection does not occur inside the community; insiders are not outsiders to be destroyed, as in biblical traditions of constructive family violence. Salvation for the community rather comes through withdrawal from sin and sinners in order to pursue study of the law.[108] By reshaping the narratives of Genesis in these ways, the stories of *Jubilees* allow readers to question the acceptability of constructive violence within the covenant community espoused in ancient Israelite and early Second Temple traditions. For the narratives of *Jubilees* (if not the laws), family violence is inappropriate, leading only to further disruption and sin.

The tendency of *Jubilees* toward nonviolence has been likened to contemporary Second Temple works.[109] Philip Davies compares *Jubilees* with the *Epistle of Enoch* and the *Damascus Document* in this respect; all three texts, he claims, foresee the salvation of Israel through instruction, not war.[110] This argument is particularly intriguing considering the political situation of the second century BCE: faced with foreign oppression and the influence of foreign cultures, the Hasmoneans and their followers responded with war rather than instruction. Although 1 Maccabees characterizes them as warriors fighting to establish the covenant as normative for Israel, a situation also desirable within the three other documents in question, the means the Hasmoneans used were questionable. Whether *Jubilees* was written in response to the Maccabean Revolt or not, its ideology is basically opposed to the conflict and violence within families and within the family of Israel that the Hasmoneans fostered; the specific uses of the Phinehas tradition in *Jubilees* and 1 Maccabees highlight their incompatible visions. In the process of clearly demarcating communal boundaries, *Jubilees* allows a place for violence against outsiders in the protection of the covenant

---

107. See also *Jub.* 1:24–25. The absence of demons may correlate with the presence of peace; demons instigate family conflict in *Jub.* 7:26–27, and even family violence in the story of the sacrifice of Isaac (17:16; 18:9–12).

108. Compare Huizenga 2002, 54–55.

109. See also Docherty 2002, 211–15.

110. P. Davies 1987, 120.

community. Unlike the Torah and 1 Maccabees, within the community Israel's relationship with God is protected by means of peace and unity, not violence.

Constructive Family Violence in the Hasmonean Era

This chapter has explored the place of constructive family violence in several texts from the Seleucid and Hasmonean period. Though these texts were written in broadly the same historical context, Sirach, 1 Maccabees, and *Jubilees* vary in their use of the biblical traditions of constructive family violence. In light of the political and social upheaval that characterized the second century BCE, perhaps the disagreement between these texts on the issue of violence is unsurprising.

Sirach adapts the wisdom tradition of Proverbs for a new era, teaching wealthy, upper-class men how to be God's people in Hellenistic society. The instruction given in the book indicates how deeply Hellenistic culture impacted Judean society. The strict control of the patriarch over his wife and daughter and the heightened physical disciplining of his son can be correlated with Hellenistic values of honor and shame. Constructive family violence in this context is a fail-safe method of protecting the patriarch's good name.

For 1 Maccabees, the traditions of constructive family violence in the Torah provide models for Mattathias and his sons as they challenge Jewish acquiescence to Seleucid rule. The first chapters of 1 Maccabees indicate that Israel faces a crisis of identity. Jewish renegades threaten the very existence of God's people by abandoning the covenant in favor of the gentile way of life. The Hasmonean Revolt can thus be pictured in terms of constructive violence against apostate Jews: Mattathias and his sons are fighting a holy war in defense of the covenant. The traditions of constructive family violence are put into practice against members of the national family, rationalizing and justifying the violence of the Hasmoneans.

Finally, in *Jubilees* constructive family violence is surrounded by ambiguity. The laws outlined in the book clearly allow for the enactment of punitive violence against members of the family who break the covenant. The narratives, on the other hand, exclude punitive violence, instead presenting constructive violence against family members as ineffective. The contrast between the laws and the stories indicates a certain discomfort with the disruption of community life through violence. Identifying study of the law as the correct method of restoring the covenant, and emphasizing communal peace and harmony as the eschatological hope of Israel—these strategies reinforce the displacement of constructive family violence. For *Jubilees*, as an alternative to the visions of Sirach and 1 Maccabees, the covenant community is protected and propagated through familial love, not war.

4

Enmity and Treason according to Philo, Josephus, and the Rabbis

The exploration of constructive family violence in the Torah, Proverbs, Sirach, 1 Maccabees, and *Jubilees* has recognized a tension within and between these texts over the usefulness and value, and perhaps ethics, of punitive violence against family members. A family member who threatens the covenant is an enemy, a traitor who must be excised from the community before the community is destroyed. Equally, however, violence against a family member, someone who should be loved and cared for, challenges social and theological expectations. The varying approaches to and appropriations of constructive family violence from the Torah to the Hasmonean era bear witness to both the communal importance and the inherent difficulty of employing laws like those in Deuteronomy.

The same tension is present in texts addressing constructive family violence during the Roman period, including the interpretation and reworking of Deut. 13:6–11; 21:18–21; and 22:13–21 by Philo, Josephus, and the Tannaitic rabbis. Philo and the rabbis write commentaries that offer interpretations of the laws of Deuteronomy for their communities, and Josephus rewrites biblical narratives and also weaves allusions to Deuteronomy's laws into his explanations of Jewish life and his histories of postbiblical times.[1] In addition to interpreting earlier texts, their works also reveal something of their own struggles with the tradition of constructive family violence. For Philo, constructive violence against a family member is morally wrong, but it is also a necessity when an

---

1. On exegesis and allusion, cf. Sommer 1998, 17–18, 29–30.

enemy infiltrates the household. Josephus supports the disciplining of children as an integral part of training them to be good Jews. Conflict and violence on the order of Deut. 13:6–11, however, are minimized as part of his attempt to justify the Jewish people to the Roman world following the failed First Jewish Revolt. The rabbis, on the other hand, severely limit the use of Deut. 21:18–21 and expand the applicability of Deut. 13:6–11 and 22:13–21. The varying treatments accorded to these texts indicate the relative importance of the laws and the people they address in the development of rabbinic Judaism.

The thread linking Philo, Josephus, the rabbis, and (in the next chapter) early Christian writers is their historical location. They lived and worked in more or less pagan societies in the Roman Empire, and this context affected their interpretation and use of the texts of the Hebrew Bible. One practical issue arises from the curtailment of Jewish communities' legal right to carry out capital punishment under Roman governance. Though arguments over the powers of self-governance among the Jews in Roman Egypt and Palestine continue (and the potential for honor killings and mob violence cannot be discounted), it is probable that Philo, Josephus, and the rabbis addressed the legal procedures for constructive family violence as theory, not reality.

These authors also may have been influenced by Roman social expectations, including the customs and laws of *patria potestas*. Before turning to Philo, Josephus, and the rabbis, then, it will be helpful to consider Roman expectations for family life and traditions of constructive violence against wives, daughters, and sons. This necessarily brief survey explores one context for understanding how the biblical traditions of constructive family violence were developed by Jews living in Roman antiquity.

Roman Families and Constructive Violence

Interest in the Roman family and Roman families has soared in recent years, and there are now many good, detailed studies of the laws, ideals, and realities of the family during various stages of the Roman Empire.[2] As in ancient Israel and Second Temple Judaism, Roman families are complex and varied, far beyond what can be covered here. This survey will focus on narratives of constructive family violence as a point of comparison and contrast with Jewish concerns.

Much like ancient Israelite and Jewish families, the Roman *familia* was a household-based unit that included spouses, children, slaves, and other dependents.[3] The primary virtue of family life was *pietas*, devotion to the family.

2. See Rawson 1986, 6–35; Dixon 1992, 26–30, etc.; Saller 1994, chap. 4; Nathan 2000, 16–37; etc.

3. On the flexibility of the *familia* in distinction to the *domus*, which referred specifically to ancestral lineage or kin, see Dixon 1992, 2–3, 7, 11; Saller 1994, chap. 4.

The *paterfamilias*, the head of the Roman family, showed compassionate *pietas* by caring for his subordinates in the household, and wives, children, and slaves were expected to show *pietas* by their submissive obedience to the *paterfamilias*.[4] The father had absolute authority over the subordinate members of his household (generally excluding his wife, who remained under her own father's authority).[5] *Patria potestas*, the traditional, ideal power of a *paterfamilias*, included economic control, legal authority, and the right of life and death.[6] Of course, as Richard Saller warns, this power was not necessarily part of the "daily reality" of Roman life.[7] The actual power of fathers would be curbed by the economic needs of the household, the political status of the family, public opinion, and ever-evolving legal restrictions.[8] In addition, the *consilium*, the family council that advised a father in the exercise of his power, could provide a check on *patria potestas*.[9] The potential violence of *patria potestas* is nonetheless evident in many stories and laws from the Roman Empire. The following survey first addresses violence against women and then turns to violence against sons in the Roman family.

The ideal Roman woman was modest, chaste, a good household manager, and loyal to her family.[10] Women could face the punitive power of their *paterfamilias* for failing to maintain these standards. As might be expected, this power was exercised in cases of adultery, which threatened inheritance and family honor.[11] It is notable, however, that Augustus's decree concerning adultery, *lex Julia de adulteriis*, in 17 BCE effectively limited the power of the father to kill a daughter who committed adultery, and husbands did not have this right at all (though leniency was encouraged if they disobeyed this prohibition).[12] Furthermore, premarital sexuality is not punished by death under Roman law.[13]

4. See further Saller 1994, 105, 114; Nathan 2000, 10, 26–27.

5. Marriage in the Roman Empire came in several forms, with different legal consequences for the woman; cf. Gardner 1986, chap. 3; Rawson 1986, 19–21; Dixon 1992, chap. 3.

6. See Saller 1994, 114–30.

7. Saller 1994, 122. See also Dixon 1992, 138, 147; Nathan 2000, 2–3; and the sharp critique of the existence of a father's "legal power of life and death" in Roman antiquity in Shaw 2001, 59–61.

8. Cf. J. Evans 1991, 187–94; Nathan 2000, 27; Cohick 2009, 42–44, 75–76.

9. The *consilium* was not legally required but was a traditional practice; cf. Seneca, *De clementia* 15.1–2; Valerius Maximus, *Memorable Deeds and Sayings* 5.8; etc. See also Rawson 1986, 16; Lacey 1986, 137; Dixon 1992, 139; Nathan 2000, 27.

10. Only wealthy women would have had the ability to realize these ideals. See Valerius Maximus, *Deeds and Sayings* 6.7.1–3; Musonius Rufus, [*Works*] 3 (Lefkowitz and Fant 2005, 50–52); Cassius Dio, *Roman History* 56.3.3; also Rawson 1986, 17–18; Nathan 2000, 10, 19; Cohick 2009, 71, 97.

11. Livy, *History of Rome* 1.58.4; Suetonius, *Tiberius* 35; Aulus Gellius, *Attic Nights* 10.23.4–5; etc.

12. Paulus, *Opinions* 2.26 (Scott 2001, 1:281–82). See Gardner 1986, 7, 127–29; Rawson 1986, 33–35; Cohick 2009, 74.

13. See, however, the story of Verginia, killed by her father when her virginity was threatened, in Livy, *History* 3.45.6–11; 3.48.5–8.

Women could face the violence of *patria potestas* for more general threats to family honor. Pliny tells two stories of families who kill women who showed too much interest in wine, which could lead to adultery and other dissolute behavior (*Natural History* 14.14; cf. Aulus Gellius, *Attic Nights* 10.23.1–3). Livy narrates the official crackdown on the Bacchanalian cults in 186 BCE. Many women (who, according to Livy, made up the majority of worshipers) were arrested, tried, and, if convicted, transferred to their families for capital punishment (39.15.9; 39.18.3–5). Livy attributes the suppression of the cults to treason against the government, abandonment of the ancestral gods of Rome, and widespread crime on the part of the participants (39.15.2, 9; 39.16.2–3, 11). For women, sexual immorality, drinking, and other Bacchanalian excesses represent rebellion against Roman custom and virtue; families have the responsibility to curb them before they threaten Rome itself.

The interplay of public and private in Livy's story is common in narratives involving constructive family violence. In stories concerning fathers who kill their sons, it is difficult to distinguish the private from the public.[14] These stories are primarily about military disobedience and treason.[15] The father acts as father because of the personal relationship with the offender, and this element is clearly important to the narrators. However, the father also acts in his official capacity as military or government official. The overlap (or elision) of the father's roles influences the way the violence is narrated and interpreted.

Dionysius of Halicarnassus reports two traditions concerning the fate of the consul Spurius Cassius, condemned for plotting treason. According to one version of the story, he was accused and executed publicly by government officials; in another version, his own father accuses him in the senate and then kills him at home on his authority as *paterfamilias* (*Antiquitates romanae* 8.78–79). Dionysius comments that the second story could be true since Brutus also condemned his own sons for treason, and the army commander Titus Manlius had his son killed for disobeying orders: "And many other fathers, some for greater and others for lesser faults, have shown neither mercy nor compassion to their sons" (8.79.3 [Cary, LCL]).

These stories appear in several other sources, including Livy, with greater detail. Though it is not identified as an instance of *patria potestas*, the account of Brutus, who, as consul, condemned his own sons and witnessed their executions, is told with emotive force by Livy in *History of Rome* 2.5.5–8.[16] A

14. See Thomas 1984, 528–29; J. Evans 1991, 177.

15. These sons, like the women in the Bacchanalian cults, are adults (at least young adults). Roman sources also address the strict physical disciplining of young children as part of their education (e.g., Seneca, *De constantia* 12.3; Suetonius, *De grammaticis* 9; J. Evans 1991, 169–70; Dixon 1992, 117–18; Nathan 2000, 33), but the punitive execution of children is not expected or recorded.

16. The connection with *patria potestas* is natural, esp. since Livy emphasizes Brutus's identity as father throughout the story (cf. Valerius Maximus 5.8.1).

father should not have to see his sons killed (5), and Brutus is visibly disturbed (8). Nonetheless, his sons have betrayed their country and their father (7). Their crime demands ultimate punishment. The tension over the exercise of *patria potestas* here is more marked in the story of T. Manlius in 8.7.1–22. T. Manlius disobeyed a command given by his father, a consul named Titus Manlius. Despite the son's ensuing bravery in battle, the consul/father accuses and condemns him. T. Manlius's one act of disobedience identifies him as a rebel against the authority of father, consul, and military. His behavior thus threatens Rome itself (14–16, 19). The consul/father condemns his own son to death in spite of his fatherly love (18); even though the son is a perceived threat to Rome, the father's command and the immediate execution shock the crowd who witnesses it (20–21). Manlius the father, according to Livy, is remembered with horror (22).[17]

Two conclusions can be drawn from these stories. First, rebellion against the authority of the *paterfamilias* is closely implicated with and even identified as rebellion against the state.[18] This association is natural in a society in which family is the cornerstone of life and state, and it was reinforced in the days of the emperor Augustus, who presented himself as the *paterfamilias* of Rome, with its citizens as his children.[19] In this larger ideological context, rebellion against the authority of the father in a household threatens the hierarchy and order within which the empire functions. This association provides a point of connection (though not an exact parallel) to constructive family violence in Israelite and Jewish traditions in which rebellion against the family is construed as rebellion against God.

Second, the use of the custom of *patria potestas* is implicitly questioned in some stories concerning fathers executing sons for treason: Livy is sympathetic to Brutus and opposed to Manlius. Fathers have the right of life and death over their sons, but it is a right that should be exercised with restraint.[20] Seneca addresses exactly this issue in *De clementia*. A father has responsibility to discipline and punish his children, but he should not treat them harshly unless repeated wrongdoing necessitates it, and then only with extreme anguish (14.1–2).[21] Seneca provides two examples to support his argument. The outraged populace of Rome stabbed one father for showing lack of restraint

17. The same tension surrounds the use of *patria potestas* in Livy 1.26.4–13; 4.29.5–6 (also cf. 1.58.8–9, in which Lucretia's family attempts to cheer her up rather than kill her following her rape, which is identified as adultery). Likewise, while Valerius Maximus praises the fathers in such stories for their resolve and emotional withdrawal, he also praises fathers who have shown restraint to their sons (*Deeds and Sayings* 5.8.1–5; 5.9.1–4).

18. See also Lacey 1986, 123; Saller 1994, 117; and Shaw 2001, 60–62, emphatically.

19. See further Lassen 1997, 111–14; Severy 2003, 158–61.

20. Cf. Saller 1994, 122.

21. Tellingly, Seneca applies his message to the emperor, the father of the country; like a father in a household, the emperor should show restraint in dealing with his children. He possesses *patria potestas* for the purpose of care, not abuse (*De clementia* 14.2).

by beating his son to death. Another father, his polar opposite, did not execute his patricidal son but exiled him, even continuing to provide for him financially (15.1–2). This notable ambivalence toward the custom of *patria potestas* can be compared with the reworkings of Deut. 13:6–11; 21:18–21; and 22:13–21 by Philo, Josephus, and the rabbis. A rebel in the household may deserve death, but a merciful interpreter of constructive family violence may find a way around the required punishment.

Roman expectations for family life and constructive family violence provide one background for the works of Philo, Josephus, and the rabbis. At some points Roman law and custom have influenced their presentations of the Jewish tradition: Josephus tells of Herod gathering a *consilium* to judge his sons, for instance. At other points Deuteronomy's laws are upheld in spite of potential Roman critique, and in some cases the laws are expanded to include new issues that arise because of Roman culture. Though it is not possible to say if Philo, Josephus, or the rabbis knew Roman stories of constructive family violence, certainly their interactions with the Jewish tradition were shaped by their Roman context.

Philo on Constructive Violence in the Family

Philo was a Jewish theologian and public servant in Alexandria in the late first century BCE and early first century CE.[22] His family, who likely held Alexandrian and Roman citizenship, as involved in governing the local Jewish community, and Philo himself was a recognized authority.[23] He is best known today through his extensive writings, which include several treatises of literal commentary on the Mosaic law (called "Exposition of the Law") and several treatises of "Allegories" on the Pentateuch. Philo explores, explains, and interprets Jewish tradition through the lenses of Hellenistic philosophy, especially Plato, and culture. His works crisscross the (hazy) dividing lines between Diaspora Jewish and Hellenistic societies, giving Jews a model of how to be Jews in the Greco-Roman world and giving non-Jews a comprehensible, admirable depiction of Judaism.[24]

Though Philo draws on Hellenistic thought in his interpretation of Jewish tradition, he clearly identifies Judaism as the best and most virtuous way of life available.[25] He thus exhorts his fellow Jews, both the educated and those who

22. Barclay (1996, 43–75, 158–80) and Hadas-Lebel (2003) provide thorough introductions to Philo, his works, and his time.

23. Cf. Barclay 1996, 159–61.

24. These aims can be connected to Philo's historical context, in which growing tensions between the various peoples of Alexandria erupted in riots against the Jewish community. See Philo's *On the Embassy to Gaius* and *Against Flaccus*; Barclay 1996, 52–59.

25. Dawson (1992, 73–74) and Barclay (1996, 173) argue that, far from hellenizing Jewish tradition, Philo gives Greek culture a Jewish flavor.

know little of Judaism, to follow their ancestral traditions. He also implicitly addresses all the world, calling people who seek discipline, wisdom, and piety to join the Jews in following the example of Moses.[26] As the hortatory element of his writing suggests, for Philo ethnicity and descent are not the only determinants of Jewishness. Being a Jew depends also on a shared commitment to a virtuous life.[27]

Philo's understanding of being Jewish entails a redefinition of kinship.[28] A person is born into a family, and the members of the family are bound together by affection and mutual responsibilities (*Spec. Laws* 1.137; 2.240; *Drunkenness* 13–14; etc.). Just as strong, however, are bonds of piety and virtue. In fact, those who are dedicated to God and a godly life are more truly kin than those who share only blood (cf. *Spec. Laws* 1.317).[29] In *Virtues*, Philo explains that kin, even parents and children, who hold opposing values are in reality strangers (195–97).[30] Virtue is the homeland (πατρίς, *patris*) of the wise, and thus foolish, wicked descendants are exiled, disinherited, and excised from their families (190, 192). Conversely, proselytes who leave their own homes and families to join the people of God should be received as kin and friends, bonded by the honor of God (214–25).[31]

Because the kinship of virtue demarcates community boundaries, the unvirtuous can be identified as enemies instead of kin.[32] For Philo, those who hold opposing values are naturally at enmity with each other: the violent, unjust, and unvirtuous are strangers, foreigners, and irreconcilable enemies (ἄσπονδος ἐχθρός, *aspondos echthros*) to the virtuous (*Spec. Laws* 3.153–56; cf. *Virtues* 195–97). Philo argues that the enemies of virtue are enemies because they live only for their own pleasure and gain, whereas a virtuous person lives for ten thousand others (*Unchangeable* 16–19).[33] Indeed, in light of the lengthy list of the wrongdoings and dangers of those who seek their own pleasure in *Sacrifices* 32, "enemy" seems almost too light a term.

The language of enmity frames Philo's interpretation of Deut. 13:6–11 and 21:18–21 in the Allegories and the Exposition. The Israelite who teaches

26. On Philo's audiences and purposes, see Barclay 1996, 108–10, 170–71, 177–78; 1998, 85–86; Birnbaum 1996, 11–13, 18–20; Mondésert 1999, 881–82; Hadas-Lebel 2003, 149.

27. So also Barclay 1996, 173–74, 404–5; Birnbaum 1996, 12–13 (contra Niehoff 2001, 13, 17–23).

28. Cf. Barton 1994, 23–35; Barclay 1996, 406–9; Birnbaum 1996, 203.

29. See further DeSilva 2000, 194; Hadas-Lebel 2003, 79. Philo also suggests that all people are kin by virtue of a common parenthood (God in *Decal.* 64, and nature in *Decal.* 41; cf. *Moses* 1.314).

30. Cf. Philo, *Spec. Laws* 3.153–56.

31. See also Philo, *Spec. Laws* 1.51–52; *Agriculture* 6; DeSilva 2000, 194.

32. The issue became more than metaphor for Philo's family. Philo's nephew, a Roman official and military commander, fought against Jews in Egypt and in Palestine during the First Jewish Revolt (66–70). In taking arms against the people to whom he owed the loyalty of blood and tradition, Tiberius Julius Alexander vividly illustrates the mutation of kin into enemy. See Josephus, *Ant.* 20.100–103; *J.W.* 2.494–98; 5.45–46; etc.; Barclay 1996, 105–6; Hadas-Lebel 2003, 80–82.

33. Cf. Philo, *Posterity* 181; *Contempl. Life* 47; *Virtues* 131–32.

foreign ways is a "public and general enemy," and the disobedient son is the
"common and . . . national enemy of all" (*Spec. Laws* 1.316; 2.248 [Colson,
LCL]; cf. *Drunkenness* 14). Such enemies should be admonished and physically
disciplined in order to save them from themselves and to train them to be good
members of humanity, living for others (*Drunkenness* 14, 29; *Hypothetica* 7.3;
Migration 116; *Joseph* 74; etc.). Yet sometimes reeducation is not possible: the
unvirtuous person may be too far gone. In such cases violence becomes the
way to protect communal boundaries and identity—to protect the virtuous
community from the enemy within.

"Family" Violence in Philo's Allegories

In his allegorical commentaries on the Pentateuch, Philo interprets the
details on the surface of the biblical text as symbolic of the soul's journey
to spiritual maturity. His allegories are written for people who are, like Philo
himself, well educated in Judaism and Greco-Roman philosophical traditions.
This audience is exhorted to become wholly virtuous and wise, a goal reached
by strict self-discipline.[34] The resulting focus on the individual allows Philo to
interpret the families of the Pentateuch as representative of the body, senses,
and soul. Constructive family violence becomes a personal war against physical pleasures.

Philo draws on Deut. 21:18–21 and the stories of the Levites in Exod.
32:27–29 and Phinehas in Num. 25:7–8 as examples for the audience to follow as they seek the self-control necessary for spiritual maturity.[35] All three
texts are brought into conversation in *Drunkenness* 13–95. The son of Deut.
21:18–21 is representative of the undisciplined, foolish nature of a drunk who
refuses education, becoming instead disobedient, argumentative, and focused
on pleasure (*Drunkenness* 11–15). The problem such a person poses for society
must be addressed: the "parents"—symbolizing God, reason, wisdom, and
education—will discipline their undisciplined child to the point of destruction
in order to save him (29).[36] Philo therefore calls his audience to be disciplined
and controlled, submitting to the parents' authority (33–34).

The Levites in Exod. 32 enter the text as examples of those who prefer the
"father" to the "mother." The Levites are so dedicated to reason that they kill
their brothers, neighbors, and near ones. This "strange paradox" (τὸ παρα-
δοξότατον, *to paradoxotaton*) symbolically represents the priests' separation
from the interests of their bodies and physical senses (*Drunkenness* 65–72

---

34. So Birnbaum 1996, 18–19.

35. On Deut. 21:18–21, see Philo, *Names* 206; *Migration* 116; *Worse* 49; etc. Exodus 32:26–29
is explored in *Sacrifices* 130; *Flight* 90–93; and Num. 25 is examined in *Posterity* 182–83; *Alleg.
Interp.* 3.242; *Names* 108; *Confusion* 57.

36. On the identity of the parents, see also Philo, *Worse* 52; *Names* 206; *Questions and
Answers on Genesis* 4.244; etc.

[Colson, LCL]). Similarly, Phinehas's murder of Zimri and Cozbi represents an individual's victory over the sinful desires within (73–76). Philo encourages his audience to be good sons who accept the discipline of both parents (80–92), an exhortation supported by the reminder that sons who fail to honor their parents deserve to be executed (93–95). In *Drunkenness*, constructive family violence—symbolizing self-control, discipline, and submission to reason and instruction—is preventive violence, keeping the seeker of God on the right path.

The soul's search for wisdom, discipline, and maturity has an impact on society as the disciplined person gains honor and glory, and also as the undisciplined person creates havoc (*Drunkenness* 78–87). For Philo, allegorical interpretation does not replace the literal interpretation and enactment of the law of Moses (though the allegorical interpretation is identified as superior in *Abraham* 147). Rather, just as the physical body must be cared for as the house of the soul, so also the laws must be kept literally in order to be understood and kept spiritually (*Migration* 90–93).[37] The Deuteronomic laws of constructive family violence, then, are not only about the search for self-discipline and maturity. They are also directives for the common life of the people of God.

Constructive Family Violence in the Exposition

The Exposition is Philo's literal commentary on the Pentateuch, focusing on the law of Moses in *Decalogue* and *Special Laws*.[38] In these books, Philo presents a practical social vision for the community of the virtuous based on the laws of Moses. This vision complements the life of the seeker of God in the Allegories, explaining how to live for ten thousand others and how to deal with the selfish who live only for themselves (cf. *Unchangeable* 16–19). In keeping with biblical and Second Temple tradition as well as Roman expectations, the household plays a key role in Philo's social vision as the place where parents teach children to be self-disciplined, controlled, orderly members of society. The household is also the primary arena within which the constitution or way of life (πολιτεία, *politeia*) given by Moses is enacted.[39]

In the Exposition, the constructive family violence of Deut. 13:6–11 and 21:18–21 is used to protect the community of the faithful from the unvirtuous and undisciplined.[40] As in the Allegories, if a person cannot respect the authority of tradition, community, and family, they endanger the common life.

37. Cf. Amir 1988, 444–48; Dawson 1992, 113; Barclay 1996, 177–78; Hadas-Lebel 2003, 149.
38. Philo structures his commentary around the Ten Commandments, grouping the rest of the laws of the Torah under one of the ten (cf. Amir 1988, 425).
39. See further Barclay 1996, 108.
40. Colson (1937, 618) and Belkin (1940, 104–7, 113–15) argue that the Jewish community did not have the legal right of execution, making Philo's comments theoretical rather than practical. Goodenough (1929, 33–36), Dobschütz (1968, 32–36), and Seland (1995, 2, 108; 2003, 128–39), however, suggest that Philo's constructive violence is a form of lynch law against apostates (cf.

Such dangers must be eradicated, even by family members, as shocking as this pronouncement is. The shared life of the Mosaic *politeia* is more important than ties of blood, and Philo accepts preventive and punitive family violence as an effective method of protecting communal life.

Parents and Children

The commentary on the fifth commandment in *Special Laws* includes an exploration of the place of family life in the community. What God is to the world, so are parents to children: Philo elevates parents, both fathers and mothers, to an exalted position as the gods, elders, teachers, benefactors, rulers, and masters of the household (2.225–26). They are responsible for providing for their children and teaching them general knowledge, morality, and piety (228–30, 236).[41] In return, and in recognition of the authority held by parents, children owe them honor and obedience (225–27, 236). According to *Decal.* 119–20, since parents are the servants and representatives of God, to honor one's parents is to honor God (and to dishonor parents is to dishonor God).[42] Philo categorizes filial honor of parents and parental authority over children with virtues like keeping the laws, celebrating the festivals, and worshiping the gods, activities indicating that a person lives for all humanity (cf. *Unchangeable* 16–19; *Posterity* 181). The explicit connection of the parent-child relationship with the community reflects what is implicit in Jewish tradition, and also the Roman perception of how sons' and daughters' behavior has an effect on wider society.

In support of the significant parental responsibility of raising children to be wise, orderly members of society, Philo arms parents with the weapon of violent discipline. Following Deut. 21:18–21, the parents should first try to discipline rebellious sons and daughters verbally (*Spec. Laws* 2.232). Vigorous admonitions teach children to fear their parents, and fear keeps children from wrongdoing (239–41). If verbal discipline fails, though, the parents should beat and physically restrain their children; if even this physical discipline has no effect, the law allows the parents to punish such disobedient children to death (232).

Philo suggests that the prerequisite agreement of both father and mother to the accusation of the child in Deut. 21:19 limits the law to only the most serious

---

Morin 1973, 342; Berthelot 2007, 127–28). The evidence is slim on both sides; whatever the reality, Philo does incorporate constructive violence in his interpretation.

41. Compare Reinhartz 1993, 73–74; Barclay 1996, 106–8; Niehoff 2001, chap. 6.

42. This exaltation of parents is known in Greco-Roman philosophy (see, e.g., Cassius Dio, *Roman History* 56.3; Dionysius of Halicarnassus, *Antiquitates romanae* 26.1–27.1; Goodenough 1929, 67–70; 1962, 127). Jewish thought also likens parents to God, and Philo is a major exponent of this view (e.g., *Spec. Laws* 2.223–25; *Decal.* 51, 106–7; *Heir* 171–72). On Philo's interpretation of the fifth commandment, see Reinhartz 1993, 66–67, 76–77; Jungbauer 2002, chap. 16; D'Angelo 2007, 72–74; Wold 2008, 294–95, 300.

problems. The child's offenses must be great to overcome the parents' natural love (*Spec. Laws* 2.232), a comment that betrays some discomfort with the law. In the face of a child's insubordination, rebellion, and incurable wickedness, though, the parents do have this final option (234). Disobedient children face execution because they are enemies within the *politeia* of Moses. If a person cannot respect the agents of God in the household, they will not honor the God of the universe (*Decal.* 119–20; *Flight* 83–84). Since the honor of God is foundational to a pious, virtuous life (*Decal.* 52), those who dishonor God and God's agents must die. Second, Philo argues that if children fail to honor and obey their parents, they will not respect anyone at all (*Decal.* 111–12; cf. *Spec. Laws* 2.237–38). Children who do not show kindness to their parents are condemned as common and public enemies of the community, worthy of execution for the security of a society that cares for its own (*Spec. Laws* 2.243, 248). This discussion of Deut. 21:18–21 may reflect the connection of a son's rebellion against a father with treason in Roman sources (a relationship also implicit in Jewish tradition). Philo's identification of rebellious children as enemies would thus connect biblical constructive family violence with *patria potestas*.[43]

Patria potestas, however, is employed against "children" who are young adults or older; Philo's "children" are παῖς (*pais*), which technically refers to young children (cf. *Creation* 103–5; *Decal.* 117; *Cherubim* 114; etc.). Furthermore, while only the *paterfamilias* of a Roman family has the power to discipline to death, Philo emphatically includes mothers in the process. *Special Laws* 2.232–34 is not a straightforward example of *patria potestas*. Philo also revises Deuteronomy's gendered presentation of sons and daughters. Because daughters are included in his discussion of children's duties to their parents (2.227), surely daughters and sons are intended by "child," παῖς, throughout the ensuing presentation of Deut. 21:18–21.[44] This interpretive move recognizes that daughters as well as sons can be disobedient, rebellious, and undisciplined (though, based on Philo's sharp distinctions between the genders, perhaps in different ways).[45]

The blurring of Deuteronomy's separation of children into rebellious sons and sexually foolish daughters continues in Philo's commentary on Deut. 22:13–21 in *Spec. Laws* 3. Much like the undisciplined child, adulterers are the "common enemies of all people." An adulterer destroys the family, the center of

43. So Goodenough 1929, 69–72; Reinhartz 1993, 76–77; Niehoff 2001, 176–77; Jungbauer 2002, 223.

44. The term παῖς (*pais*) refers to a son specifically in, e.g., *Drunkenness* 93 (quoting Deut. 21:18–21); *Sobriety* 31; *Heir* 49; Reinhartz (1993, 65) suggests that "son" is the primary meaning of παῖς for Philo. However, παῖς refers to sons and daughters together in *Moses* 1.330; *Spec. Laws* 2.129–30; *Rewards* 134; etc.

45. Compare Sly 1990, chap. 3 (esp. 51–54); 1991, 305–6; Mattila 1996, 106–7; Conway 2003, 473, 475; D'Angelo 2007, 81–84.

society, thus threatening society as a whole. Such a person should be executed
before they disrupt more families or teach others their ways (11; cf. *Decal.*
126–27).[46] Likewise, a prostitute teaches men and women to be unvirtuous,
licentious, and shameful; as "a pest, a scourge, a plague-spot to the public,"
she deserves death (*Spec. Laws* 3.51 [Colson, LCL]). This conclusion extends
no further, however. Contrary to Deut. 22:13–29, for Philo, women who face
rape or accusations of sexual indiscretion are not enemies but victims.[47]

The laws of Deut. 22:23–29 are covered in *Spec. Laws* 3.65–78. Philo indicates that in these cases the women are nearly always innocent, whether
(contra Deut. 22:23–27) the rape happens in the city or the countryside. There
may be some women who willingly participate, and they should be punished
to death for adultery; otherwise, the woman is innocent (73, 76). The man,
on the other hand, is always guilty—of "reckless and shameless effrontery,"
"treacherous snares," and rascally behavior (66 [Colson, LCL]; cf. 76). This
assumption also guides Philo's interpretation of Deut. 22:13–21.[48]

Philo assumes the first case presented in Deut. 22 is true: the bride has been
slandered by her misogynist husband, who is vainly seeking a reason to divorce
his new wife (*Spec. Laws* 3.79–80).[49] The husband is punished financially and
physically. His desire for a divorce is most definitely not granted. However, he
is not identified as an enemy to be executed because his offense is limited in its
effect to the woman and her family (80–81; cf. 65). More generously than Deuteronomy, Philo allows the bride to remain with her husband or divorce him at her
own will and pleasure, and the man must abide by her decision (82). For the first
time in interpretive history, the bride is allowed a voice in the proceedings (cf. 71).[50]

Philo does not address Deut. 22:20–21.[51] The husband's accusation is false
from the beginning of the commentary on this law to the end, and so the
consequences of a truthful accusation against a foolish bride are not admit-
ted. The bride and her parents remain innocent. As in the reading of the law
of the rebellious son, the interpretation of the law of the foolish daughter in
Special Laws recognizes the mercy inherent in the text in Deuteronomy: the
primary assumption of the girl's innocence. For Philo, Deuteronomy's laws
concerning disobedient children naturally limit their own applicability.

46. See further Sly 1991, 307; D'Angelo 2007, 77–78.
47. How Philo's presentation of the laws of Deut. 22:13–29 fits into his understanding
of sexuality and gender deserves further exploration; cf. Philo, *Cherubim* 49, 51–52; Mattila
1996, 105–6.
48. According to Sly (1990, 189), Philo counts men as responsible for maintaining "sexual
morality."
49. This is not a case of adultery for Philo. Virginity, however, is still a prized state in women
(cf. *Spec. Laws* 1.105–6; 3.169; J. Wegner 1991, 58).
50. The suspected adulteress of Num. 5 is also given a voice in the proceedings against her
in *Spec. Laws* 3.52–62.
51. Sly (1990, 200n31), however, connects Philo's pronouncement of a death sentence on
prostitutes with Deut. 22:20–21.

The Enemy within the Walls

Philo addresses Deut. 13 in *Spec. Laws* 1.315–18.[52] The first book of *Special Laws* is concerned with the first two commandments of the Decalogue, including the prohibition of polytheism and idolatry, the directions for the lawful worship of the one God, and an exploration of the pious lifestyle demanded by God. Obedience to this way of life is central to the God-loving *politeia* (πολιτεία φιλόθεος [*philotheos*]), but the community is endangered when its members turn away from the laws and the education or discipline (παιδεύω, *paideuō*) given by their leaders (*Spec. Laws* 1.314 [Colson, LCL]). The potential crisis of disobedience brings Philo to Deut. 13:6–11 (7–12 LXX).[53]

According to *Spec. Laws* 1.316, if a close relation or friend promotes (ἐνάγω, *enagō*) the worship of other gods, that person must be treated as a hostile enemy. The law of Deut. 13:6–11 applies to brothers, sons, daughters, wives, true friends, and any other apparently friendly person who leads the pious to worship and offer sacrifices in pagan temples. The encouragement to associate with idolaters represents the attempt to mislead the faithful from devotion to God, marking this so-called relative as "a public and common enemy" (*Spec. Laws* 1.316), just like the undisciplined child in 2.248. In 1.317–18, Philo reminds the reader that true kinship depends not on blood or ancestry, but on dedication to God.[54] This sort of kinship is holy (σεμνός [*semnos*], ἱεροπρεπής [*hieroprepēs*]); it is kinship with God the Father, who will treat those who please him as children (cf. *Prelim. Studies* 177). Anyone who reneges on kinship with God must be punished immediately. According to Philo, the announcement in Deut. 13:9 (10 LXX) is an announcement of execution; the pious respond by joining in the execution, which is identified as a holy act (εὐαγής [*euagēs*]; *Spec. Laws* 1.316).[55] The actual execution is not otherwise discussed, leaving the method and manner open to interpretation.

In conjunction with the redefinition of kinship in *Spec. Laws* 1.316–18, the command to execute the internal enemy without trial connects Philo's commentary on Deut. 13 with *Spec. Laws* 1.51–55. In the earlier text, Philo addresses the welcoming of proselytes into the holy family (51–52) and, conversely, the punishment of those who turn away from the traditions of the law to "betray" (καθυφίημι, *kathyphiēmi*) God (54–55 [Colson, LCL]). The virtuous must show their love for God and, significantly, their zeal by punishing

---

52. On this text, see Barton 1994, 24–25; Seland 1995, 136–60.

53. The commentary focuses on Deut. 13:6–11 (7–12), condensing Deut. 13:1–5 (2–6) into a brief warning (*Spec. Laws* 1.315) and entirely omitting verses 12–18 (13–19), perhaps because they have no relevance in Philo's Diaspora setting.

54. Cf. Hadas-Lebel 2003, 79. Barton (1994, 24–25) points out that Philo's discussion of true kinship goes beyond the (merely) punitive measures of Deut. 13.

55. In the Exposition, εὐαγής (*euagēs*) and εὐαγῶς (*euagōs*) frequently refer to sacrificing, keeping festivals, and other cultic activities (e.g., *Decal.* 96; *Spec. Laws* 1.68, 159; *Moses* 2.147). See Seland 2003, 132.

the traitor without mercy or even recourse to a legal trial: they themselves
are judge, jury, witnesses, and all.[56] All the virtuous should join in killing this
person, thus following the example of Phinehas.[57]

Philo emphasizes the problem of misleading in Deut. 13:6–11 by making
it a prominent element in the stories of Phinehas and the golden calf (*Spec.
Laws* 1.56, 79). The retelling of Num. 25 in *Spec. Laws* 1.56–57 highlights
the sexual relationships that led the Israelites away from their own traditions
to follow foreign customs. Phinehas kills Zimri, a leader of the lawlessness,
and the woman who taught him to do such wicked things (she is a διδάσκαλος
κακῶν, *didaskalos kakōn*). He thereby prevents anyone else from following
Zimri's example, instead setting an example for the true worshipers of God to
follow.[58] In fact, in the renarration of Num. 25 in *Moses* 1.300–303, many zealous Israelites do follow Phinehas's example and kill their relatives and friends,
sparing none of their blood relatives who have been seduced into impiety.[59]

Phinehas is rewarded for fighting for God's honor (*Spec. Laws* 1.57; *Moses*
1.304), just as the Levites are rewarded for their zeal in the holy act (εὐαγής)
of slaughtering the worshipers of the golden calf (*Spec. Laws* 1.79).[60] Philo
explores the story of the Levites' "righteous slaughter" more thoroughly in
the discussion of the cities of refuge in *Spec. Laws* 3.124–27 (Colson, LCL).[61]
When the Israelites turn to impiety, idolatry, and reveling (125), the Levites,
inspired like Phinehas (3.126; 1.56), become enraged.[62] In their zeal they arm

56. Though the absence of a trial in these laws could relate to the underlying biblical traditions, Goodenough (1929, 33–34) reads the "lynch law" as resulting from the inability to try
such a case in a Roman court. Philo also demands immediate execution without a trial in the
case of the poisoner to prevent their intentions from coming to fruition (*Spec. Laws* 3.93–96);
a similar justification could be behind *Spec. Laws* 1.55, 316; cf. Berthelot 2007, 124.

57. Cf. Goodenough 1929, 34; Seland 1995, 108. Dobschütz (1968, 33) suggests that Philo has
hellenized Num. 25 by making Phinehas zealous for reason (ζῆλος ἀρετῆς [*zēlos aretēs*] in *Spec.
Laws* 1.55; cf. also *Alleg. Interp.* 1.34; *Confusion* 57; *Names* 199; etc.). In the Allegories, Philo
does describe Phinehas's action in terms of reason (as in *Alleg. Interp.* 3.242; *Posterity* 182–83;
cf. Hengel 1989b, 60). In light of recent scholarship on Philo's subordination of non-Jewish
philosophies to the Mosaic writings and the primacy of virtue and piety as characteristics of
the Jewish community (see, e.g., Barclay 1996, 173–76), however, it may be better to reverse
Dobschütz's judgment: Phinehas's zeal rewrites Greek reason (cf. *Spec. Laws* 2.253). See further
Morin 1973, 341; Berthelot 2007, 123–24.

58. Compare fighting against impiety in Philo's *Spec. Laws* 1.55 with Phinehas, the one who
fights for God's honor, in 1.57.

59. Compare Num. 25:5 LXX; Barton 1994, 34; Dorival 1994, 460. Dobschütz (1968, 33–35)
identifies Philo's inclusion of youth in lynch mobs as a sign of historical reality. Although Philo's
addition of youth (in *Spec. Laws* 1.79; 3.124–28; *Moses* 1.300–303) is interesting, there does not
seem to be enough evidence to support his theory (cf. Seland 1995, 29).

60. Note that these worshipers were misled by a few fools (ἀγνώμων, *agnōmōn*) in Philo's
Spec. Laws 1.79.

61. See also Philo, *Moses* 2.160–73.

62. Phinehas and the Levites are inspired to slaughter apostates; they directly counter the
inspiration of the prophets who teach their people to worship idols (Philo, *Spec. Laws* 1.315).

themselves and, even without Moses's command, slaughter the impious. Philo emphasizes that the first to die are the Levites' friends and members of their households. Though these people should be "their nearest and dearest," the Levites recognize true kinship only with the lovers of God (3.126 [Colson, LCL]). As in the case of Phinehas's execution of Zimri and Cozbi, the Levites' violence prevents further impiety among God's people (3.126), and God the Father rewards his faithful followers (127).

As in Livy's narratives of *patria potestas*, Philo displays overt discomfort with these laws and stories of constructive family violence. The slaughter of kin is, under normal circumstances, considered wicked and impious (cf. *Spec. Laws* 1.312–13; *Virtues* 131). Phinehas and his emulators face an accusation of murder in *Moses* 1.313 (cf. *Drunkenness* 65–76), and in *Moses* 2.172 the bystanders witnessing the Levites' violence pity the dead and fear the executioners. The execution of close relatives apparently violates "family affection" (φιλόστοργος [*philostorgos*] in *Spec. Laws* 3.153). However, Philo subordinates natural emotions to what are, in his view, more essential issues of community tradition and piety. In fact, he suggests that only abnormal, excessive affection would seek to protect an enemy within the family (153–56).[63] In each case, Philo justifies the acts of violence with reference to the good of the community.[64] What looks like murder in these biblical stories is actually righteous vengeance against the enemies of God, and violence against enemies within the family thus protects the wider community from the insidious influence of a bad example and from false teaching (*Spec. Laws* 1.56–57, 79). By heightening the danger for the community, the threat of false teaching emphasized in Philo's explanations of Deut. 13:6–11; Num. 25; and Exod. 32 makes the use of violence against family members more justifiable.

Interpreting Kinship and Enmity

Philo represents Phinehas and the Levites as heroes of the faith who allowed no earthly ties to mislead them from pious living. He strongly exhorts the godly community to follow both their allegorical model of self-control and their literal example of zealous violence. The case of the rebellious son likewise provides an example of allegorical self-discipline and literal constructive family violence. That Philo includes family violence in both his allegorical and literal interpretations indicates the continuing place of violence in the protection of his vision for the Jewish community.

The Exposition and the Allegories provide evidence of Philo's recognition of the social and emotional repulsiveness of constructive family violence. He

63. Philo also describes these overly affectionate people as weak, "unmanly," and unreasonable (*Spec. Laws* 3.156).

64. See also Seland 2003, 129; Feldman 2005, 260.

is able to justify violence against kin by redefining kinship. Shared blood does not make someone kin; rather, shared piety is the marker of true kinship.[65] The one who dishonors God and disrupts society with uncontrolled, undisciplined, or impious behavior, therefore, is not kin but an enemy of the godly community, an identification that resonates with Mic. 7:1–7. Such behavior threatens the well-being of the community, and so the community must treat the enemy within as they would treat enemies of state.

Philo's commentaries draw together the violent disciplining of disobedient children and apostates. Disobeying a parent is of a piece with disobeying God. In either case, the offender uses the license of freedom to give in to insidious desires that disrupt the social life of the pious and virtuous. The disciplined person accepts and abides by the traditions and rules of the community. Those who are undisciplined, rebellious, and apostates must be physically removed from the community to protect its righteousness, justice, and virtue.

The Ambiguity of Family Violence in Josephus's Works

As in the case of Philo, the works of Josephus bridge Jewish and Greco-Roman cultures. Born and raised in a wealthy, priestly family in Roman Palestine, Josephus lived through the First Jewish Revolt and spent his last decades in Rome, supported by the patronage of the Flavians.[66] The failure of the revolt against Rome left the surviving Jews in a precarious position. In the *Jewish War*, written in the late 70s CE, Josephus defends Judaism against Roman hostility by denigrating the rebels as wicked and impious.[67] The *Jewish Antiquities*, finished about twenty years later, continues the defense by explaining Jewish law and retelling biblical stories and more recent history. *Against Apion* can be described as an apology for Judaism as an ancient, virtuous, and estimable way of life.[68] The Judaism presented in these works is Josephus's own understanding of Judaism. Each thus has an apologetic slant as Josephus seeks to convince the readers that his depiction of Judaism is correct and that the Judaism so depicted is good and virtuous.[69]

Family and community form a major part of Josephus's Judaism. He repeatedly emphasizes the value of family unity. Children obey and honor

65. Compare Barton (1994, 35), who understands Philo's use of kinship as a metaphor for loyalty.
66. Barclay (1996, 346–68) and Feldman (1999, 901–15) provide general introductions to Josephus and his works.
67. See, e.g., Barclay 1996, 346; Mason 1998, 73.
68. It has been suggested that Josephus wrote to explain Judaism to non-Jews (so Feldman 1998, 543; Spilsbury 1998, 18–19; Mason 1998, 67, 79, 97), to teach Jews how to be Jewish in the Roman world (Spilsbury 1998, 21–22), or to defend his thought against knowledgeable Jewish critiques (Gerber 1997, 89–91); perhaps a combination of these purposes and audiences is the best answer.
69. See also Barclay 1996, 367; Mason 1998, 84–85.

their parents. Parents provide for their children, and adult children in turn support their parents (e.g., *Ant.* 1.222; 4.261; *Ag. Ap.* 2.204, 206). Brothers and sisters and wider circles of kin care for each other (*Ant.* 1.176; 2.161; etc.). As for Philo, the unity of the family extends from blood to behavior and belief: family ties include a shared commitment to the Mosaic law, and so the Jewish community welcomes proselytes (*Ag. Ap.* 2.210). Unlike Philo, however, Josephus does not explicitly place those who do not share the same values outside the family. Transgressors may be impious, lawless, and apostate (cf. *J.W.* 7.259–73), but they are never identified as enemies rather than kin.[70]

The language of enmity instead describes the behavior of less salubrious characters in the Jewish story toward their kin: Laban in *Ant.* 1.315–19; Joseph's brothers in *Ant.* 2.20; Absalom in *Ant.* 7.255; and the rebels in the Jewish revolt in *J.W.* 5.529; 7.254, 263. People like this disregard the importance of kinship (*J.W.* 7.266). They foment rebellion and strife within families and the wider community (*Ant.* 6.126, 238; 9.95; 13.301–3; etc.). They are definitely not good, virtuous Jews.[71] Along with the emphasis on family and community unity as a key value of Judaism, Josephus identifies Jews who encourage disunity as bad Jews in an effort to counter Roman perceptions of Jewish society as fragmentary and disrupted due to the behavior of the rebels during the revolt (cf. *J.W.* 4.15; 6.121, 217; etc.). This argument effectively prevents Josephus from placing the rebels or other lawless Jews out of the "family": since they treat their kin as enemies, Josephus must treat them as kin.

The focus on family unity leaves little room for constructive family violence. Rebellious children and unchaste brides may still meet a violent end, as they also do under the Roman *patria potestas*. Since conflict within the community is wicked and impious, however, Josephus minimizes other stories and laws that incorporate violence against family members or Jews in general. Deuteronomy 13:6–11 and the stories of Phinehas and the Maccabean Revolt are reworked to justify these acts of constructive violence to an audience living after the failure of the First Jewish Revolt.

Parents and Children

In the *Jewish Antiquities*, Josephus develops a positive portrayal of Jewish families through praising obedient sons whose lives follow the examples set by their good, righteous fathers (e.g., 1.68, 232). Sons like these model the effective

---

70. Note, for instance, Josephus, *Ant.* 12.286, in which Judas (Maccabeus) drives out the enemy, the Seleucids, and destroys the apostates, his fellow citizens. Although they have abandoned the ancestral law, these Jews are not "enemies."

71. Nor would they be good Romans (see Josephus, *J.W.* 2.211; 3.349).

training and disciplining of children outlined in *Ag. Ap.* 2.204, 206.[72] Josephus emphasizes the importance of the fifth commandment: honoring parents is second only to honoring God (206).[73] Parents in turn are responsible for the transmission of Judaism to their children.[74] The explanation of child rearing in 204 reads like a measure to prevent the situation of Deut. 21:18–21 (a connection supported by the punishment of stoning for disobedient children in 206). A birth should not be celebrated with riotous drunkenness: from the first days of their children's life, parents should raise them to be sober and virtuous. The child should be taught general knowledge, the laws (to keep the child from ignorance and sin), and stories about the ancestors (to inspire imitation; cf. 173).[75] In the context of *Against Apion*, these regulations for parental and filial responsibilities provide evidence of the piety and virtue of the Jewish life.[76]

Unfortunately, not all children imitate their fathers (cf. *Ant.* 4.289), and for these Josephus prescribes harsh punishment. In *Against Apion*, even intending to wrong parents or God demands immediate destruction (2.217): a child who is ungrateful or otherwise fails in the honor owed to parents must be stoned to death like the rebellious son of Deuteronomy (206).[77] Josephus's more thorough explanation of Deut. 21:18–21 in *Ant.* 4 applies the law to young people (νεός, *neos*) who fail to honor their parents, instead insolently rising up against them (260–64). The stubborn rebellion represented in Deut. 21:18–21 is emphasized by a lengthy speech in which the parents outline expectations for family life: "'When you were born,' they shall proceed, 'it was with joy and deepest thankfulness to God that we raised you up and devoted our utmost care to your upbringing, sparing nothing that appeared profitable for your welfare and training in all that was best'" (261 [Thackeray, LCL]). The parents deserve the child's respect and obedience because of their care and also because they are like God, the Father of all (262), and thus hold absolute authority over their children. The young people in 260–64, however, do not uphold their responsibility. They break the fifth commandment. Their rebellion (ἐξυβρίζω, *exybrizō*) echoes the behavior of the Israelites in the wilderness and foreshadows the wickedness of Samuel's sons

72. The family laws in *Ag. Ap.* 2.199–206 are part of an overview of the law; Josephus claims that these laws encourage piety, good intracommunal relations, and general humaneness to outsiders (2.145–286). Cf. Gerber 1997, 77; Barclay 2007, xx–xxi.

73. Josephus also compares the law to a father controlling every element of his child's life (*Ag. Ap.* 2.174), a description that weaves together obedience to a father with keeping the law.

74. See also *Ant.* 4.209–11; *J.W.* 7.343; Barclay 1996, 404–5, 412–13.

75. Josephus often uses "child," παῖς, to refer to sons alone (e.g., *Ant.* 1.52; *J.W.* 1.312; *Ag. Ap.* 1.36; 2.270), but also occasionally to daughters alone (*Ant.* 1.286; 13.81–82; etc.). When used as a collective, as here, it can refer to sons and daughters (e.g., *Ant.* 4.209–11; *J.W.* 7.101).

76. Cf. Barclay 1996, 367; Mason 1998, 189, 213.

77. Barclay (2007, 289) comments on the enhanced severity of *Ag. Ap.* 2.206 in comparison with the Deuteronomic law and *Ant.* 4.260–65; he suggests that Josephus may be polishing Jewish customs with Roman ideals. For Jungbauer (2002, 237), in *Ag. Ap.* 2.206 Josephus replaces the reward of the fifth commandment with the penalty of Deut. 21:18–21.

in disobeying their father and God (4.13; 6.33–35).[78] The behavior of the young in *Ant.* 4.260 represents the rejection of their role in Josephus's Jewish society. The young people, called sons in *Ant.* 4.260, explicitly include sons and daughters in 263. For Josephus, a young person is someone between childhood and adulthood (cf. 14.158). The young are not yet skilled, learned, or wise in decision making (5.214; 7.336), and thus they should be forgiven their misdeeds (2.156; 8.278). In 4.262 the parents tell the disobedient son or daughter that the sins of youth will be forgiven if their behavior changes (cf. 263). However, children who dishonor their parents also dishonor God the Father and will be punished accordingly (262). Such children are, according to Josephus, either shameless or witless (260). If these children refuse to heed their parents and continue to rebel, thus making the law their irreconcilable enemy (ἐχθρὸς ἄσπονδος, *echthros aspondos*),[79] the parents must take them out to be executed (264). Although the people of the town join in the stoning, the elders of Deut. 21:18–21 are not involved in trying or condemning the child. Rather, the authority for the execution rests with the parents alone as, according to Josephus, the judge (δικαστής, *dikastēs*) of their child (260).[80] Josephus adds that the body should be left visible all day and be buried in the evening, as should be done with the corpse of anyone executed for lawlessness (264; cf. Deut. 21:22–23).

The presentation of Deut. 21:18–21 in *Ant.* 4.260–64 insists on both the necessity of the execution of an unrepentant disobedient child and the parents' reluctance to use this law against their children (cf. 262–63). Herod the Great's attempt to do away with his sons in *Ant.* 16.356–69 and *J.W.* 1.536–43 provides a narrative example of this tension and in so doing echoes Roman stories of fathers executing treasonous sons.[81] When Herod accuses Alexander and Aristobulus of treason against him as father and king, he follows the emperor's advice and gathers a council of advisers to aid in judging his sons (*Ant.* 16.356–58).[82] Yet Herod, described throughout the account of the trial as unpaternal (cf. 362–63), manipulates this council. His indictment of his sons leaves no room for opposition, and he directly informs the gentile council that he has the right to execute his sons in accordance with Jewish law (365–66). The council somewhat reluctantly affirms his decision (367–69), and he eventually does kill both sons (394).

As in Roman expectations for *patria potestas*, the manner in which Josephus narrates this story suggests that fathers' power over the household should

---

78. See Levine 1993, 76.

79. Enmity arises on behalf of the rebellious one, not as an identification of the rebellious one (and furthermore, the enmity is against the law, not those who abide by the law); cf. *Ant.* 4.319.

80. See also Feldman 2000, 434.

81. The accusations against Herod's sons fit Josephus's requirements for the execution of a disobedient child in *Ag. Ap.* 2.206, 217, as well as *Ant.* 4.260–65. On the parallel between *Ant.* 4.260–65 and 16.365, see also Feldman 2000, 432.

82. This council (συνέδριον, *synedrion*) reflects the Roman *consilium*; cf. Sivertsev 2002, 97–98.

not be abused. Herod's use of the law of the rebellious son, if this is indeed the law to which Herod refers in 365, is unjust. An earlier installment of the saga reinforces this conclusion. In *Ant.* 16.261–65 Alexander's father-in-law, Archelaus, deviously condemns Alexander and expresses a wish to kill his own daughter for merely being married to an attempted patricide. Herod is thus tricked into experiencing the emotions of a father toward Alexander and begs Archelaus to forbear and forgive their children. This vignette and its parallel in *J.W.* 1.499–501 suggest that paternal affection should properly restrict the execution of a disobedient child. Thus one of Herod's counselors argues, "While he condemned Herod's sons, he did not think it right to put them to death, since he himself had sons, and such a penalty was too great, even granted that all his misfortunes were due only to them" (*Ant.* 16.368 [Thackeray, LCL]).[83]

The characterization of the Herodians in the *Jewish Antiquities* influences the presentation of family violence in these stories. Even so, the reluctance to discipline disobedient children to death resonates with the chance for repentance in 4.260–64. Josephus suggests that even a (failed!) patricide can be forgiven by a loving father (cf. Seneca, *De clementia* 1.15). On the other hand, parents are responsible for training their children in piety and virtue, and the reflection of God's authority and honor in the world within the family makes good family life imperative. Children must fulfill their role in the household; those who neglect their role draw down on themselves the wrath of the law.

Husbands and Wives

Marriage is a serious affair in Josephus's Judaism. In *Ant.* 4.244–45, he identifies an appropriate bride as a freeborn virgin daughter of good parents. Widows, divorcées, slaves, and prostitutes are forbidden. The children of such a marriage would not be good, virtuous Jews, a considerable problem since Josephus sees the purpose of marriage as procreation (cf. *Ant.* 4.258, 261; *Ag. Ap.* 2.199).[84] These instructions are addressed to men alone. Women, according to Josephus, are under the control of male relatives until they pass into the God-given authority of their husbands at marriage (*Ag. Ap.* 2.200–201). As such, they can have no say in the matter of their marriage. Their responsibility is solely to guard their virginity in order to protect their husband's rights (cf. *Ant.* 4.248).

Before and after marriage, a woman's sexual relationships with any man to whom she is not engaged or married disrupts male authority over her and threatens the procreative purposes of marriage. Josephus outlines several laws

83. In *J.W.* 1.540, Herod himself comments that a guilty verdict against his sons, though a victory, would be a defeat.
84. Compare Barton 1994, 36–37; Kasher 2005, 95–96.

relating to the punishment of adultery. In *Against Apion*, a man who seduces someone else's wife or rapes someone else's fiancée is executed (2.201; cf. *Ant.* 4.252). *Against Apion* does not mention the punishment of the woman involved; in *Ant.* 4.252 Josephus pardons a woman who was raped when she was out of reach of help. In *Ant.* 4.251 he does condemn a betrothed woman who has been persuaded to have sex with another man, explained as "giv[ing] herself over to shame [ὕβρις, *hybris*] because of pleasure or because of gain."[85] This woman is corrupted and dishonored by the act. If the woman is not engaged, however, neither party dies. Instead, the man must marry her or pay her father for shaming her (252).

These regulations provide the rationale for the law concerning the virgin accused of harlotry in *Ant.* 4.246–48. The concern is, first, with a bad bargain. The girl is supposed to be a virgin, but she is not (246): she is corrupt and unchaste (248). In accordance with the rules for legal cases as stated in 214–19, Josephus requires the husband to produce unspecified proof of his accusation in an official trial (246). The girl, who as a woman is incapable of providing legal evidence (219), is defended by father, brother, or other male kin (246); the mother has no place here both as a woman and because the girl is under male authority with respect to marriage (*Ag. Ap.* 2.200–201). If the husband's case is disproved, he is punished with a beating and a fine, and he can only divorce the woman with a very good reason (μεγάλη αἰτία, *megalē aitia*). On the other hand, if the woman is proved guilty, she is stoned (or burned if she is the daughter of a priest; *Ant.* 4.248).

Josephus's presentation of this law focuses attention on the woman, who is assumed to be guilty. The possibility that the husband is lying only arises after the explanation of the legal procedure for accusation. The words and actions of the parents' defense of the girl in Deut. 22:15–17 are omitted, as is the location of the execution at the door of her father's house. The shame that accrues to the parents, according to Deut. 22:13–21 and Philo's interpretation of the law, is absent from Josephus's account. The girl alone is the guilty party: "She did not preserve her virginity" (*Ant.* 4.248 [Thackeray, LCL]). This interpretation of Deut. 22:13–21 thus affirms women as social agents even as it identifies them as little more than incubators. For Josephus, in addition to a concern with honor and shame relating to female sexuality, women play a key role in the propagation of Jewish blood. Their responsibility for preserving their sexuality for one partner is paramount.

Violence in Family Life

In a sermon on the nature of the family in *Ant.* 2.20–28, Reuben tries to dissuade his brothers from their wicked plan of killing Joseph, the brother

---

85. On hubris in this text, cf. *Ant.* 4.206; *Ag. Ap.* 2.212; etc.; and see Levine 1993, 52, 76–77.

they perceive to be their enemy, by warning that God would punish them. Desisting from their murderous intent would be good in God's sight, for even killing a brother who has erred is wrong. As Josephus indicates in this speech, the ideal Jewish family is a harmonious unit of mutual care. Close kinship is sacred (cf. *J.W.* 1.465), and violating family relationships is the height of impiety.[86] The rebels display precisely this impiety throughout the *Jewish War*. The Romans, who according to Josephus treat their kin and fellow citizens virtuously and piously even in times of civil disruption (2.201–14, 581–82; 3.349), were horrified as they witnessed the wicked internecine violence of the Jewish rebels (e.g., 6.121).[87] As part of his attempt to salvage Judaism in Roman eyes, Josephus strongly critiques the rebels for fighting against close friends and kin instead of their common enemy (*J.W.* 4.131–32; cf. 7.259–65).[88]

Exalting family unity and condemning dissent allow Josephus to judge the behavior of the rebels as inimical to the Jewish way of life. And yet according to the *Jewish War*, the behavior of the rebels has some correspondence with biblical traditions of constructive family violence. When rebels fight pacifists and those who submit to Rome in their households and country, they are taking up arms against those whom they identify as enemies and traitors (2.264; 4.131–34). During the census of Quirinius, the Sicarii treated Jewish collaborators as enemies (πολέμιος, *polemios*) and foreigners (ἀλλόφυλος, *allophylos*), killing them and "plundering their property, rounding up their cattle, and setting fire to their habitations" (7.254–55 [Thackeray, LCL]), actions that resemble the destruction of the apostate city in Deut. 13:15–16 (16–17 LXX). Though Josephus clearly presents the rebels as bent on evil (particularly in taking arms against their nearest and dearest; cf. *J.W.* 7.256–74), they did apparently seek to protect what they understood as God's honor and Israel's identity as the people of God (cf. *J.W.* 2.118, 169–74, 192–98, 258–59; etc.).[89]

Reading between the lines of Josephus's rhetoric, it is possible to place the rebels' acts of violence against family and friends within the Jewish tradition of constructive violence.[90] Josephus's excoriation of the rebels for their acts of family violence therefore necessarily challenges the constructive nature of family violence on the pattern of Deut. 13:6–11 (cf. *Life* 171). Notably, in his retelling of Jewish history, Josephus condenses Deut. 13:6–11 into a passing

86. Halpern-Amaru (2001) suggests that Josephus knew *Jubilees*. Is it possible that *Jubilees* had some influence on Josephus's opinion of constructive family violence? It is certainly interesting that they share a focus on familial unity and a condemnation of familial violence as impious.

87. Josephus claims this viewpoint for himself as well (*Life* 26, 100, etc.).

88. Josephus identifies the divisiveness in Jewish society as the cause of the destruction of Israel (*J.W.* 1.10; 2.472–76; etc.). On stasis in the *Jewish War* and comparative Greek literature, see Rajak 1983, 81–83, 91–96; Mader 2000, 65, 72.

89. See Hengel 1989b, esp. 140–41, 183–86; D. Schwartz 1992, 29–38; J. Taylor 1998, 106.

90. On Josephus's obfuscation of the rebels' ideology, see further Mader 2000, 10–15.

remark, downplays the violence in Num. 25 and 1 Macc. 2, and omits Exod. 32 entirely.[91] These editorial moves reinterpret biblical and Second Temple tradition to support Josephus's presentation of Judaism as an admirable way of life in direct opposition to the Judaism of the rebels and contemporary Roman critique.

A greatly abbreviated version of Deut. 13 is integrated into the covenant oath ceremony of chapter 29 in *Ant.* 4.309–10.[92] Moses's people swear obedience to the law even if and when family members encourage disobedience: fidelity to the law takes precedence over kinship. Furthermore, if a family member or an entire city chooses to disobey the law and destroy the constitution (πολιτεία, *politeia*),[93] the rest of the family or nation should destroy the rebels if possible; if impossible, then they should simply express their disapproval![94] Josephus reports that all the people swore to keep the law, including this forceful condition. In referring to Deut. 13:6–11, Josephus gives the family the responsibility of ensuring communal faithfulness to the law. In compressing Deut. 13 into such a small narrative space, though, he limits its relative importance.

Josephus's version of Num. 25 in *Ant.* 4.131–49 includes a long speech in which Zimri accuses Moses of inventing God's laws in order to further his (Moses's) own wicked aims (145–49). Zimri's protest on behalf of freewill, personal inclination, and the right to worship whatever gods one chooses would lead to nothing less than a complete abandonment of Israel's unique way of life.[95] After Moses retires from the debate to avoid provoking further apostasy, Phinehas saves the day by killing Zimri and his lover, an act of violence on behalf of God immediately mimicked by a crowd of youths. Human violence and a divine plague eradicate the guilty from the camp, including the intermarriers, the idolaters, and the relatives who encouraged their sin (*Ant.* 4.150–55).[96]

In light of *Ant.* 4.310, the inclusion of the transgressors' kin among the victims of constructive violence reflects the role of the family in guarding communal obedience. The absence of the cultic language of atonement and Phinehas's priestly rewards, though, diminishes the glorification of violence

91. On the omission of Exod. 32, see Feldman 1999, 906; 2000, 7.

92. Compare Horbury 1998, 56; Feldman 2000, 469.

93. Josephus avoids the language of covenant; see Barclay 1996, 359; Spilsbury 2005, 216–18.

94. This addendum recognizes the difficulty with keeping the Mosaic law under foreign political rule. Horbury (1998, 56) suggests that excommunication is the alternative to execution in *Ant.* 4.309–10.

95. Feldman (2000, 382) notes that Zimri's accusations contrast with Josephus's praise of the law in *Ag. Ap.* 2.174 (cf. Barclay 1996, 367). Unnik (1974, 259), Barclay (1998, 86), and Feldman (1998, 130–31) suggest that Zimri's speech represents the arguments of Jewish assimilators in Josephus's own day and, Feldman adds, reflects Greco-Roman critiques of Jewish separatism (544).

96. The involvement of many Israelites in this violence is a tradition shared with Philo (*Moses* 1.300–303) and may reflect the command in Num. 25:5 (esp. in the LXX).

notable in other tellings of this story.[97] Josephus's story also omits Phinehas's zeal (cf. also *Ant.* 8.343, 350; 9.132–33). Zeal is present but muted in Josephus's version of the Maccabean Revolt in *Ant.* 12.267–71 (cf. *J.W.* 1.36–37). Instead of the violent, wrathful zeal of 1 Macc. 2:24–26, Josephus's story describes the Maccabees' zeal as pious, righteous, and nonviolent (cf. esp. *Ant.* 12.271).[98] This interpretation of zeal is supported by Mattathias's deathbed exhortation to his sons to be unified with each other and with all who are righteous and pious, and to be faithful in their war on behalf of the ancestral traditions (12.279–84).[99]

In separating zeal from wrath and excising the biblical models of constructive violence listed in 1 Macc. 2:26, 51–60 from his story, Josephus impedes the connection of these ancestral heroes with the Zealots of his own day. His editing protects Phinehas and Mattathias from imputations of wickedness and limits the justification of the cause of their spiritual descendants.[100] But despite Josephus's obfuscation, it seems that the rebels were only following the example set by their ancestors like Phinehas and Mattathias, turning against family and fellow Jews with violence in order to protect the community against perceived threats to Israelite identity (cf. *Ant.* 12.285).

Josephus does support violence, even against kin, on behalf of God's law (*Ant.* 4.309–10). Violence against the apostasy at Baal of Peor protects the national way of life; Mattathias's band fights a holy war.[101] The simultaneous condemnation of violence between relatives as the cause of divine punishment in 70 CE, however, leaves the reader unsure of Josephus's stance on family violence. This ambiguity is reflected and explained to some extent in the story of the Transjordanian altar in *Ant.* 5.100–113. The kinship of the Israelite tribes on both sides of the Jordan is emphasized in this narrative (102, 105, 111–12; cf. 97), as is the willingness of the majority of the people to overlook kinship in order to defend the lawful worship of God (cf. 102). The surge toward violence is dampened, however, by the leaders. The people should not rush to commit an act of violence without first ascertaining the purpose the Transjordanian tribes had in building the altar. In Josephus's narrative world, violence against kin is a serious business that should not be lightly undertaken, and therein lies his judgment on the rebels of the first century.[102]

97. See particularly Bernat 2002, 140–41.
98. Compare Hengel 1989b, 60.
99. See Feldman 1994, 50.
100. Compare Hengel 1989b, 155.
101. See D. Schwartz 1992, 33; Feldman 1994, 48.
102. Note also Bernat (2002, 146) and Spilsbury (2005, 213–15), who identify pacifist leanings in Josephus. Barclay (1996, 357) and Spilsbury (2005, 215) also draw attention to Josephus's reliance on divine punishment and reward (cf. Solomon's dream in *Ant.* 8.125–29).

Josephus on Constructive Family Violence

Josephus's presentation of Jewish law, traditions, and history is influenced by his historic context in the Roman world following the First Jewish Revolt. In response to potential Roman critique of Judaism as impious due to the behavior of the rebels during the revolt, Josephus develops a depiction of Judaism that Romans can understand and appreciate. Family values—virtuous obedience, mutual care, and above all, unity—hold a primary place in Josephus's Judaism, and biblical and Second Temple traditions of constructive family violence are reworked to support these values.

As in the Roman custom of *patria potestas*, constructive family violence is used to punish errant children and adulterous women. While Josephus maintains a difference between the laws of Deut. 21:18–21 and 22:13–21 and the Roman customs, these examples of constructive family violence are comprehensible within the Roman world, and the story of Herod the Great's accusation of his sons as patricides shows clear influence from Roman tradition. However, corresponding to his emphasis on family unity, Josephus rarely encourages violent discipline on the model of Deut. 13:6–11. Only the total apostasy and disruption of the Jewish way of life represented in *Ant.* 4.131–49 can justify this sort of dissent and conflict within the household.

In place of family violence, Josephus's writings show a preference for protecting internal boundaries by promoting Judaism as virtuous and pious. He makes the Jewish past a national treasure (*Ag. Ap.* 2.171–75), even perhaps an international treasure. The laws and customs are worth dying for, and Josephus's narration of the Roman response to Jewish martyrdom for the sake of the law emphasizes its inherent value (*J.W.* 2.174, 196–98). Josephus's all-pervasive praise of the Mosaic law and ancestral traditions guards the Jewish family against the corruption of apostasy by making Judaism a way of life of which Jews can be proud, even in post-70-CE Rome.[103]

The Tannaitic Rabbis

Like Josephus, the Tannaitic rabbis lived after the First Jewish Revolt and the destruction of the temple (ca. 70 to 200 CE).[104] Their work, preserved (though edited by later rabbis) in the Mishnah and some of the midrash, became the foundation of rabbinic Judaism. The Tannaitic period witnessed a growing

103. Compare Barclay 1996, 364–67; Mason 1998, 84–85.
104. The early rabbinic material is notoriously difficult to date, particularly because it contains layers of tradition and editing that developed over time. The focus of this section is on two of the earliest rabbinic texts, the Mishnah, which dates to between 200 and 220 CE, and the slightly later *Sipre on Deuteronomy* (cf. Hammer 1986, 7–8; Fonrobert 2000, 13; and the timeline in Fonrobert and Jaffee 2007, xiv–xv).

Roman presence and authority in Palestine; cities and societies became in-creasingly paganized.[105] The writings of the Tannaitic rabbis therefore show particular interest in how to live as Jews, without the temple, in the Greco-Roman world. In this sense, though they are not as concerned with making Judaism understandable or admirable to Greco-Roman audiences, they are comparable with Josephus and Philo.

For the Tannaitic rabbis, Jewish identity centers on the study of the law and acts of charity (e.g., *m. 'Abot* 1:2).[106] Jewish identity can be adopted by proselytes, but it is realized fully only in those who are Jews by descent (cf. *m. Bik.* 1:4). Since Jewish identity and its associated membership in the family of God are passed on through families (*m. 'Abot* 3:15), family life is of great interest to the rabbis.[107] The literature records detailed discussions concerned with identifying proper marriage partners, determining dowries and bride-prices, explaining the responsibilities of husbands and wives, and exploring the end of marriage in death or divorce. The rabbis also identify the household as one place in which the law is enacted and passed on to new generations, though teachers are equally important in this process (cf. *m. B. Meṣi'a* 2:11 and *Sipre Deut.* 32).[108] In fact, Deut. 6:4–9, which locates instruction in the covenant within the household, is interpreted in *Sipre Deut.* 34 as a reference to the rabbis' instruction of their disciples.[109] The overlapping responsibilities of the family and of the rabbis and their disciples in embodying and preserving Jewish identity shape the rabbinic understanding of Deut. 13:6–11 (7–12 MT); 21:18–21; and 22:13–21.

The rabbis' historical context is also important here. Under Roman rule, the Jews likely did not have the legal right to execute wrongdoers, and recently, some scholars have questioned the existence of a Sanhedrin during the Tannaitic era.[110] As marginal figures in society, moreover, the rabbis would not have had the authority to institute their system outside their own group.[111] Nonetheless, throughout the Mishnah, especially in giving directions for the sanhedrins, the rabbis establish strict requirements for conviction and detailed

105. Compare Halbertal 1998, 159; Berkowitz 2006, 7; S. Schwartz 2006, 25–27, 46–49; 2007, 77.

106. J. Wegner (1988, 4) identifies the Mishnah as a "model of sanctity": its instructions teach Jews how to be sanctified and to preserve sanctity in their daily life and work (cf. Neusner 1988, xvii, xxix). See also Kraemer 2006, 313.

107. Peskowitz (1993, 14–18, 21–24, 28–34) and Kensky (1996, 74–83) address family life in rabbinic texts.

108. On the family as agent of the covenant, see Kensky 1996, 77; and on the rabbis, see Cohen 1999, 975; Slater 2002, 17, 21.

109. This teaching may have occurred in the rabbis' homes, further blurring the identity of rabbinic groups and families; see Rubenstein 2007, 59.

110. So, e.g., Hezser 1996, 186–90; Berkowitz 2006, 15; Grabbe 2008, 14–15.

111. Compare Hezser 1996, 186–95, 462; Cohen 1999, 975; Berkowitz 2006, 6, 15; S. Schwartz 2007, 77–79.

procedures for carrying out executions (cf. *m. Sanh*. 4:5; 5:4–5; 6:1). These regulations often make instituting the law impossible, as in the commentary on Deut. 21:18–21. Instead of a practical directive for family life, the law becomes a theoretical exercise in biblical interpretation (cf. *t. Sanh*. 11:6). It has been suggested that this sort of interpretation is intended to make capital punishment impossible.[112] The rabbis' presentation of Deut. 21:18–21 would then provide an example of their overall humanism and mercy.[113]

This conclusion is challenged by the rabbinic interpretation of Deut. 13:6–11 and 22:13–21, which expands these two laws to incorporate more situations than absolutely necessary. In contrast to a humanist reading of rabbinic commentary, Beth A. Berkowitz argues that the rabbis actually strengthen the death penalty by regulating its processes.[114] The contrast between the rabbis' explanations of the laws of Deuteronomy thus becomes quite important: why does the son get off lightly, while the seducer and bride continue to face harsh penalties? The varying rabbinic interpretations of Deuteronomy's laws open a window into the developing roles of family members in their construction of Jewish identity. The exploration of constructive family violence in the Mishnah and *Sipre on Deuteronomy* begins with the rebellious son as an entry and counterpoint to the other two laws.

Deuteronomy 21:18–21 in the Mishnah and Sipre on Deuteronomy

According to the Tosefta, a commentary on the Mishnah, "there has never been, and there never will be, a rebellious and incorrigible son" (*t. Sanh*. 11:6 [Neusner 2002]). Indeed, the requirements listed in the precise, detailed interpretation of Deut. 21:18–21 in Mishnah tractate *Sanhedrin*, a collection of instructions for the Jewish courts, effectively prevent the use of the law. The limitations placed around the law of the rebellious son can be related to the rabbis' understanding of its significance. According to *m. Sanh*. 8:5, the son is tried and potentially executed "on account of [what he may] end up to be" (Neusner 1988). The shift in the motivation for the law from the nation to the individual sharply distinguishes the rabbis' treatment of the law from that of their exegetical predecessors.

The commentary on Deut. 21:18–21 in *m. Sanh*. 8 begins with a lengthy, detailed explanation of when, precisely, this law can be implemented. This son is, first of all, a son, not a daughter (8:1). He must be past the age of sprouting "two hairs" but not yet have a fully grown beard (8:1 [Danby 1933]). The hair here is pubic hair, indicating that the son has entered puberty and is thus responsible for keeping the law (cf. *m. Nid*. 6:11; *b. Sanh*. 69a), but he

---

112. So Bamberger 1961, 284; see also *m. Mak*. 1:10; *m. Ketub*. 3:1; etc.
113. See, e.g., Bamberger 1961, 290; Gevaryahu and Sicherman 2001, 250–51, 253.
114. Berkowitz 2006, esp. 4–7.

has not matured into adulthood.[115] It has been suggested that the allowable age range covers only approximately three months.[116] This law is not, for the rabbis, applicable to all sons at all times. The rabbis next specify how much meat and wine must be consumed before the son qualifies as a glutton and a drunk. There is disagreement over the precise amounts, which range from six to twenty ounces of meat and one to two liters of wine. The eating and drinking cannot fulfill or break a commandment (8:2). Furthermore, the son must steal the food and drink from his father but consume it outside his father's home (8:3; Rabbi Yose adds a further limitation that the food should be stolen from both father and mother).

Like Philo, the rabbis emphasize the challenging need for the parents to condemn the son together (*m. Sanh.* 8:4). They add that the parents' marriage must be lawful and proper, presumably so that the child is legitimate and thus liable for the law (cf. *m. Qidd.* 3:12). A strictly literal reading of Deut. 21:19–20 suggests that neither parent can be maimed (because they grab their son), lame (because they bring him to the gate of the city), blind (because they identify the son as their own son), or deaf (because they know the son has not listened to or obeyed them; *m. Sanh.* 8:4). The parents' attempts to discipline the son are also carefully detailed. They must warn their son and beat him in the presence of three judges; if he misbehaves after this treatment, he is put on trial before twenty-three judges (as in other cases of capital punishment). He can only be condemned to execution, however, if the original three judges are present. Finally, if the impossible is done and these prerequisites are all met, the rabbis provide one last loophole (8:4 [Neusner]): the son can run away before sentence is passed and thus be "exempt" from execution once he is fully grown! (If, however, he runs away after the sentence is passed, he is still condemned.)

The Mishnah's lengthy list of conditions that must be met for Deut. 21:18–21 to be implemented would, as the Tosefta suggests, severely limit the use of the law. The rabbis' discussion of the purpose of the law in the Mishnah helps explain this treatment. The execution of the son is a "benefit" to him; he dies "innocent," before he becomes guilty of greater lawbreaking (*m. Sanh.* 8:5 [Neusner]). Wider society is also benefited, but only as in the death of any wicked person. Unlike earlier explanations or even Deuteronomy itself, the rabbis do not identify the son as a danger to Israel's identity. A rebellious son is an enemy only to himself.

In the commentary on Deut. 21:18–21 in *Sipre on Deuteronomy*, piska 218, the rabbis draw more attention to the son's stubborn, rebellious behavior. They suggest that the son may be guilty of planning to kill his father,

115. See Bamberger 1961, 281.
116. Compare Bamberger 1961, 290, citing *b. Sanh.* 69a; Maimonides, *Mishneh Torah Mamrim* 7:6.

apostasy, rebellion against the law and prophets, or turning against community leaders. These accusations indicate that the son's case is serious, deserving of capital punishment; he faces condemnation and death because of what he may become in the future (piska 220). Despite the seriousness of the problem, however, as in *m. Sanh.* 8, the potential implementation of the law is strictly limited in *Sipre on Deuteronomy*. In addition to the requirements listed in *m. Sanhedrin*, a second disciplining and beating are included (piska 219), and the rabbis allow the parents to forgive their son's wrongs rather than put him on trial for his life (218). Once again, the rebellious son can slip through the system without punishment.

The rabbinic commentary on Deut. 21:18–21 in the Mishnah and *Sipre on Deuteronomy* recognizes the seriousness of the son's crime. His death benefits him and potentially the whole community because the execution prevents him from sliding further into rebellion. At the same time, the woodenly literal interpretation of the law constrains its use. In the end, although the rabbis admit that a guilty son should die, the cases in which the law could actually be enforced would be few. This presentation of Deut. 21:18–21 accords with the control over capital punishment in the Mishnah and other rabbinic writings. But perhaps there is another reason as well: the rabbis can restrict the applicability of Deut. 21:18–21 because in their sort of Jewish society, the son threatens himself, not the people of God. The law is now passed on through the rabbis and their disciples; the family is no longer the only, or perhaps even the primary, means of inculcating Israelite identity. The rebellious son's behavior is a threat to the son, but he is not a national enemy to threaten the continuity of the people of God.

The Rabbis and the Shameful Daughter

The rabbinic interpretation of Deut. 22:13–21 in the Mishnah and *Sipre on Deuteronomy* is more ambiguous than the commentary on the rebellious son. The limitations on the law of the disobedient son are present to a certain extent in the law of the shameful daughter and bride, but the rabbis also expand the applicability of the law on a few points. The differences between the presentation and potential use of each law draw attention to the different social values and positions held by sons and daughters in the days of the Tannaitic rabbis. Ironically, the harsher treatment of the daughter identifies her as more significant than the son because her (mis)behavior can threaten society, inheritance, and the identity of her husband and offspring. For the rabbis, though fathers and sons may lose some of their theological importance, women remain key players in the propagation of Jewish identity.[117]

117. So Slater 2002, 21. On actual practices of betrothal and marriage in this period, which likely did not follow rabbinic directives, see Satlow 2001, chaps. 4 and 7; 2006, 612, 617–18.

Some scholars have compared the rabbinic interpretations of Deut. 21:18–21 and 22:13–21, suggesting that both laws are made theoretical, impossible to institute. A major plank in this argument is the rabbis' interpretation of the cloth spread before the elders as witnesses in support of the husband's accusation and the wife's defense (*Sipre Deut.* 235–37).[118] The requirement for witnesses would limit the chance of condemning a bride.[119] The bride herself is given voice as a witness in the proceedings in *m. Ketub.* 1:6–7. If she claims she was raped after her betrothal or lost her virginity through an accident (and thus is not eligible for punishment), her testimony can be accepted, according to some rabbis (though not all).[120] Furthermore, like the son, the daughter's age matters. She is not a child nor a woman; as a "young woman" (נַעֲרָה, *na'ărâ*) she falls in the time between, a mere six-month period according to *y. Ketub.* 4:4 (cf. *m. Ketub.* 3:8 on Deut. 22:28–29).[121] According to *b. Ketub.* 11b and 46a, the young woman must have engaged in adultery during her betrothal period; Deut. 22:13–21 does not apply to women who had sex before betrothal.[122] Finally, most of the rabbinic discussion of Deut. 22:13–21 in *m. Ketubbot* is concerned with the financial settlement on the bride, not capital punishment.[123] For Bernard J. Bamberger and Joshua Kulp, these regulations add up to a law that is a theoretical exercise and impossible to implement.[124]

Some of the texts used to support Bamberger and Kulp's interpretations come from later sources, though. In the Mishnah and *Sipre on Deuteronomy*, the evidence is not as clear as this analysis suggests. In comparison with the detailed, specific regulations laid out for the law of Deut. 21:18–21, the Tannaitic presentation of this passage does not limit the law. The bride's age and the timing of her indiscretion are not emphasized in the Mishnah or *Sipre on Deuteronomy*.[125] The presence of both parents in the girl's defense is not

118. The possibility that the cloth of Deut. 22:17 is a literal cloth is also mooted (*Sipre Deut.* 237).

119. Compare Tigay 1993, 130; Shemesh 1998, 256; Kulp 2006, 36. Bamberger (1961, 284–85) suggests that, though it is not mentioned in *Sipre Deut.* 235–37, the normal procedures for witnesses would be followed here, so the husband's witnesses would have had to warn the woman not to have sex with another man and then had to have witnessed the act itself.

120. See further Kulp 2006, 38–39.

121. See Bamberger 1961, 281–82, 284. Kulp (2006, 46) further suggests that "many" women would have been married as adults and thus would not have been liable under this law (cf. Satlow 2006, 618); however, J. Wegner (1988, 15) argues that most women would have been married before adulthood, while they were still under the control of their fathers.

122. Compare Bamberger 1961, 285; Kulp 2006, 36.

123. See, e.g., *m. Ketub.* 1:2–5. Kulp (2006, 37–38) suggests that there are two types of virginity cases for the rabbis, one theoretical (based on Deut. 22:13–21) and one "potentially effective" (relating to the payment of the *ketubbah*). That there are two distinct cases is not obvious in *m. Ketubbot* (cf. 1:1 with 4:3), though; Bamberger (1961, 285) and J. Wegner (1988, 21) both refer *m. Ketub.* 1 to Deut. 22:13–21.

124. Bamberger 1961, 285; Kulp 2006, 37.

125. By contrast, the age of the husband is specified in *Sipre Deut.* 238.

mentioned. Moreover, the law is expanded to include more situations than Deut. 22:13–21 explicitly demands. According to *m. Ketub.* 4:3, a bride (in this case, the daughter of a proselyte) can be executed whatever her personal circumstances are: in sharp contrast to the son's situation in *m. Sanh.* 8:4 and *Sipre Deut.* 219, if the bride has a father without a house, or a house but no father, she can nonetheless still be executed as a foolish daughter (cf. *Sipre Deut.* 235, 239). She dies, "whatever her circumstances may be" (*Sipre Deut.* 239 [Hammer 1986]).

The Mishnah tractate *Ketubbot* opens with a declaration that the wedding of a virgin should take place on a Wednesday so that her husband can go to court on Thursday, one of the biweekly court days, to "lodge a virginity suit" (1:1 [Danby]).[126] In other words, the accusation should be brought as quickly as possible.[127] In conjunction with the expansion of Deut. 22:13–21 to include women without fathers or houses, the recommended timing of marriages indicates the seriousness of a virginity case. Unlike a rebellious son, a bride who has not preserved her virginity is a threat to the rabbinic understanding of Jewish identity.

The punishment of a slandering husband and shameful bride are explained in *Sipre on Deuteronomy* with respect to all the women of Israel. The husband "has defamed all Israelite virgins" by falsely accusing the one virgin whom he has married (238 [Neusner 1987]). The guilty bride likewise shames all the virgins in Israel with her misbehavior (240). The wife's shame can be related to her role in protecting and propagating Israelite identity.[128] If the wife has had a sexual partner before her official marriage, she has committed adultery against her future husband and thus also forces him to commit adultery.[129] However unwittingly, the husband becomes a sinner and thus brings his own identity into question.[130] Any potential children of the marriage are also threatened. If the woman is an adulterer, her children become mamzer, not fully Israelite (so *m. Yebam.* 4:13; 10:1; *m. Giṭ.* 8:5; and esp. *m. Hor.* 1:4).[131] The position of the mamzer in (rabbinic) Jewish society is marginal: they cannot legally marry an Israelite (*m. Yebam.* 2:4; *m. Qidd.* 3:12; 4:1; *m. Mak.* 3:1), nor do they have the right or responsibility to participate fully in keeping the law (*m. Maʿaś. Š.* 5:14; *m. Yebam.* 8:3; *m. Soṭah*

---

126. Again, Kulp (2006, 37–38) limits the "virginity suit" (טַעֲנַת בְּתוּלִים, *taʿănat bětûlîm*) in *m. Ketub.* 1:1 to cases concerned with financial settlement, but Danby (1933, 245), Bamberger (1961, 285), and J. Wegner (1988, 21) connect it with Deut. 22:13–21.

127. But see also *t. Ketub.* 1:1.

128. See esp. Stott 1992, 25, 33.

129. So Kulp 2006, 48, referring to *m. Soṭah* 5:1; *t. Soṭah* 4:16; *Sipre Deut.* 270. According to Kulp's analysis (48–51), the later rabbis compared the case of the bride in Deut. 22:13–21 with an unproved but suspected adulteress; in both cases, the husband is not allowed to keep the woman as a wife lest he commit adultery.

130. A point particularly emphasized by J. Wegner (1988, 5, 29) and Stott (1992, 30–31).

131. Compare Satlow 2001, 149; McKnight 2003, 86–97.

4:1; 8:3).[132] For the rabbis, women have a prime role in the propagation of the identity of God's people through the bearing of legitimate children in legal marriages. Daughters have taken precedence over sons in the passing on of identity, and their supremacy leads to the strengthening and tightening of Deut. 22:13–21.

Deuteronomy 13 in Rabbinic Interpretation

Idolatry is of serious practical and theological concern to the rabbis. Idolatry leads to exile, according to *m. 'Abot* 5:9. Following 70 CE, however, Palestinian Jews were necessarily surrounded by idols, idol worshipers, and idolatrous practices.[133] In this context, idolatry could potentially include much more than simply worshiping an idol. If a Jew sells incense to a gentile, who then offers it to an idol, is the Jew implicated in idolatry (*m. 'Abod. Zar.* 1:5)? What if a Jew goes to a public bath that is decorated with a statue of Aphrodite, buys a house that once had an idol in it, or walks under the shade of a tree used for worshiping idols (*m. 'Abod. Zar.* 3:4, 7, 8)? For the rabbis, keeping the second commandment entails a complex, detailed set of guidelines for conducting business, decorating the home, buying food and cooking, walking down the street, taking baths, and all other aspects of life in a pagan environment (*m. 'Abod. Zar.*).[134] These guidelines would provide a way to protect the traditions of Judaism from corruption and keep Jews from inadvertently sinning, while allowing Jews to live, work, and socialize with gentiles.[135]

According to Moshe Halbertal, the regulations in *m. 'Abodah Zarah* create a neutral space for Jews to encounter and interact with gentiles by establishing passive resistance to pagan practices.[136] When these practices enter the home, however, passive resistance is abandoned in favor of violence. References to Deut. 7, 12, 13 weave throughout Mishnah tractate *'Abodah Zarah*, but the major treatment of the laws of Deut. 13 occurs in tractate *Sanhedrin*. As in the case of the foolish daughter, the rabbis expand the applicability of Deut. 13:6–11 (7–12 MT) beyond a strictly literal reading, even beyond the guidelines for court procedures established in *m. Sanhedrin*.[137]

In *Sipre Deut.* 87, the rabbis emphasize the intimate relationships represented by the list of family members in Deut. 13:6. The list is expanded to include half and full brothers, betrothed and married wives, proselytes (an interpretation

---

132. But see also *m. Hor.* 3:8.
133. Compare S. Schwartz 2006, 46–47.
134. See further Halbertal 1998, 163–65; Hayes 2007, 247–48.
135. So Halbertal 1998, 159; C. Hayes 2007, 245.
136. Halbertal 1998, 163–65.
137. Note, however, that the commentary on the law of the apostate city in Deut. 13:12–18 (13–19) limits the potential for its use (*m. Sanh.* 1:5; 10:4–5; cf. *Sipre Deut.* 92–94).

of "friend"), and fathers (an interpretation of "as your own soul"). The one secretly seduced by a family member toward idolatry must not love, pity, spare, or conceal the seducer: "Do not seek excuses for him [or her]." "If you know grounds for convicting him [or her], you do not have the right to remain silent." "It is a religious duty incumbent upon the one who has been subject to enticement to put him [or her] to death" (piska 89 [Neusner]). The seducer is an enemy within, and the threat of this enemy must not be taken lightly.

Such a seducer is subject to an official trial with testimony from the witnesses of the crime (*m. Sanh.* 7:10; cf. *Sipre Deut.* 89), which, it might be thought, would protect the accused from injustice. Although the rabbis are generally very strict concerning proper procedure in legal cases, however, they bend their own rules for the idolatrous seducer.[138] Because the seduction to idolatry happens secretly (Deut. 13:6), the two witnesses necessary for conviction may not be forthcoming. Thus in *m. Sanh.* 7:10 the rabbis recommend that the target of the idolatrous seduction try to trick the perpetrator into seducing in the presence of another person. If that does not work, the targeted person should hide a witness and then trick the seducer into repeating the seductive action: "They may not place witnesses in hiding against any that become liable to the death-penalties enjoined in the Law save in this case alone" (Danby). If the seducer does not repent, the witnesses immediately bring him or her before the court to be stoned.[139] The seducer to the worship of other gods is caught in a rabbinic trap.

This unusual, even unjust, treatment of the seducer can be explained with reference to *Sipre Deut.* 85–89. The interpretation of Deut. 13:5 follows the text closely, emphasizing that nothing less than Israelite identity is at stake:

> After the Lord your God you shall walk—this refers to (following the pillar of) cloud—and him you shall fear—meaning that the awe of the Lord shall be upon you—and his commandments—referring to positive commandments— you shall keep—including the implied negative commandments—and unto his voice you will listen—meaning the voice of his prophets—and him you shall serve—serve him according to his torah and his sanctuary—and unto him you shall cleave—separate yourselves from idolatry and cleave unto the Lord. (*Sipre Deut.* 85 [Hammer])

The basis of and motivation for this identity in the character of God in Deut. 13:5 also comes into play. The rabbis comment, "Even if [God] had no other claim upon you than that he had taken you out of the land of Egypt, that would have been sufficient; . . . even if he had no other claim on you than that he had redeemed you from the house of bondage, that would have been sufficient"

---

138. Compare Neale 1993, 92.

139. The witnesses "bring him [the seducer] to the court and stone him" (*m. Sanh.* 7:10 [Danby]). Neale (1993, 93) suggests that this instruction bypasses the due processes of law (cf. *b. Sanh.* 33b), though perhaps the processes are assumed in the Mishnah.

(*Sipre Deut.* 86 [Hammer]). For the rabbis, these two verses of Deut. 13 represent the core of Judaism, and challenges to this core demand a strong response. In *Sipre Deut.* 89, they recognize that killing a family member grates against expectation and even against the Torah (cf. Lev. 19:18), but they do not on that account lessen the demands of Deut. 13:8. In a time in which the potential to imitate the gentiles all around was great, the Tannaitic rabbis demanded radical faithfulness to the ancestral laws and traditions and the God at their center.

Constructive Family Violence and the Tannaitic Rabbis

Overall, the Tannaitic rabbis have a reputation as peaceable people who limit punitive violence, a tendency that is obvious in their interpretation of Deut. 21:18–21. The strictly literal interpretation of the Deuteronomic law leads to a list of demands that, in effect, protect the rebellious son from prosecution, since cases in which all the requirements are met would be rare. For the rabbis, this particular law is unnecessary. While family remains important to the embodiment of and enculturation in Jewish tradition, it is no longer essential to the inheritance of Jewish identity, a responsibility shared by the rabbis themselves as teachers of the law and ancestral traditions. In the Judaism of the Tannaitic rabbis, the rebellious son no longer poses a major threat to identity.

The rabbinic tendency to control and limit capital punishment throws their treatment of Deut. 13:6–11 and 22:13–21 into sharp relief. Far from playing down the violence in these laws, the rabbis actually increase their scope, thus indicating that the foolish daughter and the idolatrous seducer are still dangers to Jewish identity. By engaging in sexual activity with a man who is not her future husband, the daughter casts doubt on the inheritance of property and Jewish identity. To counteract this threat, she must be executed. Likewise, the one who encourages idolatry is dangerous because of the threat to the maintenance of Jewish identity in a pagan environment. Idolatrous seducers become even more dangerous as they try to teach their own sin to others. In reference to Num. 25 in *Numbers Rabbah* 21.4, Rabbi Simeon comments: "How do we know that one who causes a man to sin is even worse than the one who kills him? Because one who kills him does so only as regards this world but leaves him a share in the world to come. One who causes him to sin, however, kills him in this world and in the next" (trans. Slotki). The seducer must be executed because she or he threatens the life of God's people now and in the future.

Constructive Family Violence according to Philo, Josephus, and the Rabbis

This chapter has traveled from an early first-century Diaspora Jewish thinker influenced by Greco-Roman philosophy and culture, to a Jew trying to make a new life for Jews after the disaster of 70 CE, to rabbinic circles reading the

Torah in a posttemple, paganized society. These men are not as disparate as might be thought. Philo, Josephus, and the Tannaitic rabbis were all engaged in defining what it meant to be God's people in their times—times that brought Jews ever more into contact with gentile customs, traditions, and culture. Their common context in the Roman Empire affected their interpretations of biblical texts and traditions, including the use they made of Deuteronomy's constructive family violence.

A notable feature of the interpretation of Deut. 13:6–11; 21:18–21; and 22:13–21 across the writings of Philo, Josephus, and the rabbis is ambiguity. Explicitly and implicitly, the interpreters recognize tensions and conflicts between what the laws demand and normal expectations for family relationships. The use of the traditions is limited in various ways, some that develop out of careful reading of the texts, as exemplified in the presentation of Deut. 21:18–21 in Philo's Exposition, and some that were likely influenced by Roman tradition, as in Josephus's story about Herod's family council. Each of the laws is even abandoned by different interpreters: Philo omits the death of a shamed bride, Josephus neglects the law against the idolatrous seducer, and the rabbis effectively pardon the rebellious son. *Jubilees* tends to reject constructive family violence in favor of unity and peace, a trend that comes to fruition in these first- and second-century authors. Constructive family violence becomes a dangerous tool, to be wielded with care.

It is still to be wielded, however. Philo, Josephus, and the rabbis each uphold parts of the laws and traditions of constructive family violence. Like 1 Maccabees, Philo even celebrates the violence in the stories of the Levites and Phinehas. The continued support of Deuteronomy's laws despite their distastefulness marks their importance to the particular constructions of Jewish identity proposed. For Philo and Josephus, the obedience of children is necessary to the proper functioning of family life and to the education of children to be good Jews. Philo and the rabbis stress the threat of false teaching and idolatry, and for Josephus and the rabbis, adultery endangers the passing on of Jewish identity: idolaters who seduce others into idolatry and women who cast their children's identity into question receive the full measure of the law. Even in the midst of reinforcing these laws, though, the interpretations provided recognize their inherent offensiveness and the difficulty of enacting them. Again, ambiguity marks the use of traditions of constructive family violence.

The next chapter investigates the allusions to and adaptations of constructive family violence in the New Testament. The context is still the Roman Empire inside and outside Palestine, including Jewish and gentile communities. The use of the laws of Deuteronomy and other traditions of constructive family violence at some points in the New Testament echoes earlier and contemporary interpretations. The marginal position of the early church in society and the church's self-identification as family and as righteous sufferers, however, influence the way constructive family violence is adopted and adapted.

5

Constructive Family Violence
and the Early Church

In Roman Palestine in the late first century BCE, a certain young woman was betrothed to be married. Her affianced husband one day added up the signs that had recently appeared and realized that his bride was pregnant with someone else's child. The groom did not want to accuse her according to the law of Deut. 22:20–21. Instead, acting perhaps under a custom not otherwise known until the rabbinic period or on his own initiative, he decided to end the betrothal with divorce.

The young woman gave birth to a son who became a teacher and was known to teach things the official leaders did not teach. He kept company with the poor, the unrighteous, and the ritually unclean, teaching them, touching them, and even sharing meals with them. He gained a reputation as a glutton and drunk. Stories circulated about the time when his family tried to discipline him but he rejected them, saying they were not his mother, brothers, and sisters at all. The community agreed: such a son deserves death.

The mother and son in these stories, of course, are Mary and Jesus, and the sources of the picture are the Synoptic Gospels.[1] According to Matt. 1:18–19,

---

1. This chapter is concerned with the Jesus(es) of the Gospels and the church in the New Testament. Although the texts covered here may well relate to the historical Jesus and the historical experience of the early church, attention remains focused on their literary development of the traditions of constructive family violence.

when Mary became pregnant before marriage, her betrothed husband decided
to divorce her rather than shame her (δειγματίζω, *deigmatizō*). Although there
are no verbal links, it is possible that hiding behind Matthew's language is
a practice like that in Deut. 22:20–21, involving the public accusation of a
"foolish" bride: Mary has given an obvious indication that she has committed
adultery during her betrothal period, and she should thus be shamed to death.[2]

Several clues in the Gospels suggest that Jesus can be identified as a rebellious son. The description of Jesus as a glutton and drunk in Matt. 11:19 and
Luke 7:34 bears obvious resemblance to Deut. 21:20 (cf. Prov. 23:20–21; 28:7).[3]
In Mark 3:21, Jesus's people, "the ones from (or with) him" (οἱ παρ' αὐτοῦ, *hoi
par' autou*), come to the house where he is teaching in order to seize him; other
people are saying that he has gone out of his mind. In light of the household
setting, the developing picture of the opposition to Jesus in the chapter, and
the presence of Jesus's mother and brothers in verse 31, it is likely that Jesus's
people are his natural family, coming to take control of their out-of-control son
and brother.[4] Jesus apparently rejects their discipline. The spatial distancing of
the mother and brothers from Jesus in verses 31–32 identifies them as outsiders, a state confirmed by Jesus's definition of family in verses 34–35. For Jesus,
family relationships depend not on blood, but on mission: those who do the will
of God are his mother, brother, and sister (cf. Matt. 12:46–50; Luke 8:19–21).

The tension between Jesus and his family is developed further in Mark
6:1–6. When Jesus preaches in his hometown, the people of Nazareth stumble.
They know his mother, brothers, and sisters; they know where he comes from.
They do not know where he received authority to teach and heal (cf. 1:27).
Jesus interprets their reaction as the dishonoring of a prophet by hometown,
family, and household (6:4; cf. Matt. 13:54–58). In Luke 4:16–30, this story
ends with the angry people of Nazareth attempting to throw Jesus off a cliff,
possibly in preparation for stoning (cf. *m. Sanh.* 6:1). Luke's version of the
story has been interpreted as an enactment of the law of the seducer in Deut.
13. Jesus misleads the people by teaching new things, and the people respond
by attempting his execution.[5]

2. Cf. *Protevangelium of James* 14.1 (Ehrman 2003, 68); Meier 1980, 6; Luz 1989, 119; Kirk-
Duggan 2006, 69; Marohl 2008, 64 (and throughout).

3. So Kee 1999, 331; McKnight 2003, 74; Modica 2008, 63 (cf. May 1987, 86). Sanders (2002,
120–21) also suggests the parable of the prodigal son as an interpretation of Deut. 21:18–21 that
gives fathers a nonviolent option for dealing with a rebellious son. It is an interesting connection:
if the prodigal son is a rebellious, stubborn son, the story has more in common with Sirach's
focus on the son's ability to shame the patriarch and the rabbis' limitation of the danger to the
son himself, than with the broader understanding of the son as a danger to Israelite identity.

4. The expression οἱ παρ' αὐτοῦ (*hoi par' autou*), "those with him/her," and similar phrases
refer to family members in Prov. 31:21 LXX and Sus. 33, but to more general associates in
1 Macc. 9:58; 12:28–29; etc. On Mark 3:21, see Wansbrough 1972, 234–35; Painter 1997, 70–71;
Barton 1994, 70–71, 74; etc.

5. So Derrett 1985, 111; Neale 1993, 99–100; Green 1997, 218.

As it is for the teacher, so it will be for the disciple. In the Gospels, Jesus warns his disciples that they will be subject to violent attacks from the members of their households. In conjunction with the Gospels' presentation of Jesus's own story, these warnings suggest that the disciples will face constructive family violence because the teachings of and about Jesus threaten the identity of God's people. Biblical traditions of constructive family violence are also apparent in several New Testament texts concerned with the punitive disciplining of members of the church. As the early church becomes more established, the errant member of the church family becomes the enemy within, threatening the identity of the church as the people of God.

The texts addressed in this chapter do not provide commentaries on Deuteronomy's laws, but they do appropriate and rework biblical constructive family violence for new purposes. The misleading prophets in some texts—including Mark 13; 2 Pet. 2:1; Jude 8; and Rev. 2:20—echo Deut. 13:1–5, connecting the experience of the disciples or the early church with the story of Israel.[6] Other texts show the influence of Deuteronomy's models of constructive family violence through a collocation of themes, sometimes supported by verbal allusion (Mark 13:9–13; Matt. 10:17–22; 1 Cor. 5). These texts add to the ongoing tradition of constructive family violence, but in so doing they also reinterpret biblical tradition.[7] Like *Jubilees*, then, the New Testament texts may not primarily or explicitly exegete Deuteronomy, but they do provide a witness to important developments in the practices of constructive family violence.

This chapter begins with a brief survey of definitions of the family in the New Testament before turning to a study of the use of constructive family violence against Jesus's disciples in Mark and Matthew. Mark 13:9–13 and its parallels in Matt. 10 provide a unique opportunity to investigate the tradition of constructive family violence from the viewpoint of its victims.[8] Attention then turns to the potential for constructive family violence within the church family. The models of church discipline in Matt. 18 and 1 Cor. 5 and the instructions for dealing with false teachers across the New Testament witness to the development of group identity in the early church as the victims of violence adapt the structure of violence for their own use.

Defining the Family in the Early Church

Across the New Testament, the church is identified as a family. In Matthew, Mark, and Luke, Jesus defines "family" as those who do the will of God the

---

6. Compare Sommer 1998, 31.

7. Sommer 1998, 27, comments on the interpretive effects of textual influence.

8. Though Luke also includes a parallel to this text in 21:16, the role of the family is minimized. For clarity, this discussion will focus on the Gospels of Mark and Matthew.

Father by following Jesus (Mark 3:31–35; Matt. 12:46–50; Luke 8:19–21).[9] In Acts 2:44–47; 4:32–37, the church functions as a family. Family language in the Epistles commonly describes relationships between members of the community (1 Cor. 1:10; 4:15; 1 Thess. 2:7, 11; James 4:11; 1 John 2:9–11; etc.). This language extends to the relationship between members of the church and God: following Jesus brings with it birth or adoption into the family of God (Rom. 8:22–23, 29–30; Gal. 4:5–6; Heb. 2:10–18; John 1:11–13; etc.). In 1 Tim. 3:15; 5:1–2, the church is the household of God, and thus the members of the church are family (cf. Gal. 6:10; Eph. 2:19). The extent to which this language reflects reality can be debated, and certainly family language in the New Testament also represents traditional ties based on blood, marriage, or living situations.[10] According to the literary evidence, however, churches in the first century identified and operated (or were encouraged to identify and operate) as families.[11]

The pervasive use of family language to describe relationships within the church across the New Testament is influenced by the identification of Israel as the family of God. In 2 Cor. 6:16–18, Paul draws on the imagery of temple and family to explain the identity of the church. A string of quotations and allusions to the Hebrew Bible—including Lev. 26:11–12; Ezek. 37:27; Isa. 52:11; and 2 Sam. 7:14—indicate that for Paul, the church is the family of God just as Israel is the family of God.[12] Family language in the New Testament also resembles its use by comparable groups, including Jewish communities like the Essenes and Greco-Roman voluntary organizations.[13] Indeed, as Philo and Josephus suggest, becoming a Jewish proselyte meant leaving one family to join a new family, a potential reality for the followers of Jesus as well (cf. 1 Cor. 4:14–15; Philem. 10; etc.). For the early church, family would be a natural and significant identity to adopt.[14]

---

9. See also Mark 10:30 (paralleled in Matt. 19:29 and Luke 18:29); Matt. 10:37; and Luke 14:26–27. The calling of disciples away from their families in the Gospels is part of the redefinition of family for Jesus's followers (Mark 1:16–20 and parallels; 10:21 and parallels; Matt. 8:21–22; Luke 9:59–62). On the biblical, Jewish, and Greco-Roman background of separation from the traditional household for the purpose of devotion to a cause, see Barton 1994, 20–54; 1997, 82–98; Bockmuehl 1998, 558–61, 567; Ahearne-Kroll 2001, 2–9.

10. Compare Mark 7:9–13; Eph. 5:1; Heb. 13:4; Col. 3:18–4:1; etc. See further Barclay 1997, 72–78; deSilva 2000, 226–29; Ahearne-Kroll 2001, 10–11, 19.

11. See esp. Sandnes 1994, 109–11, 130, 170, 181; deSilva 2000, 212–25; Burke 2003a, 173–74, 250–53.

12. Compare M. Thompson 2000, 117.

13. Compare Duling 1999, 7–9; Meeks 2003, 77–80, 87.

14. The identification of the church as family in New Testament texts has often been taken as an example of fictive kinship (e.g., Bossman 1996, 163, 168–70; Duling 1999, 7–9; Malina 2001, 214–15). I prefer to avoid this descriptor because of the underlying assumption that "family" entails biological or marital connections. Because family is socially and culturally defined, family language, structure, and responsibilities indicate how a particular society understands family (cf. Bourdieu 1996, 19–21; R. Schwartz 1997, 78); either all kinship is fictive or none is.

Family language permeates the New Testament and is used in a variety of ways. More traditional social constructions of the family and household coexist with the association of family terms and functions with the church. Members of the church family would most probably be members of traditional households also, and the two families do not necessarily coincide. Constructive family violence, then, has two potential arenas, the church and the home, and allusions to the traditions of constructive family violence can be found in both across the New Testament.

Being the Enemy Within: The Disciples as Victims of Constructive Family Violence

In Mark 13:9–13, Jesus warns his disciples that they will face deadly opposition from the members of their families. They will be handed over for execution by their siblings, parents, and children, and they will be hated by all on account of Jesus's name. Biblical and Second Temple traditions of constructive family violence provide a powerful lens for interpreting this text: the disciples are subject to violence as those who teach other Jews to follow Jesus, a blasphemer and false teacher. The identification of the disciples as threats to Judaism is even stronger in the parallel text in Matt. 10:17–22, in which violence arises in the context of the disciples' mission. In this reading, the disciples, themselves misled by Jesus, mislead the people of God, and they face constructive family violence as a result.

Neither Mark 13:9–13 nor Matt. 10:17–22 cites Deut. 13 (though there are allusions to Deut. 13 in the misleading false prophets and teachers who appear in the context of each text). Moreover, the Gospels do not identify Jesus or the disciples as false teachers. From the standpoint of the Gospels, the family violence is not constructive, but rather represents destructive persecution. Reading these texts as examples of constructive family violence requires reading inside out, seeking to understand the motivation of the opponents of Jesus and the disciples. As will be seen, clues throughout the Gospels do suggest that the opponents can be placed within the tradition of constructive family violence, acting against Jesus and the disciples as enemies who threaten Jewish identity.[15]

Support for this interpretation of Mark 13:9–13 and Matt. 10:17–22 comes from John 16:1–3, in which the disciples are warned that they will be turned

---

The early church's description of itself as a family witnesses to one definition of family for that community (cf. Donahue 1983, 42; and Sheffield 2001, 56, briefly).

15. Or, rather, Jewish identities. In the first century CE, as witnessed by the multiple Judaisms known from Philo, Josephus, the Pharisees, Sadducees, Essenes, Zealots, and others, there was no single way to be Jewish. There was enough of a center, however, for Jewish leaders like the priests, scribes, or Pharisees pictured in the Gospels to identify and respond to threats to Jewish tradition; cf. Barclay 1998, 91–92; Horbury 1998, 1, 44.

out of synagogues and killed as acts of worship to God (cf. Exod. 32:29; Num. 25:13). Paul, who famously began his career by prosecuting the followers of Jesus, exemplifies this attitude. In Phil. 3:5–6, Paul gives his résumé: "circumcised on the eighth day, from the people of Israel, from the tribe of Benjamin, a Hebrew of Hebrews, a Pharisee according to the law, a persecutor of the church according to zeal, and blameless according to righteousness in the law." The use of "zeal" here recalls the zeal of Phinehas, the Levites, and the Maccabees, and indeed Paul seems to identify with the tradition of constructive violence against internal threats to Jewish identity (cf. Gal. 1:13–14).[16] According to Acts 8:1–3; 9:1–2; 22:3–4; and 26:9–11, Paul as a Pharisee imprisoned, condemned, and witnessed the deaths of the disciples of Jesus. Although Acts describes Paul's actions as persecution, from Paul's perspective he was zealously and violently protecting Judaism from the false teaching of Jesus.[17]

After becoming a follower of Jesus himself, Paul identifies his earlier activity as the persecution of the church. Paul's reinterpretation of constructive violence against the enemies of God as persecution of the followers of Jesus is comparable to the situation in the Gospels. The perpetrators of the violence in Mark 13:9–13 and Matt. 10:17–22 may understand Jesus and the disciples as enemies of Jewish identity, but according to the Gospels they are themselves the enemies of God. This polyvalence is a good reminder that the victims of constructive family violence have their own story to tell. Reading Mark 13:9–13 and Matt. 10:17–22 as examples of constructive family violence provides the opportunity to see constructive family violence from the perspective of its (self-identified) victims.

Suffering like Jesus in Mark 13:9–13

Discipleship in the Gospel of Mark is no easy task. Jesus's followers must leave their homes, jobs, and families (1:16–20; 10:29–30). They must deny themselves and take up their own crosses, giving up their lives for the sake of Jesus and the message he preaches (8:34–37). They must drink the cup of suffering that Jesus drinks (10:38–40; cf. 14:36). And in Mark 13:9–13 they must be prepared to suffer and die as they witness to Jesus:

> Watch out for yourselves. They will hand you over to the courts, and you will be beaten in synagogues, and you will stand before governors and kings on account of me for a witness to them. It is necessary for the gospel first to be preached to all nations. When they take you and hand you over, do not worry beforehand about what you should say, but whatever is given to you in that hour, say it, for

16. Compare Bammel 1995, 358–60; Légasse 1995, 383; J. Taylor 1998, 105, 109.
17. In Acts 21:20–21, Paul faces the same charges he earlier brought against the disciples: Jews who are zealous for the law accuse him of breaking the law and teaching apostasy to others (ἀποστασίαν διδάσκεις ἀπὸ Μωϋσέως, *apostasian didaskeis apo Mōyseōs*).

you are not the ones speaking, but the Holy Spirit. Sibling will hand sibling over
to death, and a father, a child; and children will rise up against parents and put
them to death; and you will be hated by all because of my name. But the one
who endures to the end, this one will be saved.

The inclusion of violence originating from family members with official action against the disciples personalizes the warning of suffering: everybody will
hate the disciples, even their own brothers, sisters, children, and parents. The
somewhat abrupt shift from the general to the specific is surprising, though.
Why do the disciples' families turn against them, even to the point of putting
them to death?

Family conflict in Mark 13:9–13 is sometimes identified as an allusion
to the historical experience of the Markan community during the Caligula
crisis in Palestine in the mid-40s, Nero's persecutions in Rome in 64, or the
Jewish Revolt of 66–70.[18] While the historic reality of persecution cannot be
discounted, though, it may not be the only, or even the primary, reason for the
presence of family violence in Mark 13. The conflict is perhaps more frequently
related to its location in Mark's Little Apocalypse, the extensive discourse in
chapter 13 concerning the destruction coming on the temple.[19] As one of the
birth pains of the end (vv. 5–13), the family violence in Mark 13:9–13 echoes
the severe social conflict in the last days in texts like *4 Ezra* (2 Esd.) 13:30–32;
Jub. 23:16, 19; *1 Enoch* 56:5–8; 100:1–2; and *m. Soṭah* 9:15.[20] However, as is
the case with *Jub.* 23, family violence in Mark 13 does not exactly line up with
the other texts. Instead of representing general social upheaval, the conflict
is focused on the followers of Jesus. Rather than exemplifying the devolution
of the world into utter, total sin, the conflict in Mark 13:9–13 is suffered by
Jesus's followers on account of and in order to provide testimony to him.
Biblical and Second Temple traditions of constructive family violence provide
a stronger, more theologically relevant explanation for the presence of family
conflict in Mark 13.

Interpreting Mark 13:9–13

The birth pains of the end in Mark 13:5–13 shift from general wars and
unrest to the persecution of the disciples, and then to even more specific violence from family members. This section is held together by the warnings to

---

18. On the Caligula crisis, see Theissen 1992, 156–57; N. Taylor 1996, 29–30; on Nero's
persecutions, see Hengel 1985, 23; Iersel 1996, 244–45; 1998, 40–41; on the First Jewish Revolt,
see A. Collins 1996, 7; Marcus 2000, 32–35.

19. Many excellent studies of Mark 13 are available; notable are Beasley-Murray 1957;
Hartman 1966; Hooker 1982; A. Collins 1996. Dyer (1998) helpfully surveys the history of
scholarship on this chapter.

20. Compare (among others) Beasley-Murray 1957, 49–50; Grelot 1986, 363–64; A. Collins
1996, 20–21; Marcus 2009, 887–88.

beware in verses 5 and 9. The first warning concerns deception by those who claim to be Jesus; the second relates to the danger of being turned over to the courts (sanhedrins), being beaten in the synagogues, and standing before governors and kings. In both cases, the warning encourages endurance: do not be deceived; do not renege on your witness.

In the second warning, the disciples are handed over to the sanhedrins, the Jewish courts for legal matters and for trying offenses relating to the Jewish law. In the system pictured in the Gospels, small courts would operate locally, somewhat like the institution of the elders in the city gate in Deuteronomy, with a major court, the Sanhedrin, in Jerusalem. The reference to sanhedrins (συνέδρια, *synedria*) in Mark 13:9 makes the disciples' experience an official concern, as does the beating of the disciples in the synagogues. A beating in this instance is most likely a disciplinary measure taken by the authorities, as in Deut. 25:2–3; Acts 5:40; 22:19; 2 Cor. 11:23–24 (though see also Mark 12:3, 5).[21] Appearances before governors and kings round out the disciples' experience (cf. Acts 5:27; 22:30; 24:20). They will be held accountable for their behavior and their teachings.

Official action is taken against the disciples on account of Jesus and as testimony to the courts, synagogues, governors, and kings.[22] Witness or testimony (μαρτύριον, *martyrion*) in this context has legal overtones (cf. Mark 14:55–64; Acts 6:13). The phrasing in Mark 13:9, "on account of me for a witness to them," also echoes "on account of me and the gospel" in 8:35; 10:29. The earlier texts are concerned with giving up one's life, home, and family to follow Jesus. In chapter 13, those who have given up everything for Jesus and the gospel are warned that they will themselves be given up on account of Jesus and as a testimony. Standing in the place of the gospel in 8:35; 10:29, the witnessing in 13:9 is the disciples' testimony about Jesus and his teaching. The witness, in other words, is preaching the way of Jesus, and the official action against the disciples to stop their witness ironically leads to the spreading of their teaching (cf. vv. 10–11).[23]

In Mark 13:9, 11, an unspecified "they" hand the disciples over to the officials. The general turns specific in verse 12 with the identification of the disciples' opponents as their siblings, parents, and children.[24] In Mark's Gospel,

21. Compare Cranfield 1974, 397; Marcus 2009, 882. In *m. Makkot*, the rabbis prescribe beatings as a disciplinary measure in the case of false witnesses (1:1–3), illicit sexual relationships (3:1), cultic transgressions (3:2–3), unlawful haircuts (3:5), and other crimes. The ceremony for the synagogue leader who carries out the beating is described in 3:12–14. Although the age of these traditions is unknown (the tractate itself postdates Mark by some time), the discussion does provide an interesting analogy to Mark 13:9.

22. Or possibly a testimony against the courts, synagogues, governors, and kings (see Mark 6:11; Gaston 1970, 19; Cranfield 1974, 397–98).

23. See also Dupont 1978, 97–98; Gundry 1993, 738.

24. Iersel (1998, 396) suggests that there are no female relatives in view in Mark 13:12 (as there explicitly are in 3:34–35; 10:29–30). Though this may be true of fathers, "brother" (ἀδελφός,

the family can be either the household of origin (1:29–30; 6:3; 10:19) or the redefined family of Jesus's followers, those who do the will of God (3:31–35; 10:30). Which family is intended in Mark 13? In the parallel text in Matt. 24:10, the disciples' opponents are other disciples who stumble and fall away from the redefined family of Jesus.[25] The analogy between the handing over of Jesus by Judas in Mark 14:43–46 and the handing over of the disciples by family members seems to support the location of 13:12 within the new family of the disciples.[26] Judas is one of Jesus's twelve disciples, his closest circle of associates, perhaps present when Jesus identifies his followers as his family in Mark 3:34–35. If Jesus can be betrayed by Judas, one of his true family, the disciples should certainly expect no less.

On the other hand, the disciples are not the only ones to fail Jesus in Mark. As already noted, his family and hometown also reject him (3:21; 6:2–6). Accordingly, the siblings, parents, and children of 13:12 could be blood or marital relatives and cohabiting people, as in the parallel text in Luke 21:16.[27] The presence of fathers in the list of betrayers in Mark 13:12 makes this option more probable. In 3:33–35 Jesus does not identify his disciples as "father." This absence could be due to the absence of a father among the family members present in verse 31, but fathers are also omitted from the list of restored family members in 10:30, and Jesus explicitly identifies God as the Father of the new family in 11:25. If 13:12 refers to the church, the father and one of the parents would be God. It would certainly be unusual for God to be referenced as a parent (γονεύς, goneus), one of a pair. Furthermore, although it is not impossible that God the Father would hand children over to their deaths (cf. 14:36), it would be an unexpected and unparalleled pronouncement in the case of the disciples. The family language in Mark 13:12, therefore, likely indicates the traditional household, not the family of Jesus and the disciples.[28]

The allusions to Mic. 7:5–7 in Mark 13:12–13 support this interpretation. Micah 7 begins in a lamentation over the rampant unrighteousness of society, including the deterioration of household relations. In verse 2, brother hunts down brother (or, as in the LXX, a neighbor oppresses a neighbor). A man cannot trust his wife or his best friend (v. 5). Verse 6 details a scene of total household disruption: the son dishonors his father, and the daughter turns against (ἐπαναστήσεται ἐπί, epanastēsetai epi) her mother, daughter-in-law

---

adelphos) can refer to sisters as well as brothers, parent (γονεύς, goneus) includes mothers and fathers, and τέκνον (teknon) is used for children of either sex.

25. Cf. Didache 16.3–4; Cyril of Jerusalem's Catechetical Lectures 15.7 (NPNF² 7:106).

26. Mark identifies Judas as Jesus's betrayer eight times (3:19; 14:10, 11, 18, 21, 41, 42, 44). See also Hooker 1982, 86; Hengel 1985, 24; Graham 1986, 21; Iersel 1996, 256; 1998, 397.

27. Compare Justin Martyr, Dialogue with Trypho 35.7 (ANF 1.212).

28. Although the disciples are integrated into a new family in Mark 3:33–35, layers of family language continue throughout the Gospel; for instance, James and John are identified as the sons of Zebedee in 10:35 although they were called to leave their father in 1:20. On Mark 13:12 as the natural family, see also Wellhausen 1903, 109; N. Taylor 1996, 34; Incigneri 2003, 78; etc.

against mother-in-law. The focus on family relations and the specific image of children turning against parents may have influenced Mark 13:12.[29] Yet the purpose of the disruption in Mark 13 is quite different from Mic. 7. Rather than being part of the unrighteousness of the people of God, the conflict in Mark 13 represents family division over the contentious person of Jesus.

In addition to specifying the opponents of the disciples, Mark 13:12 also ratchets up the seriousness of the attack. The disciples are no longer handed over just to testify, but to death (cf. 10:33), and their children turn against them and put them to death. In light of verse 9, "putting to death" (θανατόω, *thanatoō*) may be better translated as "execution" (see Mark 14:55; Exod. 21:12, 14–15; Lev. 20:2; Deut. 17:7; etc.). That this violence originates in the family makes the situation much more dire. As Jesus comments in verse 13, the disciples are hated by everyone on account of his name.[30] If the members of your own family—your siblings, parents, and children—turn against you, who will be for you? Perhaps the disciples' opponents would add, "Who *should* be for you?" In Mark 13:9–11, the disciples face official sanctions on account of their testimony to Jesus. This context suggests that the violent attack on the disciples by their families in verse 12 is an instance of constructive family violence. Members of households take action against the enemy within—the disciples of Jesus.

Constructive Family Violence in Mark 13:12

Mark's Little Apocalypse is located at the transition from Jesus's challenge to the temple and religious authorities in chapters 11–12 to their move to arrest him in chapter 14, ending with the crucifixion in chapter 15. Many verbal and thematic links tie Mark 13:9–13 to the passion of Jesus.[31] The handing over of the disciples is repeated for Jesus throughout Mark 14–15 (παραδίδωμι [*paradidōmi*] in 13:9–12; 14:10–11; 15:1; etc.). Just as the disciples will be handed over by brothers, Jesus is betrayed by his "brother" Judas (13:12; 14:43–45). The disciples will be given over to the Jewish courts, or sanhedrins (13:9); Jesus is tried by the Sanhedrin, the top court in Jerusalem (14:55; 15:1). The disciples will be beaten in the synagogues (δέρω, *derō*, 13:9), and Jesus is beaten in both the Jewish and Roman courts (κολαφίζω [*kolaphizō*] and ῥάπισμα [*rhapisma*] in 14:65, φραγελλόω [*phragelloō*] in 15:15, and τύπτω [*typtō*] in 15:19). The disciples will stand before governors and kings (13:9); Jesus appears before

29. So Reicke 1967, 361, 366–67; Grelot 1986, 363–64; N. Wright 1996, 347–48; Allison 1999, 294–98.

30. In Mark 9:37, Jesus's name represents Jesus himself (cf. v. 41). Invoking Jesus's name can indicate an attempt to access his power (9:38–39); in 13:6 deceivers use the name of Jesus to lead the disciples astray. The disciples in 13:13 are hated because of their identification with Jesus.

31. The connections between Mark 13 and the passion story have long been recognized. See, e.g., Lightfoot 1950, 51–52; Tolbert 1989, 262–62; J. Heil 1992, 261–62; Painter 1997, 174–75; Hurtado 2005, 164–65.

Pilate, the Roman governor (15:1). The disciples will give testimony (μαρτύριον, *martyrion*, Mark 13:9–11). In Jesus's trial, the religious leaders seek testimony against him (μαρτυρία, *martyria*, 14:55–59); Jesus also witnesses to himself (μάρτυς, *martys*, 14:61–63). The disciples mirror their master.

The repetition of key words and images from Mark 13:9–13 in chapters 14–15 identifies the passion of Jesus as the immediate interpretive context of the disciples' suffering. The experience of Jesus, therefore, offers an explanation of the disciples' experience: they will be handed over to death, even by their own family members, for the same reasons Jesus was handed over to death.[32] According to Mark 14:61–64, the Sanhedrin officially condemned Jesus to death for blasphemy.[33] While this offense is not associated with constructive family violence, the reaction of Jesus's audiences to his teachings throughout Mark suggests that he may have also been regarded as a false teacher who seduces the people of God away from their heritage to new practices, an offense closely tied to Deut. 13.[34]

At the beginning of Jesus's ministry, the crowds are amazed at his "new teaching with authority" (Mark 1:22, 27). Jesus comes into conflict with the religious authorities over his interpretation of the way of God (cf. 2:1–3:6). In Nazareth, the crowd wonders where Jesus got his teachings (6:2).[35] In 7:1–15, Jesus critiques the teaching of the Pharisees. And on it goes, right into chapter 12, in which Jesus repeatedly questions the activities and teachings of the Jewish authorities. Finally, on the night of his arrest, Jesus establishes a covenant with his own blood (14:24), mimicking and thus potentially challenging the Mosaic covenant in Exod. 24:3–8. According to Mark 3:6, from early on in Jesus's ministry various parties began plotting to execute him on account of his lifestyle and teaching.[36] A report of the trial from their viewpoint might

32. So also Stock 1989, 334. Many studies of the crucifixion focus on the Roman condemnation of Jesus as a political revolutionary (cf. Mark 14:48; 15:1–27; Green 2001, 90–93) or on the theological explanations of Jesus's death (see Bowman 1965, 91, 314–15; Tolbert 1989, 262–63; etc.). The focus of the current study is rather on the (possible) Jewish reasons for the crucifixion.

33. Hurtado (1999, 44–48; 2005, 154–55, 162–67) argues that the accusations of blasphemy in Mark were historically mounted against the Markan community, suggesting that the disciples in 13:9–13 are punished for their faith in Jesus as a divine figure. Although Hurtado's interest in the early church's understanding of Jesus lies outside the boundaries of this study, his reading of Mark 13:9–13 supports the interpretation of the violence as a way to protect Jewish identity.

34. See also Strobel 1980, 61, 81–82, 139–40; M. Davies 1993, 190; Neale 1993, 94–101; N. Wright 1996, 439–41; Green 2001, 97.

35. In Luke 4:16–30, this Nazareth story ends in a failed execution, connected with Deut. 13:10 (11 MT) by Neale 1993, 99. Derrett (1985, 111) suggests that the story in Mark 6:1–6 could also have ended with Jesus's being stoned as a seducer (though it seems likely that he is reading Luke 4 into Mark); on the potential for violence in Mark 3:31–35, see also May 1987, 86.

36. The Pharisees and Herodians want to destroy (ἀπόλλυμι, *apollymi*) Jesus in Mark 3:6; 11:18; "destruction" translates cutting off a transgressor in the LXX of Exod. 30:38; Lev. 7:20–27; 17:10; etc. The immediate context of the plan to destroy Jesus in Mark 3:6 is breaking the Sabbath; cf. Lev. 23:30.

tell of a man who misleads the people, teaching them to break the laws and traditions of Judaism. In fact, subsequent Christian and Jewish interpretations of Jesus's story include specific accusations of deception and misleading.[37]

Identification with Jesus sets the disciples apart from those Jews who do not identify with Jesus, a point emphasized by the redefinition of family in Mark 3:34–35. Jesus's disciples share his mission (3:14–15; 6:7–13), and they drink the blood of the new covenant. Their close association with Jesus and his work will get them into the same trouble he faced.[38] In 13:9, 12, the disciples are subject to violence because of Jesus (cf. 8:35; 10:29–30). As they witness to Jesus, the disciples face the punishment about to be endured by Jesus himself. Jesus and his disciples are arrested, beaten, put on trial, and even killed for challenging the accepted identity of God's people. The brothers, sisters, parents, and children of Mark 13:12 are handed over and executed by family members as part of the long-standing tradition of constructive family violence.[39]

Read through the lens of constructive violence, family violence in Mark 13:12–13 develops out of the need to protect the community from corruption. The authorities and family members act against the disciples in order to guard the law and covenant against internal threats. From the viewpoint of the disciples, the violence against them is persecution; but from the standpoint of the perpetrators of violence, it is in obedience to the covenant. Identification with Jesus in this instance identifies the disciples as objects of hatred, enemies of the community of faith.[40] Paradoxically, of course, the gospel perspective of Mark 13:9–13 presents the persecution of the disciples as another example of God's people rejecting God's messengers, thus bringing judgment on themselves.[41]

Salvation in Mark 13:13

Placing the experience of the disciples alongside the experience of Jesus gives significance to their suffering. Just as Jesus's victory comes through suffering (e.g., Mark 8:31; 9:31; 10:32–34; 15:38–39), so must the disciples suffer as they participate in Jesus's victory (8:34–38).[42] In Mark 13:13, despite the official action, familial violence, and general hatred directed against the disciples, Jesus reassures his followers that they will be saved so long as they endure until the

37. See Matt. 27:63–65; Luke 23:2, 5, 14 (cf. Acts 13:8–10; 20:30); John 7:12, 47–48; b. Sanh. 43a; Justin Martyr, Dial. 108 (ANF 1.253); Origen, Cels. 2:1 (ANF 4.429). See further Neale 1993, 93; Stanton 1992, 172–73, 238–41; 1994, 166–79; Bauckham 1999, 225–28.

38. Compare Tolbert 1989, 263; Bammel 1995, 358 (on Acts).

39. See also Moyise 2007, 39, briefly.

40. Hatred in Mark 13:13 is comparable with enmity in Mic. 7:6 and with Philo's language of enmity and hatred in reference to apostates and other transgressors in Spec. Laws 1.55, 315–16; Virtues 191; Names 108; etc.

41. Compare Mark 12:1–12; Tolbert 1989, 262–63.

42. Compare H. Anderson 1976, 290; Hooker 1991, 301; Malbon 1996, 115; Ahearne-Kroll 2001, 19.

end (cf. Mic. 7:7).[43] It could even be argued that their salvation comes through their persecution, in that persecution provides the opportunity for endurance.[44]

Jesus's response to his arrest and trials in Mark gives the disciples a model to follow.[45] As Stephen Barton notes, Jesus's passion and resurrection meet the expectations of Mark 13:13.[46] Jesus endures by accepting his fate, witnessing to his own identity, and refusing to refute the charges brought against him (14:48–49, 60–62; 15:2–5). The disciples are called to follow his example as they face their own arrests, trials, and deaths. They must watch out, guard against misleading deception, and stay alert (13:5, 21–23, 33–37). In the midst of suffering for Jesus's sake, they must remain faithful to him. Mark 13:5–13 warns the disciples that their lives before the end will not be easy, but if they are loyal to Jesus, they will be saved.

Punishing False Teaching in Matthew 10

Biblical and Second Temple traditions of constructive family violence provide a helpful background for interpreting Mark 13:9–13. The connection is strengthened in the parallel passage in Matt. 10, in which official and familial action against the disciples occurs in the context of mission. Preaching the gospel of Jesus, an activity readily perceived as challenging and threatening the identity of God's people, meets an appropriate end in the death of the false teachers. The Gospel of Matthew developed in a community with strong ties to the Jewish community, and likely in a situation of conflict between Jewish Christians and the larger Jewish community.[47] This historical context makes the punishment of constructive family violence against false teachers even more apposite.[48]

The eschatological discourse of Mark 13 is paralleled in Matt. 24, which contains a warning concerning the betrayal of the disciples by other disciples (vv. 9–14). A closer parallel to the family violence of Mark 13:9–13, however, comes in the commissioning of the disciples for their mission in Matt. 10. This move provides a new context for family violence, though it should be noted that Matt. 10 retains an apocalyptic or eschatological flavor (cf. vv. 15, 23, 32–33, etc.).[49] The relocation of family violence may have resulted from

43. The "end" (τέλος, *telos*) has been interpreted as the end of the disciples' lives in martyrdom (so Gundry 1993, 740) and as the end of Jesus's own life in Mark 14–15 (so Tolbert 1989, 262). It may also be the end of Mark 13:7, that is, judgment.

44. Compare Rom. 12:12; 2 Tim. 2:12; Heb. 10:32; Dupont 1978, 98.

45. Conversely, the disciples who betray and abandon Jesus and fail to share the news of his resurrection in Mark 14–16 give the reader an example of what not to do.

46. Barton 1994, 111.

47. Compare Stanton 1992, 157–64; Saldarini 1994, 1–2; Foster 2004, 138–39, 253.

48. See also Harvey 1985, 81–83, 91; Neale 1993, 95–96; Sim 1998, 158, 161.

49. See esp. W. Davies and Allison 1991, 196; Allison 1998, 145–47 (contra Hare 1967, 99–100; among others).

several factors. It is not impossible that Matthew's sources included family violence in both discourses.[50] Second, the connection of family violence with the spreading of the gospel in Mark 13 may have encouraged its inclusion in Matt. 10. Finally, family conflict is inherent to the conditions of the mission in Matt. 10. The disciples are to leave everything behind (vv. 9–10): they have already left their families to follow Jesus (4:18–22; 8:21–22; 9:9), and now he sends them out with even more stringent emptiness. The necessary disregard for traditional social responsibilities could cause family tensions, as is clearly indicated in Matt. 10:34–37.[51]

As in Mark 6:7–13 and Luke 9:1–6, in Matt. 10:1, 7–8 Jesus sends the disciples out to carry on his work of preaching the kingdom, casting out demons, and healing the sick (cf. Matt. 4:23–24; 9:35). The mission discourse in Matt. 10 extends far beyond the sending out of the disciples in Mark 6:7–11, however (and unlike Mark's story, Matthew does not clearly indicate that the disciples went on their mission).[52] Matthew's additions to the Markan narrative emphasize the location of the mission among the people of Israel, deliberately excluding Samaritans and gentiles (vv. 5–6). The disciples' activities are more numerous (vv. 7–8), and the list of prohibited luggage is more extensive (vv. 9–10). Finally, in even sharper distinction to Mark 6, the majority of Matt. 10 is concerned with potential reactions to the disciples' mission.

A household may be receptive to the disciples and their message. Such a household is blessed by the disciples' peace (Matt. 10:11–13). If the disciples do not find a willing audience, however, on their way out they should shake off the dust of that city as a witness against them. Such a city will be judged more harshly than the infamously inhospitable, unreceptive Sodom and Gomorrah (vv. 13–15).[53] The next verses of Matt. 10 expand on the theme of rejection and consequent judgment. In a reversal of the imagery of verse 6 in which the disciples are sent to the lost sheep of Israel, they go as sheep to the wolves in verse 16. These wolves are dangerous, so the disciples must beware. They will be arrested, beaten, put on trial, condemned by their own families, and hated by everybody, but if they endure and remain faithful to the mission, they will be saved (vv. 17–23).

These verses in Matt. 10 closely parallel Mark 13:9–13; in fact, only one word of Matt. 10:21 differs from Mark 13:12 (substituting δέ [de] for καί

50. So Park 1995, 131 (cf. D. Wenham 1984, 225, 229).

51. Note that Wink (1998, 76) and May (1990, 144–45) argue that the disciples' abandonment of home is the cause of family violence in Mark 13; cf. also Donahue 1983, 45–46; Barton 1994, 20, 222; Malina and Rohrbaugh 2003, 65.

52. Matthew 10:5 implies that the disciples did go, but at the conclusion of the missionary discourse, Jesus himself goes to teach and preach (11:1). See further Weaver 1990, 126; J. Brown 2005, 25.

53. Neale (1993, 97) connects the refusal of entire cities to receive the disciples with Deut. 13:12–18 (13–19), though the evidence provided is not strong.

[*kai*]). Several of the modifications in Matt. 10 make the text more readable (cf. Mark 13:11 with Matt. 10:19–20), and some relate to Matthew's thematic preferences (e.g., the Holy Spirit is called "the Spirit of your Father" in v. 20). In verse 17, the word used for flogging in Deut. 25:1–3 (μαστίγω, *mastigō*) replaces the more general beating (δέρω, *derō*) from Mark 13:9, a substitution that, in conjunction with execution in verse 21, emphasizes the punitive nature of the disciples' experience (cf. Matt. 20:19).[54] Finally, the inclusion of an explicit comparison between Jesus and his disciples in Matt. 10:24–25 clarifies the connection between the sufferings of the disciples and Jesus.[55] The disciples can expect nothing more nor less than the treatment Jesus himself receives.

As is the case with Mark 13:12, questions have been raised concerning the identity of the family members listed in Matt. 10:21. On the basis of the related text in Matt. 24:10–12, the close parallel between Jesus and his disciples, and the references to God as Father and the household of Jesus and his followers in 10:20, 25, it has been argued that the family members in verse 21 must be other members of the church.[56] On the other hand, the redefinition of the family as those who do the will of God the Father does not happen in Matthew's narrative until 12:46–50. God, identified as the only Father for Jesus's disciples (23:9), cares for God's children (e.g., 5:43–48; 7:11), a characterization that would be called into question if God handed the children over for execution in 10:21. The imagery of verse 25 identifies Jesus and his followers as a household in order to emphasize the external origin of the attacks they suffer, and the family conflict in verses 34 to 39 indicates that the disciples do still have traditional families from which they can separate. As in Mark 13:12, the people listed in Matt. 10:21 are best understood as the members of the disciples' own families.[57]

The inclusion of Matt. 10:34–39 in the mission discourse draws attention to the danger involved in following Jesus. Far from bringing peace on earth, Jesus brings a sword to divide the members of a household from each other (vv. 34–36).[58] The specific relationships mentioned here come from Mic. 7:6–7: Jesus divides a man against his father, a daughter against her mother, and a daughter-in-law against her mother-in-law, and turns the members of the household into enemies.[59] This conflict and enmity arise from the radical nature of Jesus's call to discipleship. His followers must love him more than

54. Compare Hare 1967, 104.

55. See further Allison 2005, 223–25.

56. So Ascough 2001, 107–8.

57. As assumed by the majority of interpreters, including M. Davies 1993, 83.

58. The relationship between this text and the parallel passages in Luke 12:51–53 and *Gospel of Thomas* 16 has oft been examined; see, e.g., Lambrecht 1967, 135–37; C. Heil 1997, 214–21.

59. Matthew 10:35–36 is not a direct quote of Mic. 7:6–7. W. Davies and Allison (1991, 217–20) suggest that Matt. 10 is the fulfillment of Mic. 7 (cf. Beasley-Murray 1993, 405; Allison 1998, 146–47).

their families, they must take up their cross to follow, and they must lose their life for his sake (vv. 37–39). Jesus's disciples are called to prove themselves worthy of him and of life by privileging their relationship with Jesus over their responsibilities to their families (cf. 4:18–22; 8:21–22).

The association of swords, division, and enmity with family in Matt. 10:34–39 is quite striking. Otto Betz and Matthew Black connect these verses with the story of the Levites in Exod. 32:27–29, girding on their swords to kill their brothers, relatives, sons, and neighbors: Jesus is calling his followers to war (though Matt. 10:34–36 and Exod. 32:27–29 use different words for "sword," and do not share other words or images).[60] It is also possible to see these roles reversed: the disciples' families are the Levites, strapping on the sword against the disciples themselves (cf. enmity in Matt. 5:43–48). In either case, the violence of Matt. 10:34–39 brings the reader back to verses 21–22. Jesus causes division in their households as he calls his followers to put him above their families, to imitate him in his mission, and to march to death. The families left behind by the disciples in turn hand them over to the authorities for execution. The heavenly Father of the disciples will support them in their coming ordeal (10:20, 29–31); their birth parents, siblings, and children will turn them over to it.

As with Mark 13:12–13, we can effectively read Matt. 10:17–22 within the tradition of constructive family violence.[61] The changes in the setting and in the wording noted above make the connection even more clear, as does the explicit comparison with the experience of Jesus in 10:24–25. If Jesus is regarded with suspicion and eventually rejected because of his teaching and miracle working (Matt. 9:3, 34; 11:19; 12:9–14, 24; etc.), so also his household of followers will be subject to violence. Placing family violence in the context of the mission to Israel allows the disciples to be identified as apostates and false teachers.[62] The seducers in Deut. 13 are executed not only because of their own decision to worship other gods but even more because they have tried to spread their foreign ways throughout Israel, an issue emphasized in Num. 25:6 LXX; 1 Macc. 1–2 (cf. 2 Macc. 6:24–25); and Philo, *Spec. Laws* 1.316. It is also a notable reason for the persecution of the church leaders in Acts 6:14; 18:12–13; and 21:20–24.[63] The missionary activity of Jesus's followers in Matt. 10 leaves them open to the charge of counseling rebellion against the covenant God of Israel, and the treatment they receive sets them within the traditions of violence against idolaters, apostates, and false teachers.

From the perspective of the disciples, this treatment is an honor that brings heavenly rewards (Matt. 5:10–12). Following Mark 13:13, constructive

---

60. See O. Betz 1957–58, 129–30; Black 1970, 118; 1984, 289.

61. See also Weaver 1990, 94 (cf. Neale 1993, 95–98).

62. Compare Dupont 1978, 102: in Mark 13, persecution provides the opportunity to witness. In Matt. 10, the witnessing leads to persecution.

63. See Bammel 1995, 358; Barclay 1998, 89–90.

family violence in Matt. 10:22–23 ends on a note of hope: the one who endures to the end, remaining faithful to the mission even under persecution, will be saved. Moreover, in 10:28–31 Jesus reminds his disciples that their heavenly Father, who has ultimate authority, knows and cares for them. If the disciples stand firm, endure persecution, and continue to confess Jesus, then Jesus will confess them before God (v. 32). As in Mark, Jesus himself provides a model of faithful endurance for the disciples to follow. He accepts the violence brought against him even to the point of refusing the armed protection of his disciple or heaven (26:52–54). The disciples are likewise called to accept and endure the violence they will face on account of their devotion to Jesus.

Constructive Family Violence against the Disciples in Mark and Matthew

In the story of the early church in the book of Acts, the Jewish leaders accuse Jesus's disciples of misleading the people by teaching them ways of living and believing that go against the law of Moses and the traditions of the ancestors (6:11–14; 21:20–21, 27–28; etc.). The same could be said of Jesus in Mark and Matthew, and if said of Jesus, so also of the disciples who share his mission. Jesus's warning of official and familial opposition in Mark 13 and Matt. 10 can be read within this context as an indication that the disciples will suffer under the tradition of constructive family violence.

The issue at stake is identity. The new teaching and covenant announced by Jesus and his disciples threaten more traditional understandings of the identity of the people of God. Jesus and his disciples therefore become enemies within, and the threat they raise must be addressed. The official and familial actions against the disciples in Mark 13:9–13 and Matt. 10:17–22 seek to stamp out their devotion to Jesus and preaching of the gospel before more people can be misled. For the early church, expecting to become the victims of constructive family violence is also an issue of identity: identity as those who suffer for Jesus's sake, a powerful image across the New Testament, and one that empowers the group and individuals in the group (as in Matt. 5:11–12).[64] Suffering is the way of discipleship (Mark 8:34–38), and so experiencing suffering is proof that the sufferer is one of Jesus's followers, identified with Jesus himself.[65] Disciples are called to accept suffering just as Jesus accepted the cross; vengeance belongs to God alone.[66] Within Mark and Matthew, constructive

---

64. See also John 15:18–16:4; Phil. 1:29–30; Heb. 12:1–13; 1 Pet. 1:6–7; 2:18–23; 4:12–19; Rev. 1:9; 12:17; etc.

65. On the place of suffering and martyrdom in the early church, cf. Bauckham 1993, 234–37; Zerbe 1993, 290; Hays 1996, 326, 329–33; Desjardins 1997, 31.

66. See Rom. 12:14–21; Rev. 6:9–11. The ideological tension between accepting persecution, loving enemies, and awaiting divine judgment has often been noted; see, e.g., Zerbe 1993, 209, 268; Desjardins 1997, 90–91, 119–21; Carter 2005, 98–99.

family violence enacted against the disciples further develops the identity of the church as righteous sufferers, following the model of Jesus.

Disciplining the Family

In Mark 13 and Matt. 10, Jesus's disciples face constructive family violence as threats to Jewish tradition and identity. Attention now turns to the potential allusions to the use of this violence against enemies within the family of Jesus's followers. These references are few and minor; considering the use of constructive family violence to support group identity as righteous sufferers in Mark and Matthew, perhaps it is not surprising that traditions of constructive family violence are not extensively or thoroughly employed for relationships within the community.

The few references to the use of constructive family violence in the New Testament relate to the church family rather than households.[67] Like the rabbis, the church passed on its identity, both belief and way of life, primarily through teaching in the community. Teachers and leaders act as parents, "feeding," caring for, and forming their children into members of the church (cf. 1 Cor. 4:14–21; 1 Thess. 2:7, 11–12; 1 Tim. 3:14–4:16; Heb. 5:12–14; etc.). Within this system, false teachers pose a significant danger, and echoes of Deut. 13 appear in some of the New Testament texts that address this problem. Despite the grave danger of false teaching, however, the punishment prescribed in Deut. 13 is not encouraged in these texts. Members of the church should withstand the temptation offered by the false teachers, but they are not instructed to use violence against them.

The church is given responsibility for identifying and punishing errant members in Matthew and 1 Corinthians. In Matt. 18, the disciplining of straying members of the church is framed within family language, and later interpreters of this text connected its instructions with Deut. 13:6–11. First Corinthians 5 applies the purge formula found in Deut. 21:21 and 22:21 (among other texts) to the disciplining of an offender, a "so-called brother" or sister (v. 11 NASB). Although these connections with biblical and Second Temple traditions of constructive family violence are minimal, the potential for violence in each text allows them to be compared with the disciplining of family members in earlier traditions.

The rhetoric of constructive family violence within the church family in the New Testament is incomplete. The limited, partial use of biblical and Second Temple traditions of constructive family violence is itself an interesting

---

67. Texts that give directions for household life seem to discourage the use of harsh treatment in disciplining wives, children, and slaves (Eph. 5:21–6:9; Col. 3:18–4:1; 1 Pet. 3:7), though see also 1 Tim. 3:4–5, 12.

development in the tradition. Reference can be made to the historical improbability of enacting punishment and execution in explaining this gap. Perhaps more apropos is the importance of community identity as righteous sufferers. The allusions to Deuteronomy's traditions of constructive family violence without extensive use of violence in the community gives insight into the process of self-definition in the early church.

False Teachers in the Church

The story of the early church in the New Testament is in part the story of teachers traveling from city to city, preaching the gospel and instructing new believers (cf. 2 Cor. 11:4; Gal. 2:12; 2 John 7–11; 3 John 5–10). In this context, the question of distinguishing between acceptable and unacceptable teachings becomes quite serious, as indicated by the numerous references to false teaching through the New Testament.[68] The use of language drawn from Deut. 13 to describe the false teachers emphasizes the danger. Despite the importance of false teaching for a group in the process of developing identity, though, violent punishment based on traditions of constructive family violence is absent from these texts. Instead, the Gospels, Epistles, and Revelation call for faithfulness to the teaching of Jesus expressed by separation from false teachers.

A number of New Testament texts recognize the danger of false teaching for the community. False teachers encourage behaviors that defile the community in Jude and 2 Pet. 2:10–22. They disrupt the love that is the central mark of the Johannine community (1 John 4:20–21). They pervert Paul's gospel, leading to the loss of those who accept their teachings (Gal. 1:6–9; 5:4). They were on the way of Jesus but stepped off (2 Pet. 2:20–21). They destroy Matthew's ideal obedient, loving community from within (24:10–12). Accepting false teaching entails the loss of communal identity. Occasionally, these texts describe the false teachers with language and imagery of prophecy and misleading drawn from Deut. 13. The false prophets who try to mislead Jesus's followers as well as others in Mark 13:5–6, 21–23 resemble the prophet of Deut. 13:1–5.[69] False teachers are again false prophets in 2 Pet. 2:1; in Jude 8, they are "dreamers" (ἐνυπνιάζομαι, *enypniazomai*, as in Deut. 13:1–5 [2–6 LXX]). The prophet Jezebel "teaches and misleads" (διδάσκει καὶ πλανᾷ, *didaskei kai plana*) the church of Thyatira (Rev. 2:20).

James 5:19–20 addresses the possibility of bringing back a sibling who has gone astray, or been led astray, from the truth (πλανηθῇ ἀπὸ τῆς ἀληθείας, *planēthē apo tēs alētheias*). Only two New Testament texts use family language

---

68. Compare Lieu 1986, 125–32; 1991, 11–12.
69. "Misleading" (πλανάω, *planaō*) in Mark 13:5–6 echoes Deut. 13:5 (6 LXX), but shifts to the relatively rare ἀποπλανάω (*apoplanaō*) in Mark 13:22. These texts are paralleled in Matt. 24:4–5, 11, 23–26; Luke 17:23; 21:8.

of the false teachers themselves, and in both cases the descriptor is "false sibling" (ψευδάδελφος, *pseudadelphos*, in 2 Cor. 11:26; Gal. 2:4). In Galatians, these false kin do not even originate in the community; they are outsiders who sneak in to disrupt community life (cf. Jude 4). Although the teachers themselves may have identified with the community, these texts disavow the connection (see esp. 1 John 2:18–19). As in Philo's understanding of enmity and kinship, the actions and words of the false teachers show they are not true kin at all.[70]

The directives given for dealing with false teachers across the New Testament repeat the instructions concerning false prophets in Mark 13:5, 21, 23: watch out and do not be led astray (cf. Luke 17:23; 21:8; Matt. 24:13, 26).[71] Attention remains focused on the churches' reception of the message, and only a few texts address what to do with the false teachers themselves. In 1 Tim. 1:3–4, the leader of a church has the responsibility to command or instruct (παραγγέλλω, *parangellō*) the false teachers not to teach, and in Titus 1:10–14, false teachers should be silenced and rebuked so that they may be reeducated in true doctrine.[72] Galatians 1:8–9 is the only text in which a consequence drawn from Deut. 13 is applied to false teachers: those who preach a different gospel than Paul does, even if the preacher is an angel or Paul himself, should be "accursed" (NRSV; ἀνάθεμα, *anathema*). *Anathema* in the Septuagint is the translation of the ban (חֵרֶם) in the Hebrew text, and therefore Gal. 1:8–9 accesses the violent destruction visited on the misled city in Deut. 13:15–17 (16–18 LXX). Notably, however, Paul does not instruct the Galatians to destroy a false teacher. He rather says, "let him or her be accursed": here, as in other New Testament texts, judgment on the false teachers is reserved for God (e.g., James 3:1; Jude 5–16; Rev. 2:16, 22–23; etc.).[73] No New Testament text instructs the church to execute or otherwise physically punish false teachers.

The dearth of instructions regarding the punishment of false teachers in the church could have several explanations. Part of the answer may lie in the church's precarious position in Jewish Palestine and the wider Roman Empire. Churches did not have the legal clout to carry out executions or other

70. Frankfurter (2007, 116) identifies the false teachers as the "intimate enemy" of the Johannine community. The language of enmity does not enter the New Testament's own references to false teaching. Those outside the group can be enemies (Rom. 8:7; Phil. 3:18; James 4:4; etc.), but so were the members of the group before they changed their identity (Rom. 5:10; Col. 1:21). Enemies are sometimes persecutors of the church (Matt. 5:44; Rom. 12:20). Troublemakers in the community are not called enemies, however, and in 2 Thess. 3:15 they are specifically to be treated as kin, not enemies.

71. See Gal. 1:6–9; 3:1–5; Rom. 16:17–18; Eph. 4:14; 1 John 2:24; 4:1–3; 2 John 7–11; Jude 20–23; Rev. 2:2, 16, 24–25; etc.

72. Cf. "rebuke" (ἐλέγχω, *elenchō*) in Lev. 19:17, and see further below on Matt. 18:15.

73. So Bruce 1998 (1982), 83; see also H. Betz 1979, 53–54; Ciampa 2007, 99. On the slippage between announcing, awaiting, and enacting God's judgment, see Desjardins 1997, 91, 108; Frankfurter 2007, 120; and on divine eschatological judgment in the Second Temple period, Kuck 1992, 61–95; Berthelot 2007, 120–21.

punishments and so instead awaited divine punishment.[74] This cannot be the full reason, however, for several of the Jewish traditions surveyed here also developed within communities that lacked the power to enact their own decrees. The pervasive instructions to love and forgive insiders, outsiders, and even enemies across the New Testament may have been another factor discouraging the violent punishment of offenders.[75] More precisely yet, perhaps the early church did not command violence against false teachers because Jesus and his earliest followers were themselves subject to violence as false teachers within the Jewish community. As noted above, the church in the New Testament is identified as a body of righteous sufferers. The acceptance of violence for the sake of, in imitation of, and to identify with Jesus may preclude the use of violence against enemies within as much as against enemies without (cf. Matt. 5:38–48; Rom. 12:14–21).[76]

In any case, the New Testament texts do not have a place for constructive family violence against misleaders within the church family. Their fate lies in the hands of God as judge and executioner (which is violence, but of a different sort). The absence of constructive family violence in response to false teaching does not mean the tradition is never used in the New Testament. The cases of sinning members of the church in Matt. 18 and 1 Cor. 5 offer a different approach to internal disruption.

Disciplining the Stray Sheep

Church discipline in Matt. 18 is set within language of family, violence, and forgiveness.[77] Two situations of discipline are addressed: the first is concerned with the person who causes another member of the church to stumble; the second deals with the church member who sins (or, in the textual variant, who sins against a brother or sister).[78] In each case, the immediate response to the enemy within the church is punitive: better to be drowned or mutilated than be a cause of stumbling (18:6–9); the unrepentant sinner should be treated as a tax collector or gentile (vv. 15–20). However, each example of discipline is also

74. Compare Frankfurter 2007, 125–26. In later centuries, Christians did take up arms against each other over doctrinal disputes; see, e.g., Walzer 1968, 4–8; Pásztor 2005, 50–52; Galvao-Sobrinho 2006, 324–26, 331.

75. These instructions are balanced by the connection of the kingdom with violence in Matt. 11:12; Luke 22:36; etc., and the expectation of the violence of future judgment. See esp. Desjardins 1997, 109–10.

76. Compare McGinn 2005, 216–17.

77. "Church" is used advisedly; Matt. 18:17 is one of the two places in the Gospels where the word "church" (ἐκκλησία, ekklēsia) appears (cf. 16:18).

78. Love (1993, 29) and Saldarini (2001, 158) suggest that only men are in view in Matt. 18, but there is no strong reason to limit the gender of "sibling" (ἀδελφός, adelphos) in this way. The twelve disciples directly addressed in the narrative may be all men, but the text clearly extends the instructions to the church as a whole.

followed by exhortations to seek out and forgive a straying brother or sister (vv. 10–14, 21–35). Church discipline turns out to be an ambiguous matter.

The first situation of discipline concerns the follower of Jesus who causes self or others to stumble (Matt. 18:6–9; cf. Mark 9:42–48). Stumbling (σκανδαλίζω, *skandalizō*) and stumbling block (σκάνδαλον, *skandalon*) are identity-changing issues: the one who stumbles may be lost from the flock (Matt. 18:12–14; cf. 16:23; 24:10).[79] The one who causes stumbling therefore poses a serious danger, and indeed the violence envisioned for the source of stumbling in 18:6, 8–9 indicates how seriously the threat is taken. Rather than cause a "little one" to stumble, it is preferable to drown in the depths of the sea with a millstone around the neck (v. 6).[80] Counting drowning as beneficial is a remarkable statement in light of traditions like Ps. 69 (68 LXX), which associates drowning with the absence of God.[81] This dire pronouncement is followed in Matt. 18:8–9 by a command for a person to cut off a hand or foot or put out an eye that causes stumbling, an echo of Matt. 5:29–30.[82] It is again better to be maimed, lame, or blind than to stumble, a claim that gains power from social reality. In the first century, these conditions would have immeasurably increased the difficulties of life, potentially even restricting participation in the Jewish community.[83] Physical conditions like these could be interpreted as signs of sin or the absence of God (Deut. 28:29; Zeph. 1:17; cf. Matt. 9:2–6; 23:16–26; John 9:1–2), and their reversal was a sign of the kingdom (Isa. 29:18; 35:5–6; etc.; cf. Matt. 11:4–6).[84] The commands in Matt. 18:8–9 are, of course, rhetorical,

79. Compare Josh. 23:13; Judg. 2:3; Ps. 106:36 (105:36 LXX); 1 Cor. 8:7–13. Most often in Matthew, Jesus himself causes stumbling (11:6; 13:57; 15:12; 26:31). These references may allude to Isa. 8:14. They may also relate to Jesus's opponents' identification of him as a false teacher who leads the people away from the law and traditions.

80. The "little one" (μικρός, *mikros*) could indicate the children of Matt. 18:1–5, or more likely the followers of Jesus in general (cf. 10:42; W. Davies and Allison 1991, 763; Saldarini 2001, 161). In either case, the little one who believes in Jesus is given high regard in heaven (18:10) and should therefore be protected, not led into sin or even allowed to fall away from Jesus. Along with Mark 9:42–48, the texts of Matt. 5:27–30 and 18:6–9 could refer to sexual relations with children (see, e.g., Sir. 9:5; A. Collins 2007, 450, on Mark 9), but such a limited meaning may miss the larger connotations of identity in the texts (cf. Marcus 2009, 696–97). On the power relations in this text and their implications for the rest of Matt. 18, see Ramshaw 1998, 403; Saldarini 2001, 161; Gibbs and Kloha 2003, 7; Foster 2004, 5.

81. Note also the sea as a place of danger and chaos in Matt. 8:24–27, 32; 14:22–24 (cf. Gen. 1:2; Jon. 2:3; Rev. 13:1; etc.); see further W. Davies and Allison 1991, 763 (who also identify the millstone as a large donkey-driven millstone, not a handheld version).

82. Compare Lev. 24:19–20; Deut. 25:11–12; Josephus, *Life* 34–35; *b. Ta'anit* 21a; A. Collins 2007, 450–53; Marcus 2009, 690.

83. Indicative of perceptions of disability, the blind and lame are prohibited from entering the "house" (possibly temple) in 2 Sam. 5:8 (cf. Olyan 2008, 31–32); priests who are blemished, blind, lame, mutilated, maimed, etc., are restricted from full participation in temple service in Lev. 21:16–23. These conditions also limited participation in the Qumran community (e.g., CD-A [*Damascus Document*] 15.15–17; 1QM [*War Scroll*] 7.4–5). See further Olyan 2008, 31–35, 102–8.

84. Cf. Olyan 2008, 42, 78.

but in light of social reality and theological interpretation, the instructions to maim, lame, or blind oneself intentionally are surprising to say the least.[85]

In Matt. 18:6–7 the stumbling block causes another member of the community to stumble. The danger to the community here is answered by the removal of the threat, drowned in the depths with a heavy millstone to keep the body down. In 18:8–9, however, the victim of the stumbling and the source of stumbling are the same person: the enemy within is a person's own hand, foot, or eye (cf. 5:29–30).[86] The response again removes the stumbling block, but in this case the person is not necessarily lost to the community and can still "enter life." [87] Cutting off the offending body part is rather self-discipline comparable to Philo's allegorical interpretation of Deut. 21:18–21. The shocking claims of Matt. 18:8–9 emphasize the danger of stumbling, requiring strict preventive discipline to protect the identity of individuals in the group and avoid suffering the eternal fires or the Gehenna of fire. "Woe to the world because of stumbling blocks! Occasions for stumbling are bound to come, but woe to the one by whom the stumbling block comes!" (Matt. 18:7 NRSV).

Being drowned in the depths of the sea, self-mutilation, and burning in eternal fire are the only options provided for the stumbling block. Notably, despite the danger of stumbling for self or others, there is no instruction for members of the church to drown or perform surgery on the stumbling block.[88] This omission is rectified by Origen's commentary on Matt. 18. Origen understands severing an offending hand, foot, or eye as casting off a member of the church who, through attachment to the world, sins (*Comm. Matt.* 13.24 [*ANF* 9.489]). Despite the violence inherent to the imagery of Matt. 18:8–9, Origen indicates that physical separation rather than punishment is in order. Excommunication protects the rest of the body, the church, from falling. The personal nature of hands, feet, and eyes also leads Origen to connect Matt. 18:8–9 with Deut. 13:6–11. If someone as near as an eye—a parent, child, wife, or dear friend—tempts a member of the church to sin, thus rebelling against Christ, such persons too must be cast off as "enemies of our salvation" (πολεμίους ἡμῶν τῇ σωτηρίᾳ, *polemious hēmōn tē sōtēria*, in *Comm. Matt.* 13.25 [*ANF* 9.489–90; PG 13.1161a]).[89]

85. See also Keener 1997, 285; Neyrey 1998, 198–99.

86. The individualization of enmity reflects the internal demands of the law in Matt. 5:21–30 (cf. 15:1–20). W. Davies and Allison (1991, 765) also connect this text thematically with Matt. 7:1–5: it is necessary to take care of one's own stumbling blocks (or logs in the eye) before dealing with a sibling's sin.

87. Life in Matt. 18:8–9 represents the kingdom (cf. 19:16–17, 23–24; 7:13–14; 25:46).

88. Note that hanging a millstone on the neck and drowning in Matt. 18:6 are in the passive voice (κρεμασθῇ [*kremasthē*] and καταποντισθῇ [*katapontisthē*]); the agent of these actions is not identified.

89. See also Augustine, *Sermon on the Mount* 13.37–38 (*NPNF*[1] 6:16–17); John Chrysostom, *Homilies on Matthew* 59.4 (*NPNF*[2] 10:349). In *Salvation of the Rich* 22, Clement of Alexandria similarly interprets the command to hate family members in Luke 14:26 as a command to break

The individual focus of Matt. 18:8–9 is problematic for Origen's inter-pretation. However, drawing Deut. 13 into Matt. 18 can be supported by the association of stumbling blocks with misleading, from πλανάω (*planaō*) in Matt. 18:6–14. The straying sheep in verses 12–14 has either wandered off or been misled.[90] In light of the stumbling blocks of Matt. 18:6–9 and the danger of being misled by false prophets and messiahs in 24:4, 11, 24 (cf. Deut. 13:5 [6 MT]), it is perhaps more likely that this sheep has been led astray. This misled sheep is in danger of losing a place in the flock, just as the one who is caused to stumble may be lost to eternal fire or Gehenna. Equally, there is hope for life in each case, that the stumbler will cease stumbling through self-discipline and that the lost sheep will be found.

In Matt. 18:15–20 attention shifts to detailed, specific instructions for deal-ing with erring members of the church, brothers or sisters who have sinned (or possibly sinned "against you," εἰς σέ, *eis se*).[91] This member of the church could be the straying sheep of verses 12–13, the stumbling block or the one who has stumbled in verses 6–9, or another case altogether: the details of the sin are lacking in verses 15–20.[92] The response to the unspecified sin is more precise. The first step is a private reproof (ἐλέγχω, *elenchō*; cf. Lev. 19:17–18).[93] If the sinner in Matt. 18:15 heeds the reproof (listens to the discipline), then all is well: the sinner has been gained.[94] If the sinner will not listen, the reprover is instructed to bring in one to two witnesses and eventually the entire church if resistance continues (vv. 16–17; cf. Deut. 19:15).

As many have pointed out, this process resembles the Qumran and later rab-binic procedures for judging wrongdoing in the community, involving reproof,

ties with fathers, sons, or brothers (πατήρ, υἱός, ἀδελφός [*patēr, huios, adelphos*]) who are a hindrance and impediment, κώλυμα and ἐμπόδιος (*kōlyma, empodios*), to a person's faith. Such a relationship is enmity (ἔχθρα, *echthra*) rather than kinship.

90. With reference to literal and metaphorical livestock, the passive of πλανάω (*planaō*) often carries an active meaning (Deut. 22:21; Ps. 119:176 [118:176 LXX]; 1 Pet. 2:25). Matthew's stray sheep could then be compared with the lost sheep of Isa. 53:6 or Luke 15:4. However, sheep can also be led astray by their shepherds (Jer. 50:6 [27:6 LXX]).

91. The longer reading is in Codexes D and W, along with a few other manuscripts and the majority text; the shorter appears in Codexes ℵ and B, etc. "Against you" may have sneaked into Matt. 18:15 from verse 21 or Luke 17:4, but the longer reading may be supported by the use of the second-person singular in this section of Matt. 18. See further Gibbs and Kloha 2003, 20–25.

92. "Sin" per se is not a major topic in Matthew. In this Gospel the verbal form (ἁμαρτάνω, *hamartanō*) appears only here (18:15, 21) and in 27:4. The noun "sin" (ἁμαρτία, *hamartia*) oc-curs more frequently, along with "sinner" (ἁμαρτωλός, *hamartōlos*), but the references are vague and general with respect to the nature of the sin (1:21; 3:6; 9:2; 11:19; etc.). Sinning against a particular person is not mentioned elsewhere in Matthew, though Duling (1999, 11) draws at-tention to Matt. 5:22–23 and 7:3–5 as potential examples of wronging a community member.

93. Note also reproof as part of discipline in 2 Sam. 7:14; Prov. 3:12; Job 5:17; and throughout the Psalms (6:1 [2 MT]; 38:1 [2]; 94:10; etc.).

94. As Gibbs and Kloha (2003, 16) emphasize, the sibling's identity as a group member is in danger; cf. Mathew 1985, 123.

opportunities for repentance, and witnesses to the reproof before official rec-ognition is given.[95] The punishment for the crime, however, is rather different than those prescribed at Qumran or by the rabbis. Instead of straightforward execution, excommunication, or even a beating or fine, the sinning brother or sister in Matt. 18 becomes like a gentile or tax collector to the reprover (v. 17).[96] The significance of this treatment is debatable. Gentiles and tax col-lectors provide a negative example in Matt. 5:46–47 and 6:7, so perhaps the unrepentant sinner is to be shunned as a form of excommunication.[97] On the other hand, Jesus associates with sinners and tax collectors throughout Mat-thew (9:10; 10:3; 11:19), and he tells the religious leaders in Jerusalem that the sinners and tax collectors will enter the kingdom before they do (21:31). The unrepentant sinner in 18:17 may thus be an object of ministry, someone to be invited into the community.[98] The second option is perhaps more likely, as the omission of the potential punishment of the sinner in Luke's condensed version of this text suggests (17:1–4; cf. 6:37).[99]

The context of the punishment for the sinner in Matt. 18 also supports this interpretation. In the parable preceding verses 15–20, the strayed sheep is sought and returned to the flock. Immediately following the teaching on disci-pline, Jesus tells Peter to forgive a brother or sister over and over again (v. 22). Finally, echoing and heightening Matt. 6:14–15, the parable in 18:23–35 ends with a warning for the disciples to forgive their brothers and sisters, or God will punish them. In this context, the sinner in verse 17 would be identified as an outsider for the purpose of being restored as an insider.[100] Forgiveness, not community-inflicted punishment or retaliation, is the enduring mark of Matthew's community.[101]

Violent (self-)discipline, strong warnings against leading others in the church astray, rebuking sinners to encourage them to repent, and forgiveness: these

95. See 1QS (*Community Rule*) 5.24–6.1; CD-A (*Damascus Document*) 9.1–8; 9.16–10.3; *m. Sanh.* 5:1; cf. Carmody 1989, 150–58; Duling 1999, 10, 12–13, 15–17.

96. Though witnesses and the entire church have been involved in disciplining the sinner at this point in the process, "you" in Matt. 18:17 is in the singular (σοι, *soi*).

97. So Lampe 1967, 345; Meier 1980, 205; Mathew 1985, 123; Duling 1999, 17–18 (noting a tension with the context of forgiveness and love). The reference to binding and loosing in Matt. 18:18 may support this interpretation: the person is bound to or loosed from the church on earth and in heaven with the power of Jesus (vv. 19–20; cf. Lampe 1967, 244; Meier 1980, 206; etc.).

98. Gentiles are emphatically not objects of ministry in Matthew until the Great Commis-sion in 28:19–20 (cf. 10:5–6; 15:24).

99. The closest parallel in Mark omits all mention of rebuking, instructing the disciples only to forgive (11:25).

100. Compare *Didache* 15:3; Carmody 1989, 152–53, 156–57; Ramshaw 1998, 397–98, 402; Ascough 2001, 115. This interpretation is reinforced by James 5:19–20, in which the reader is instructed to bring back brothers or sisters who go astray (πλανάω, *planaō*) from the truth. The one who brings back the sinner saves a life, as the one who reproves a brother or sister in Matt. 18:15 gains them (cf. Gal. 6:1).

101. So also Pfitzner 1982, 37; N. Wright 1996, 290, 296.

are Matthew's instructions to the church faced with an enemy within. The association of the violence of self-mutilation and drowning with forgiveness in this chapter makes its overall effect rather ambiguous. Elsewhere in Matthew, of course, Jesus instructs his followers not to judge a brother or sister lest they themselves be judged (7:1–5).[102] Anger at a brother or sister is unacceptable, and forgiveness is necessary even in the context of an official case to be tried before a court (5:21–26; cf. 1 Cor. 6:1–11). Jesus warns his followers against taking vengeance for wrongdoing, instead teaching them to love their enemies, pray for persecutors, and be perfect as God their Father is perfect (Matt. 5:38–48). While this broader context draws attention away from punishment toward the role of forgiveness in church discipline, the violent language in the chapter remains strong, leaving Matt. 18 an internally conflicted collection of teachings.

Hand Such a One Over to Satan . . .

Like Matt. 18, Paul in 1 Corinthians is less than clear on the place of judgment and punishment in the church. In this letter he addresses multiple problems in the church in Corinth, ranging from divisions between members of the church to critiques of his apostolic authority to incidents of sexual immorality and more. The process of addressing problems and exhorting the church to change represents Paul's attempt to form the Corinthians, living in the midst of a pagan society, into a sanctified, unified community.[103] Family imagery and expectations support his message. Paul admonishes the Corinthians like a father, calling on them to imitate him as children should (1 Cor. 4:14–16). And like the father of Proverbs, he has a rod of discipline at hand (v. 21; cf. Prov. 10:13; 23:13–14; 26:3; etc.).[104]

The particular child threatened with this rod in the next verse is a man who is in a sexual relationship with his stepmother.[105] For Paul as for the Torah, this is sexual immorality of the worst sort (cf. Lev. 18:8; 20:11; Deut. 22:30 [23:1 MT]; 27:20), compounded by the church's reaction: instead of mourning (and thus repenting and disciplining the man), the Corinthians have taken perverse pride in this man's sin (1 Cor. 5:1–2; cf. 4:6, 18–19; 8:1).[106] This one sin may infect the entire church, as the metaphor of yeast leavening flour in verses 6–8

---

102. Compare James 4:11–12; Rom. 14:1–12. In Rom. 14:13–23, judging a member of the church is connected with causing that person to stumble, thus bringing them under God's judgment; instead of harming a brother or sister in this way, members of the church are instructed to love, work for peace, and build each other up (vv. 15, 19).

103. See further Furnish 1999, 49–50; Hays 2005, 21, 23.

104. Compare Joubert 1995, 217–18; Burke 2003b, 107–12; Wanamaker 2006, 344–45.

105. See C. Barrett 1968, 122.

106. The church's reaction is seen as the major problem in 1 Cor. 5 by John Chrysostom, *Hom. 1 Cor.* 15.1–2 (NPNF[1] 12:83–84); and Donfried 1976, 150.

suggests (cf. 6:18–20).[107] The church must therefore judge the sinner with the support of Paul and Jesus himself (5:3–4; cf. Matt. 18:17–20). In 1 Cor. 5:5, Paul announces his judgment, commanding the church "to give this person over to Satan for the destruction of the flesh in order that the spirit might be saved in the day of the Lord"—an instruction that raises more questions than it gives clarification on the issue of church discipline.[108]

In context, handing the sinner over to Satan represents cutting them off from the community. In verse 2, the person should be removed from the community, also symbolized in the metaphor of clearing out the old yeast of wickedness and sinfulness in verses 6–8. The prohibition of associating with those who are called brothers or sisters but are sexually immoral, greedy, idolaters, revilers, drunkards, or swindlers—thus by implication not true siblings at all—in verse 11 also supports this interpretation of verse 5. The chapter ends with a command: "Drive the evil one away from yourselves" (1 Cor. 5:13). This order echoes the Septuagint's version of purging the evil from the midst of Israel in Deut. 17:7; 21:21; 22:21, 24.[109] The parallel directly connects Paul's instructions on church discipline with the tradition of constructive family violence, but instead of execution, excommunication purges evil from the community.[110] The man who has had sex with his father's wife should be cut off from fellowship and relationship. He is no longer identified as a member of the church, but with Satan.[111]

Handing the man over to Satan is clearly related to his excommunication, but the meaning of "destruction of the flesh" is less certain. It may indicate that excommunication leads to physical suffering and even death. The judgment on the sinner is thus comparable to the deaths of Ananias and Sapphira in Acts 5:1–11, and with Greco-Roman magic texts in which giving over (παραδίδωμι, *paradidōmi*) indicates giving someone over to demons to prevent particular behaviors or actions.[112] Destruction (ὄλεθρος, *olethros*) sounds quite final, as in the similar language in 1 Cor. 10:10; 1 Thess. 5:3; and 2 Thess. 1:9.[113] If "flesh" (σάρξ, *sarx*) in 1 Cor. 5:5 represents a living being, as it does in 1 Cor. 15:50;

107. See Tertullian, *Modesty* 13 (*ANF* 4:86–88); John Chrysostom, *Hom. 1 Cor.* 15.5 (*NPNF*[1] 12:85); Rosner 1991, 137, 145; Obenhaus 2001, 4–5.

108. The various interpretations suggested for 1 Cor. 5:5 are helpfully (and briefly) surveyed in Campbell 1993, 331–32.

109. Compare also Deut. 13:5 (6 LXX); see further Rosner 1994, 63.

110. The church in Corinth surely could not legally execute a member; cf. Horbury (1998, 55–59) on the move from execution to excommunication as punishment in the Second Temple period.

111. Compare C. Barrett 1968, 126; Furnish 1999, 53. The use of family language in 1 Cor. 5:1–13 to refer to "someone who is called brother or sister" (τις ἀδελφὸς ὀνομαζόμενος, *tis adelphos onomazomenos* [v. 11]), with the implication that they are not truly kin (cf. 2 Cor. 11:26; Gal. 2:4), ironically emphasizes the lack of relationship with evildoers.

112. See Deissmann 1927, 301–3; A. Collins 1980, 255–56; Shillington 1998, 36–37.

113. See A. Collins 1980, 259; Rosner 1991, 139–40; also cf. 1 Cor. 5:5 with 3:17.

Phil. 1:22; Gal. 1:16; and Rom. 3:20, then the destruction of the flesh entails the death of the sinner at the hands of Satan (cf. the physical consequences of sin in 1 Cor. 11:30).[114] The spirit to be saved on the day of the Lord, then, may refer to the presence of the Holy Spirit in the church. The rest of the church is saved, or protected from destruction, by the eradication of the individual sinner who has threatened the community with his immorality.[115]

This interpretation draws 1 Cor. 5:5 in line with the claim made in Deut. 21:21 and 22:21 that the death of a wrongdoer purges evil from the midst of the people. Its focus on the consequences of punishment for the whole church is supported by the interest in the health of the church in 1 Cor. 5:6–13, the holiness and purity of the temple in 3:16–17 and 6:15–20, and on the unity of the church emphasized throughout the letter.[116] To protect the Corinthian family from impurity, Paul commands that the sinner be destroyed, not by congregational stoning but by the agency of Satan.

Alternatively, handing the sinner over to Satan for the destruction of the flesh may not mean that the sinner will die. In 1 Tim. 1:19–20, two people are handed over to Satan to be taught (παιδεύω, *paideuō*) not to blaspheme. Handing over to Satan here is a method of discipline, not execution.[117] Similarly in 2 Cor. 12:7, Paul's thorn in the flesh is a messenger of Satan (ἄγγελος Σατανᾶ, *angelos Satana*) that God has given to keep Paul humble, weak, and dependent on Christ's power. This satanic messenger is again disciplinary, a connection that could be compared with Satan's role as a tester in 1 Cor. 7:5; Job 1:1–12; 2:1–8; Mark 1:13; and parallels.[118]

If handing the sinner over to Satan is a disciplinary measure, the flesh to be destroyed may not indicate the human being. Paul uses the idea of flesh (σάρξ, *sarx*) in several ways, including to indicate sinful human desires (see esp. 2 Cor. 7:1; Gal. 5:19–21; Rom. 7:5; 8:3; etc.).[119] This flesh is put to death in order to have life in the Spirit in Gal. 5:16–26 and Rom. 7:4–8:17. Based on

114. So Tertullian, *Modesty* 13–14 (*ANF* 4:87–89); Käsemann 1969, 71; Conzelmann 1975, 97; Shillington 1998, 39; among others. A. Collins (1980, 257) and Shillington (1998, 32) point out a parallel in the handing over of an offender to Belial to be killed in the *Damascus Document* (CD-A 8.1–2).

115. So A. Collins 1980, 259–60; Campbell 1993, 333–34; Shillington 1998, 35. Yet C. Barrett (1968, 126), Käsemann (1969, 72), and Wanamaker (2006, 355) suggest that the death of the sinner is for his own spiritual salvation. This logic could be compared with Prov. 23:13–14 and with the rabbinic commentary on Deut. 21:18–21 (that the death of the son in this world allows him life in the world to come).

116. Compare Tertullian, *Modesty* 13 (*ANF* 4:87–88); Donfried 1976, 150; A. Collins 1980, 259–60; Campbell 1993, 334, 337–40; Shillington 1998, 31, 35; Obenhaus 2001, 3.

117. Contra Tertullian, *Modesty* 13; A. Collins 1980, 258. Origen, on the other hand, brings 1 Tim. 1:20 into 1 Cor. 5:13, interpreting the destruction of the flesh as discipline (παιδεύω, *paideuō*) in *Fr. 1 Cor.* 24 (Jenkins 1908, 364); see also South 1993, 551.

118. Note also Zech. 3:1–5; see Lampe 1967, 352–53; C. Barrett 1968, 126; Thiselton 1973, 224–25; Pfitzner 1982, 47.

119. On the meaning of σάρξ (*sarx*) in Paul, see esp. Dunn 1998, 64–66.

these references, it is possible that 1 Cor. 5:5 refers to the destruction of the sinner's sinful tendencies.[120] The spirit saved by the excommunication of the sinner could still be the spirit of the church, purified by the removal of the sin and protected from imitation. Certainly the effect of excommunication in 1 Cor. 5:2, 7–8 focuses on the church, not the individual. However, turning the sinner over to Satan for discipline may also be intended to save his spirit.[121] Putting the "flesh" to death to have life in the Spirit in Gal. 5:16–26 and Rom. 7:4–8:17 would support this interpretation of 1 Cor. 5:5.[122]

The potential for the salvation of the sinner in this reading of 1 Cor. 5:1–5 echoes the gentle restoration of a sinner in Gal. 6:1 (cf. 1 Cor. 4:21) and the rebuke of a sinner as a sibling, not an enemy, in 2 Thess. 3:14–15. In 2 Cor. 2:5–6, a member of the church who sins (possibly against Paul himself, v. 5) and is punished (ἐπιτιμία, epitimia) should not be cut off from the church forever.[123] Paul encourages the Corinthians to receive this person with grace, comfort, and love (vv. 7–8). Just as Paul and Jesus are with the church in judgment in 1 Cor. 5:3–4, so they are with the church in forgiving the sinner (2 Cor. 2:10). And while the sinner in 1 Cor. 5:5 is handed over to Satan for disciplining, in 2 Cor. 2:11 forgiveness occurs in order to thwart Satan's plans. It is even possible that the same person is in mind in the two texts: the sinner who has been punished by the church can be restored by the church.[124] The equally good arguments supporting the two major interpretations of 1 Cor. 5:5 leave the question open to debate.

Matthew 18 and 1 Cor. 5 are the most detailed treatments of the disciplining of members of the church family in the New Testament. Careful reading reveals gaps and tensions in these texts between forgiveness and punishment. Seeking the lost, forgiving wrongdoing, and restoring the punished are part of the larger contexts of Matthew and 1 and 2 Corinthians. On the other hand, the punishment of sinners and the language in which it is couched in the two texts is markedly more severe than the instructions regarding false teachers; instead of waiting for the eschatological judgment of God, the church

120. See Thiselton 1973, 208–9, 214–15; Pfitzner 1982, 46; Vander Broek 1994, 5; Rosner 1999, 32–33. Alternatively, Campbell (1993, 334, 340) and Shillington (1998, 38–39) suggest that the "flesh" is the sinful nature of the church, which boasts in the case of incest.

121. So Origen, *Fr. 1 Cor.* 24 (Jenkins 1908, 364); John Chrysostom, *Hom. 1 Cor.* 15.4 (*NPNF*[1] 12:85); Kistemaker 1992, 44; Obenhaus 2001, 11.

122. So also South 1993, 552.

123. See C. Barrett (1973, 89–90) on the nature of the sin and the church's discipline (which he identifies as rebuking, not punishing) in 2 Cor. 2.

124. This point is argued by Origen, *Fr. 1 Cor.* 24 (Jenkins 1908, 364); John Chrysostom, *Hom. 1 Cor.* 15.9 (*NPNF*[1] 12:87); Lampe 1967, 354–55; Kruse 1988, 132; but denied by Tertullian, *Modesty* 13–14 (*ANF* 4:86–89); C. Barrett 1973, 89; Thrall 1987, 66–67; Obenhaus 2001, 5. Whether the offender is the same in 1 Cor. 5 and 2 Cor. 2, however, the expectation that a reproved, punished offender can be returned to fellowship in the church stands (so also Rosner 1994, 90; Furnish 1999, 53).

is called upon to judge sinners in its midst. Neither text extensively addresses or draws on the traditions of constructive family violence, and neither commands the church to violently punish or execute the offender. However, action is necessary because one person's sin can threaten the community, either by misleading others in Matt. 18 or by the spread of impurity and the potential for imitation in 1 Cor. 5. In the face of refusal to repent, the offender must be cut out of the community. This state is not necessarily permanent, but it is a serious matter for the church.

Constructive Family Violence and the Early Church

This chapter has explored the allusions to and potential uses of the biblical and Second Temple traditions of constructive family violence in the New Testament. First, the disciples in Mark 13 and Matt. 10 are warned that they will be subject to constructive family violence as Jews who teach the gospel of Jesus. Like Jesus himself, they will be identified as misleaders in the community. According to the law of Deut. 13:6–11 (7–12 MT), their own siblings, parents, and children will betray them and execute them because they endanger Jewish identity. This violence is a cause for rejoicing, according to Matt. 5:10–12: they will receive a heavenly reward.

The identification of the followers of Jesus as righteous sufferers provides a way for them to imitate Jesus, live out their forgiving and loving way of life, and find meaning in situations of persecution. This identity remains strong across the New Testament, and it provides a serious check on the use of traditions of constructive family violence against members of the community. If "we" are the ones who suffer this violence, "we" cannot enact it (much as Josephus is constrained from identifying the rebels of the Jewish Revolt as enemies instead of kin). How then should false teaching and other instances of wrongdoing be dealt with in the early church?

Throughout the New Testament, violent imagery and rhetoric does surround those followers of Jesus who mislead or sin against others. However, although the church (represented by the authors of the texts) announces the violence, the punishment itself ultimately comes from God. Members of the church are called to withstand temptation and deception, remaining faithful to the way of Jesus. They should refuse to receive false teachers. They have the responsibility to reprove and forgive sinners. They may have to cut off errant brothers and sisters from the community. They are not, however, instructed to physically discipline or execute offenders. The power to punish incorrigible sinners and false teachers rests with God. The tradition of constructive family violence here is refocused on the family of God: God as Father has the ultimate authority to punish and avenge.

6

Reading Constructive Family Violence
in the Bible

If anyone secretly entices you—even if it is your brother, your father's son or your mother's son, or your own son or daughter, or the wife you embrace, or your most intimate friend—saying, "Let us go worship other gods," whom neither you nor your ancestors have known, any of the gods of the peoples that are around you, whether near you or far away from you, from one end of the earth to the other, you must not yield to or heed any such persons. Show them no pity or compassion and do not shield them. But you shall surely kill them; your own hand shall be first against them to execute them, and afterwards the hand of all the people.

Deut. 13:6–9 (NRSV)

Three laws in Deuteronomy demand violence against family members. The execution of the seducer in chapter 13 is the most starkly stated: this law asks "you" to throw the first stone at spouse, child, or sibling (13:9–10 [10–11 MT]). The executions of the rebellious son and foolish daughter are equally harsh. The son dies because his parents accuse him before the elders of the city, and the daughter dies when her parents fail to defend her. She is killed at the door of her family home—what should be a place of safety becomes her death.

I began this study with several questions concerning Deut. 13:6–11 (7–12); 21:18–21; and 22:13–21. In light of the significance of family in the Hebrew

Bible and ancient Israel, how should we understand the Deuteronomic legislation on executing family members? Given the repugnance to family violence in the modern world, how should, or even simply should, these texts be read today? And do these texts, in the end, have anything valuable to teach readers? It is time to offer some concluding thoughts on these initial questions.

Understanding Constructive Family Violence

In Deuteronomy, Moses tells the stories of the exodus and teaches the law in order to form the heads of the tribes, the elders, the officials, and, significantly, fathers along with their wives, children, servants, and sojourners into Israel, the covenant people of God, who worship God alone and live according to God's ways (cf. 29:1–13). Families are central to the covenant: they worship together, write the words of the covenant on their houses, teach the covenant to their children, and bring to life the metaphor of God as parent and Israel as child. Families are entrusted with the embodiment and propagation of Israelite identity.

This identity is at risk in Deut. 13:6–11; 21:18–21; and 22:13–21. The member of the household who teaches idolatry misleads Israelites from the way of God to follow the ways of the nations. The son who refuses to learn and live according to Israel's identity and the daughter whose behavior calls into question her family's honor and her husband's inheritance—such persons endanger the passing on of the covenant to the next generation. As parallels to and echoes of the laws throughout the Torah and the prophets indicate, these family members represent all Israel turning away from God to their own destruction. If the errant family members are allowed to continue in their rebellion, they may corrupt the community and bring punishment on the people as a whole. Because of the family's responsibility for teaching and passing on the covenant, the family is also given responsibility for eradicating these threats. The family both embodies and guards the identity of Israel.

The question of identity remains important in ancient interpretations of, allusions to, and uses of Deuteronomy's laws of constructive family violence. In the case of Deut. 13:6–11, the worship of other gods is expanded to mean the abandonment of the covenant entirely. Since Israelite identity in Deuteronomy is based in devotion to Yahweh alone (5:6–10; 6:4–9; etc.), the association of chapter 13 with apostasy is a natural connection to make (see, e.g., 1 Macc. 1:11–15; 2:19–22; Josephus, *Ant.* 4.154–55; *Sipre Deut.* 85). That the apostate encourages others to follow their own change in identity exacerbates the problem, as seen in Num. 25:5–6 LXX; Philo's *Spec. Laws* 1.56, 79; Mark 13:9–12; Matt. 10:17–22, and the examples of false teachers across the New Testament. A seducer is a serious threat to the identity of the people of God and must immediately be met with every weapon in the arsenal (and even requires expanding the arsenal for the rabbis in *m. Sanh.* 7:10).

The significance of the rebellious son and foolish daughter is more variable in early interpretation. For Sirach, rebellious sons and foolish daughters shame their patriarch; his own identity is key in the use of violent discipline on his children (note esp. 30:1–13; 42:9–14). The rabbis limit the danger even more to the rebellious son himself (*m. Sanh.* 8:5; *Sipre Deut.* 220). Philo and Josephus retain Deuteronomy's connection between a rebellious child (son or daughter) and Israelite identity in general (e.g., Philo, *Posterity* 181). Strict discipline is an important element in the training of children into good Jews, and children who refuse to learn from their parents face death to protect the life of the community (cf. Philo, *Spec. Laws* 2.248; Josephus, *Ant.* 4.262, 264).

Women are given an expanded role in propagating Israelite identity in *Jubilees*, Josephus's works, and early rabbinic texts. They pass on Israelite blood and thus membership in the people of God to their offspring; they have the maternal power to influence the behavior of children and husbands (cf. *Jub.* 30:7–17; Josephus, *Ant.* 4.244–45; *m. Yebam.* 4:13; 10:1; etc.). In response to this development, the foolish daughter also becomes more important. For Josephus and the rabbis, the execution of the foolish bride—who, by committing adultery against her betrothed husband, endangers blood, inheritance, and behavior—emphasizes her significance (*Ant.* 4.248, *m. Ketub.* 4:3, *Sipre Deut.* 239).

It is often remarked that the execution of family members for the sake of communal identity is an example of devotion to God superseding other concerns. Family violence can be explained more precisely, however. The family in biblical and Jewish tradition, extended to the church family in Christian tradition, is an agent of the covenant. Families worship God together. The covenant, the way of life for God's people, is taught within the daily life of households. The identity of Israel as God's people is inherited through the family. The functioning of a family, then, reflects on the health of God's people as a whole. Violence against family members who endanger the people is consequent upon the family's responsibility to the identity of Israel.

Reading Constructive Family Violence

The role of the household in embodying, propagating, and protecting Israel's identity may explain the function of constructive family violence, but it does not remove the moral offense (at least, not for this reader). The question of how to read Deut. 13:6–11; 21:18–21; and 22:13–21 and other traditions remains. Careful study of the laws in Deuteronomy offers some guidelines, particularly in the tension that marks the presentation of violence and in the larger context of the laws in the book. Moreover, ancient interpreters' faithful, critical engagement with the texts and traditions of constructive family violence provides a model for modern readers. Family violence is not an easy answer, even in Deuteronomy, and this recognition allows readers space for critical reflection.

The narration of the three laws in Deuteronomy itself is marked by tension and unease. In chapter 13 the nearness of relationship to the seducer is emphasized, along with the values and behaviors that should define those relationships—obedience, listening, pitying, sparing, and concealing (vv. 7, 9). While these elements of Deut. 13:6–11 function rhetorically to heighten the violence of the law, they also balance and potentially undermine that violence by reminding the reader of normal expectations for family life. The focus on the parents' role of teaching and disciplining their son in Deut. 21:18–21 has a similar effect. The problem of family violence is also made explicit here by the inconsistency in the identity of the executioners: the parents are released from their duty of casting the first stone (contra 17:7). Finally, the case of the daughter begins with the assumption of her innocence. In contrast to the two verses that address a guilty verdict, the amount of narrative space given over to the parents' defense indicates that a primary purpose of the law is to protect brides. These internal tensions suggest that violence against family members is not the first, nor the preferred, choice for household life.

For Philo and the early rabbis, the tensions in Deuteronomy's presentation of these laws naturally limit their applicability. The rabbis extend the need for witnesses to wrongdoing in Deut. 17:6 into 13:6–11 (7–12); the inherent difficulty of finding witnesses for a secret seduction may mean that a seducer is not punished (*m. Sanh.* 7:10). The requirement for the active participation of both parents in the accusation of a rebellious child is identified by Philo (*Spec. Laws* 2.232) as a way to prevent abuse of the law, and the rabbis' expansion of the requirements for a guilty verdict in the case of the son makes the law nearly impossible to implement (*m. Sanh.* 8:1–4; *Sipre Deut.* 218–19). A few similar restrictions are brought into the case of the foolish daughter (*m. Ketub.* 1:6–7; *Sipre Deut.* 235–37). Finally, for Philo, the initial focus on the innocence of the daughter in Deut. 22:13–19 rules the use of the law: the law is about the slandering husband, not the foolish bride (*Spec. Laws* 3.79–82).

The immediate and canonical contexts of constructive family violence also balance its harsh demands. Deuteronomy's three laws are given in the midst of a book and canon that value the family and prize good family relationships (e.g., Deut. 5:16; 6:4–9; 28:4–5, 11; Josh. 24:14–15; Ps. 133:1; etc.). Deuteronomy even contains laws that prohibit certain kinds of family violence (12:31; 18:9–12). The law of the rebellious son is preceded by a law that protects the rights of sons (21:15–17), and the case of the foolish daughter is followed by a law that protects victims of rape (22:23–24). Throughout Deuteronomy, the forgiveness promised to repentant Israel following divine punishment for idolatry and rebellion implicitly provides an alternative to the absolute destruction of a son, daughter, spouse, or sibling (4:29–31; 30:1–10; 32:36, 43; etc.). The rabbis' suggestion that parents forgive a rebellious son voices this contrary context (*Sipre Deut.* 218), as, perhaps, does the New Testament's consistent teaching on forgiveness for errant members of the church family (Matt. 18:21–35; Mark 11:25; Luke 17:1–4; 2 Cor. 2:5–8; etc.).

In *Spec. Laws* 1.312–13 and *Virtues* 131, Philo warns that executing a family member could be interpreted as murder and impiety. This discomfort also appears in the denial of the constructive nature of family violence in *Jubilees* (23:16–19) and Josephus (*Ant.* 2.20–28; *J.W.* 4.131–32; 7.259–65): peace and unity instead provide the means for protecting Israel's identity. The recognition that ancient texts do not freely, unemotionally, or gleefully commend violence against family members, that ancient readers also struggled with Deuteronomy's laws and similar traditions—such recognition gives modern readers points of contact with their work. These ancient readings of the laws and traditions of constructive family violence model critical, sometimes even suspicious, interpretation. In many cases, they recognize the potential for abuse, and their interpretations and applications of the laws emphasize their limitations. For the most part, however, these interpreters are also trusting. They trust that the laws are for the good of the people of God, and they support their continued use in the service of the identity of Israel.

Learning from Constructive Family Violence

Ancient interpretations of Deut. 13:6–11 (7–12); 21:18–21; and 22:13–21 implicitly and sometimes explicitly critique the laws as ethically questionable. Demonstrating the effective use of the hermeneutic of trust, they also allow their own reactions to family violence to be challenged by the underlying message of Deuteronomy: being part of God's people means living for the community, not for self. Constructive family violence is a radical example and outworking of this principle; perhaps at this point modern readers can learn from and be challenged by these very difficult texts. (And let me preface these comments by saying that, in my opinion, readers are right to critique the use of force in "disciplining" family members. Domestic violence is not the answer to the enemy within. But, as ancient interpretation shows, there is more at stake in Deut. 13:6–11; 21:18–21; and 22:13–21 than the legalization of domestic violence.)

The three focus laws in Deuteronomy demand violence against a family member, and this cannot be forgotten: these laws and the narratives that reflect their traditions are unremittingly, horrifyingly violent. Their primary purpose is to require the execution of sons and daughters, spouses, and siblings. However, their presence in Deuteronomy also gives them a secondary purpose in discouraging the behaviors they condemn. "And all Israel will hear and fear, so that they will not again do anything like this evil thing in your midst" (13:11 [12]): by incorporating this reasoning, the law itself becomes a warning and witness to the people, reminding them of the demands of covenant loyalty (cf. 21:21; 22:19, 21). If the people heed this warning, they will not rebel against the covenant, and they will not be subject to family violence. They will rather live according to Deuteronomy's overarching theme of community before individual.

It hardly needs to be stated that the primary value in antiquity was the community.[1] In Deuteronomy, the second half of the Ten Commandments are concerned with putting others ahead of personal desires (5:17–21). Forgiveness of debts and freedom for slaves in the Sabbatical Year provides another example of how the good of the community overshadows individuals (15:1–18). Concern for the community is also evident in 19:14; 22:1–4; 23:19–20; 24:6, 10–15, 17–22; and 26:12–13. One purpose of punishing wrongdoing in Deuteronomy is to protect the community from impurity, bad examples, and ultimate judgment (cf. 17:12–13; 19:13, 20; 22:24; etc.), as is also the case for the member of the family who threatens the community (cf. 13:11 [12]; 21:21; 22:19, 21). Those Israelites who from the beginning put the life of the community above personal desires would not face this punitive, preventive violence. Deuteronomy's laws of constructive family violence in effect teach Israelites to avoid seduction, rebellion, and foolish behavior for the good of the community.

This consequence of Deuteronomy's laws is apparent in the weaving together the training of children and constructive violence in Proverbs (13:24; 19:18; 23:13–14), Philo (*Spec. Laws* 2.232, 239–41), and Josephus (*Ant.* 4.261; *Ag. Ap.* 2.204). Parents who care for, educate, and discipline their children well, and children who accept their parents' instruction, will not be faced with constructive family violence. Philo's allegorical interpretation of Deuteronomy's laws is even more apposite. The conversion of family violence into strict self-disciplining indicates Philo's understanding of its purpose: the person who lives according to these laws is a supportive, faithful member of the God-loving community, a benefit to self and others (cf. *Drunkenness* 80–92). The metaphorical violence of Matt. 18:8–9 reflects a similar goal. Members of the community are called to guard themselves against disrupting the life of the community or harming a "little one" who should be protected. The community as a whole is worth the (self-)sacrifice of its parts.[2]

The practical enduring message of constructive family violence, then, may be an exhortation for individuals to bear the burden for the life of the

---

1. On the communal focus of Deuteronomy and its significance for individuals in the community, cf. McBride 1987, 237–38; 2006, 134; McConville 2002, 26–29; Miller 2005, 135; Vogt 2008, 41.

2. Certainly there is a reciprocal relationship between community life and the lives of individuals in the community. The loss of one is a significant loss for the whole, as indicated by mourning the loss of the Benjamites to constructive communal violence in Judg. 21:2–3, or by seeking the lost sheep in Matt. 18:10–14. The focus remains on the community, however, even in attending to the individual.

community—for the seducer to choose not to seduce, for the rebellious son to choose not to rebel, for the foolish daughter to choose not to behave foolishly, as attractive as these potentials may be, for the sake of the larger community. This aspect of ancient traditions of constructive family violence can continue to challenge modern readers: the life of the community may be more important than the desires of individuals in the community. Philo's reflections on the purpose of life in *Unchangeable* 19 are helpful here:

> We must indeed reject all those who "beget for themselves," that is all those who pursue only their own profit and think not of others. For they think themselves born for themselves only, and not for the innumerable others, for father, for mother, for wife [or spouse], for children, for country, for the human race, and if we must extend the list, for heaven, for earth, for the universe, for knowledge, for virtues, for the Father and Captain of all; to each of whom we are bound according to our powers to render what is due, not holding all things to be an adjunct of ourselves, but rather ourselves an adjunct of all. (Colson, LCL)

True kin are those who live for others; enemies are those who live only for themselves. This message is implicitly a call to be true kin, living for others. The internalization of constructive family violence in Philo's Allegories and the self-discipline represented in Matt. 18:8–9 provide a way for Deuteronomy's constructive family violence to continue to speak to readers. As exhortations to be personally disciplined, these texts have implications for the individual. More important in the ancient worldview, they are also the way to live for others instead of self, to protect the "little ones," and ultimately to sacrifice those personal desires that could harm others for the good of the community.[3]

In this world it is all too easy to live for oneself, forgetting the ten thousand others. We get caught up in our own pleasures, interests, and selfish desires, neglecting the needs of the communities around us. Biblical tradition rather calls us to support the common life, bear each others' burdens, and protect others from our own stumbling blocks. In the very act of challenging our assumptions on the value of family, constructive family violence in Deuteronomy demands that we examine our priorities, put aside our self-interest, and work for the good of the whole. And that is a valuable, timely challenge indeed.

---

3. Paul's exhortation to the Corinthians to put aside their own desires to visit prostitutes, take each other to court, eat meat sacrificed to idols, and other activities for the sake of the community provides another example of this principle (see, e.g., 1 Cor. 6:1–8, 15–20; 8:1–13): "Do not seek your own advantage, but that of the other" (10:24 NRSV). Cf. Gal. 6:2; Phil. 2:4; etc.

Bibliography

Primary Sources

Aulus Gellius. 1927. *Attic Nights*. Translated by John C. Rolfe. 3 vols. Loeb Classical Library. Cambridge, MA: Harvard University Press.

Cassius Dio. 1914–27. Translated by Herbert B. Foster and Earnest Cary. 9 vols. Loeb Classical Library. Cambridge, MA: Harvard University Press.

Charlesworth, James H., ed. 1983–85. *The Old Testament Pseudepigrapha*. 2 vols. Anchor Bible Reference Library. New York: Doubleday.

Clarke, Ernest G. 1998. *Targum Pseudo-Jonathan: Deuteronomy*. The Aramaic Bible 5B. Edinburgh: T&T Clark.

Clement of Alexandria. 1919. Translated by G. W. Butterworth. 1 vol. Loeb Classical Library. Cambridge, MA: Harvard University Press.

Crawford, Sidnie White, ed. 1995. "30. 4QDeut^c (Pls. III–IX)." Pages 15–34 in *Qumran Cave 4*. Vol. 9, *Deuteronomy, Joshua, Judges, Kings*. Edited by Eugene Ulrich et al. Discoveries in the Judaean Desert 14. Oxford: Clarendon.

Danby, Herbert. 1933. *The Mishnah: Translated from the Hebrew with Introduction and Brief Explanatory Notes*. Oxford: Oxford University Press.

Ehrman, Bart D. 2003. *Lost Scriptures: Books That Did Not Make It into the New Testament*. Oxford: Oxford University Press.

Epstein, I., ed. 1969. *Hebrew-English Edition of the Babylonian Talmud*. 32 vols. New ed. London: Soncino.

Freedman, H., and Maurice Simon, eds. 1961 (1939). *Midrash Rabbah*. 10 vols. London: Soncino.

García Martínez, Florentino, and Eibert J. C. Tigchelaar, eds. 1997–98. *The Dead Sea Scrolls Study Edition*. 2 vols. Leiden: Brill.

Hallo, William W., ed. 2000. *Monumental Inscriptions from the Biblical World*. Vol. 2 of *The Context of Scripture*. Leiden: Brill.

Hammer, Reuven. 1986. *Sifre: A Tannaitic Commentary on the Book of Deuteronomy*. Yale Judaica Series 24. New Haven: Yale University Press.

Holmes, Michael W., ed. 1999. *The Apostolic Fathers: Greek Texts and English Translations*. Grand Rapids: Baker Academic.

Jenkins, Claude. 1908. "Origen on 1 Corinthians." *Journal of Theological Studies* 9:353–72.

Josephus. 1926–65. Translated by H. St. J. Thackeray et al. 10 vols. Loeb Classical Library. Cambridge, MA: Harvard University Press.

Lefkowitz, Mary R., and Maureen B. Fant, eds. 2005 (1982). *Women's Life in Greece and Rome: A Source Book in Translation*. 3rd ed. Baltimore: Johns Hopkins University Press.

Livy. 1962–69. Translated by B. O. Foster. 14 vols. Loeb Classical Library. Cambridge, MA: Harvard University Press.

Neusner, Jacob, trans. 1985. *Ketubot*. Vol. 22 of *The Talmud of the Land of Israel: A Preliminary Translation and Explanation*. Chicago Studies in the History of Judaism. Chicago: University of Chicago Press.

———. 1987. *Sifre to Deuteronomy: An Analytical Translation*. 2 vols. Brown Judaic Studies 98, 101. Atlanta: Scholars Press.

———. 1988. *The Mishnah: A New Translation*. New Haven: Yale University Press.

———. 2002. *The Tosefta: Translated from the Hebrew with a New Introduction*. 2 vols. Peabody, MA: Hendrickson.

Patrologia graeca. Edited by J.-P. Migne. 162 vols. Paris, 1857–86, 1912.

Philo. 1927–62. Translated by F. H. Colson, G. H. Whittaker, and R. Marcus. 10 vols. (+ 2 suppl.). Loeb Classical Library. Cambridge, MA: Harvard University Press.

Pliny. 1938–63. Translated by H. Rackham et al. 10 vols. Loeb Classical Library. Cambridge, MA: Harvard University Press.

Pritchard, James B., ed. 1969. *Ancient Near Eastern Texts Relating to the Old Testament*. 3rd ed. Princeton: Princeton University Press.

Roberts, Alexander, and James Donaldson, eds. 1994. *The Ante-Nicene Fathers*. 10 vols. Buffalo: Christian Literature, 1885–87. Repr., Peabody, MA: Hendrickson.

Schaff, Philip, ed. 1994. *The Nicene and Post-Nicene Fathers*. Series 1 [NPNF[1]]. 14 vols. Buffalo: Christian Literature, 1886–90. Repr., Peabody, MA: Hendrickson.

Schaff, Philip, and Henry Wace, eds. 1994. *The Nicene and Post-Nicene Fathers*. Series 2 [NPNF[2]]. 14 vols. Buffalo: Christian Literature, 1890–1900. Repr., Peabody, MA: Hendrickson.

Scott, S. P., ed. 2001. *The Civil Law: Including the Twelve Tables, the Institutes of Gaius, the Rules of Ulpian, the Opinions of Paulus, the Enactments of*

Justinian, and the Constitutions. 7 vols. Cincinnati: Central Trust, 1932. Repr., Union, NJ: Lawbook Exchange.

Seneca. *Moral Essays.* 1928–35. Translated by John W. Basore. 3 vols. Loeb Classical Library. Cambridge, MA: Harvard University Press.

Slotki, Judah J. 1961 (1939). *Numbers.* Vols. 5–6 of *Midrash Rabbah.* Edited by H. Freedman and Maurice Simon. London: Soncino.

Suetonius. 1914. Translated by J. C. Rolfe. 2 vols. Loeb Classical Library. Cambridge, MA: Harvard University Press.

Valerius Maximus. 2000. *Memorable Doings and Sayings.* Translated by D. R. Shackleton Bailey. 2 vols. Loeb Classical Library. Cambridge, MA: Harvard University Press.

VanderKam, James C. 1989a. *The Book of Jubilees: A Critical Text.* Corpus scriptorum christianorum orientalium 510. Scriptores Aethiopici 87. Leuven: Peeters.

———. 1989b. *The Book of Jubilees: Translated.* Corpus scriptorum christianorum orientalium 511. Scriptores Aethiopici 88. Leuven: Peeters.

Wintermute, O. S. 1985. "Jubilees (Second Century B.C.): A New Translation and Introduction." Pages 35–142 in vol. 2 of *The Old Testament Pseudepigrapha.* Edited by James H. Charlesworth. Anchor Bible Reference Library. New York: Doubleday.

Secondary Sources

Abu-Lughod, Lila. 1986. *Veiled Sentiments: Honor and Poetry in a Bedouin Society.* Berkeley: University of California Press.

Adam, A. K. M. 2006. *Faithful Interpretation: Reading the Bible in a Postmodern World.* Minneapolis: Fortress.

Adam, Margaret B. 1998. "This Is *My* Story, This Is *My* Song . . . : A Feminist Claim on Scripture, Ideology and Interpretation." Pages 218–32 in *Escaping Eden: New Feminist Perspectives on the Bible.* Edited by Harold C. Washington, Susan Lochrie Graham, and Pamela Thimmes. Biblical Seminar 65. Sheffield: Sheffield Academic Press.

Aejmelaeus, Anneli. 1996. "Die Septuaginta des Deuteronomiums." Pages 1–22 in *Das Deuteronomium und seine Querbeziehungen.* Edited by Timo Veijola. Schriften der Finnischen Exegetischen Gesellschaft 62. Göttingen: Vandenhoeck & Ruprecht.

Ahearne-Kroll, Stephen P. 2001. "'Who Are My Mother and My Brothers?' Family Relations and Family Language in the Gospel of Mark." *Journal of Religion* 81, no. 1:1–25.

Aichele, George. 1998. "Jesus' Violence." Pages 72–91 in *Violence, Utopia, and the Kingdom of God: Fantasy and Ideology in the Bible*. Edited by Tina Pippin and George Aichele. London: Routledge.

Allison, Dale C. 1998. *Jesus of Nazareth: Millenarian Prophet*. Minneapolis: Fortress.

———. 1999. "Q 12.51–53 and Mark 9.11–13 and the Messianic Woes." Pages 290–310 in *Authenticating the Words of Jesus*. Edited by Bruce Chilton and Craig A. Evans. New Testament Tools and Studies 28.1. Leiden: Brill.

———. 2005. *Studies in Matthew: Interpretation Past and Present*. Grand Rapids: Baker Academic.

Alter, Robert. 2004. *The Five Books of Moses: A Translation with Commentary*. New York: W. W. Norton.

Amir, Yehoshua. 1988. "Authority and Interpretation of Scripture in the Writings of Philo." Pages 421–53 in *Mikra: Text, Translation, Reading and Interpretation of the Hebrew Bible in Ancient Judaism and Early Christianity*. Edited by Martin Jan Mulder. Compendia rerum iudaicarum ad Novum Testamentum: Sec. II, vol. 1. Assen: Van Gorcum; Philadelphia: Fortress.

Anderson, Cheryl B. 2004. *Women, Ideology, and Violence: Critical Theory and the Construction of Gender in the Book of the Covenant and the Deuteronomic Law*. Journal for the Study of the Old Testament: Supplement Series 394. London: T&T Clark.

Anderson, Gary A. 1994. "The Status of the Torah before Sinai: The Retelling of the Bible in the Damascus Covenant and the Book of Jubilees." *Dead Sea Discoveries* 1, no. 1:1–29.

Anderson, Hugh. 1976. *The Gospel of Mark*. New Century Bible. London: Oliphants.

Ascough, Richard S. 2001. "Matthew and Community Formation." Pages 96–126 in *The Gospel of Matthew in Current Study*. Edited by David E. Aune. Grand Rapids: Eerdmans.

Avalos, Hector. 2005. *Fighting Words: The Origins of Religious Violence*. Amherst, NY: Prometheus.

Balch, David L., and Carolyn Osiek. 1997. *Families in the New Testament World: Households and House Churches*. The Family, Religion, and Culture. Louisville: Westminster John Knox.

———. 2003. *Early Christian Families in Context: An Interdisciplinary Dialogue*. Religion, Marriage, and Family. Grand Rapids: Eerdmans.

Bamberger, Bernard J. 1961. "Qetanah, Naʻarah, Bogereth." *Hebrew Union College Annual* 32:281–94.

Bammel, Ernst. 1995. "Jewish Activity against Christians in Palestine according to Acts." Pages 357–64 in *The Book of Acts in Its Palestinian Setting*.

Edited by Richard Bauckham. Vol. 4 of *The Book of Acts in Its First Century Setting*. Edited by Bruce W. Winter. Grand Rapids: Eerdmans.

Barclay, John M. G. 1996. *Jews in the Mediterranean Diaspora: From Alexander to Trajan (323 BCE–117 CE)*. Edinburgh: T&T Clark.

———. 1997. "The Family as the Bearer of Religion in Judaism and Early Christianity." Pages 66–80 in *Constructing Early Christian Families: Family as Social Reality and Metaphor*. Edited by Halvor Moxnes. London: Routledge.

———. 1998. "Who Was Considered an Apostate in the Jewish Diaspora?" Pages 80–98 in *Tolerance and Intolerance in Early Judaism and Christianity*. Edited by Graham N. Stanton and Guy G. Stroumsa. Cambridge: Cambridge University Press.

———. 2007. *Against Apion: Translation and Commentary*. Vol. 10 of *Flavius Josephus: Translation and Commentary*. Edited by Steve Mason. Leiden: Brill.

Barrett, C. K. 1968. *A Commentary on the First Epistle to the Corinthians*. Harper's New Testament Commentaries. New York: Harper & Row.

———. 1973. *A Commentary on the Second Epistle to the Corinthians*. Harper's New Testament Commentaries. New York: Harper & Row.

Barrett, Rob. 2009. *Disloyalty and Destruction: Religion and Politics in Deuteronomy and the Modern World*. Library of Hebrew Bible/Old Testament Studies 511. New York: T&T Clark.

Bartlett, John R. 1973. *The First and Second Books of the Maccabees*. Cambridge Bible Commentary. Cambridge: Cambridge University Press.

Barton, Stephen C. 1994. *Discipleship and Family Ties in Mark and Matthew*. Society for New Testament Studies Monograph Series 80. Cambridge: Cambridge University Press.

———, ed. 1996. *The Family in Theological Perspective*. Edinburgh: T&T Clark.

———. 1997. "The Relativisation of Family Ties in the Jewish and Graeco-Roman Traditions." Pages 81–100 in *Constructing Early Christian Families: Family as Social Reality and Metaphor*. Edited by Halvor Moxnes. London: Routledge.

Bartor, Assnat. 2007. "The Representation of the Casuistic Laws of the Pentateuch: The Phenomenon of Combined Discourse." *Journal of Biblical Literature* 126, no. 2:231–49.

Bauckham, Richard. 1993. *The Climax of Prophecy: Studies on the Book of Revelation*. Edinburgh: T&T Clark.

———. 1999. "For What Offence Was James Put to Death?" Pages 199–232 in *James the Just and Christian Origins*. Edited by Bruce Chilton and Craig A. Evans. Novum Testamentum Supplements 98. Leiden: Brill.

Beasley-Murray, George R. 1957. *A Commentary on Mark 13*. London: Macmillan.

———. 1993. *Jesus and the Last Days: The Interpretation of the Olivet Discourse*. Peabody, MA: Hendrickson.

Beck, Robert R. 1996. *Nonviolent Story: Narrative Conflict Resolution in the Gospel of Mark*. Maryknoll, NY: Orbis Books.

Beebe, H. Keith. 1968. "Ancient Palestinian Dwellings." *Biblical Archaeologist* 31, no. 2:38–58.

Begg, Christopher T. 1997. "The Destruction of the Golden Calf Revisited (Exod 32,20 / Deuteronomy 9,21)." Pages 469–79 in *Deuteronomy and Deuteronomic Literature*. Edited by M. Vervenne and J. Lust. Bibliotheca ephemeridum theologicarum lovaniensium 133. Leuven: Leuven University Press.

Belkin, Samuel. 1940. *Philo and the Oral Law: The Philonic Interpretation of Biblical Law in Relation to the Palestinian Halakah*. Cambridge, MA: Harvard University Press.

Bellefontaine, Elizabeth. 1979. "Deuteronomy 21:18–21: Reviewing the Case of the Rebellious Son." *Journal for the Study of the Old Testament* 13:13–31.

Benjamin, Don C. 1983. *Deuteronomy and City Life: A Form Criticism of Texts with the Word City ('îr) in Deuteronomy 4:41–26:19*. Lanham, MD: University Press of America.

Berkowitz, Beth A. 2006. *Execution and Invention: Death Penalty Discourse in Early Rabbinic and Christian Cultures*. Oxford: Oxford University Press.

Bernat, David A. 2002. "Josephus's Portrayal of Phinehas." *Journal for the Study of the Pseudepigrapha* 13, no. 2:137–49.

Bernat, David A., and Jonathan Klawans. 2007. "Preface." Page ix in *Religion and Violence: The Biblical Heritage*. Edited by David A. Bernat and Jonathan Klawans. Sheffield: Sheffield Phoenix.

Berthelot, Katell. 2007. "Zeal for God and Divine Law in Philo and the Dead Sea Scrolls." *Studia Philonica Annual* 19:113–29.

Betz, Hans Dieter. 1979. *Galatians: A Commentary on Paul's Letter to the Churches in Galatia*. Hermeneia. Philadelphia: Fortress.

Betz, Otto. 1957–58. "Jesu Heiliger Krieg." *Novum Testamentum* 2:116–37.

Biddle, Mark E. 2003. *Deuteronomy*. Smyth & Helwys Bible Commentary. Macon, GA: Smyth & Helwys.

Biezeveld, Kune. 2005. "The One and Only God: Reevaluating the Process of Violence and Exclusion." Pages 47–68 in vol. 1 of *Christian Faith and Violence*. Edited by Dirk van Keulen and Martien E. Brinkman. Studies in Reformed Theology 10. Zoetermeer: Meinema.

Bird, Phyllis A. 1993. "'To Play the Harlot': An Inquiry into an Old Testament Metaphor." Pages 296–312 in *The Bible and Liberation: Political and Social*

Hermeneutics. Edited by Norman K. Gottwald and Richard A. Horsley. The Bible and Liberation. Maryknoll, NY: Orbis Books.

Birnbaum, Ellen. 1996. *The Place of Judaism in Philo's Thought: Israel, Jews, and Proselytes*. Brown Judaic Studies 290. Studia Philonica Monographs 2. Atlanta: Scholars Press.

Black, Matthew. 1970. "Uncomfortable Words: III. The Violent Word." *Expository Times* 81:115–18.

———. 1984. "'Not Peace but a Sword': Matt 10.34ff; Luke 12.51ff." Pages 287–94 in *Jesus and the Politics of His Day*. Edited by Ernst Bammel and C. F. D. Moule. Cambridge: Cambridge University Press.

Blenkinsopp, Joseph. 1995 (1983). *Wisdom and Law in the Old Testament: The Ordering of Life in Israel and Early Judaism*. Rev. ed. Oxford Bible Series. Oxford: Oxford University Press.

———. 1997. "The Family in First Temple Israel." Pages 48–103 in *Families in Ancient Israel*. Edited by Leo G. Perdue et al. The Family, Religion, and Culture. Louisville: Westminster John Knox.

———. 1999. "Deuteronomic Contribution to the Narrative in Genesis–Numbers: A Test Case." Pages 84–115 in *Those Elusive Deuteronomists: The Phenomenon of Pan-Deuteronomism*. Edited by Linda S. Schearing and Steven L. McKenzie. Journal for the Study of the Old Testament: Supplement Series 268. Sheffield: Sheffield Academic Press.

Blount, Brian K. 2009. *Revelation: A Commentary*. New Testament Library. Louisville: Westminster John Knox.

Boccaccini, Gabriele. 1998. *Beyond the Essene Hypothesis: The Parting of the Ways between Qumran and Enochic Judaism*. Grand Rapids: Eerdmans.

Bockmuehl, Markus. 1998. "'Let the Dead Bury Their Dead' (Matt. 8:22/Luke 9:60): Jesus and the Halakhah." *Journal of Theological Studies* 49:553–81.

Bossman, David M. 1996. "Paul's Fictive Kinship Movement." *Biblical Theology Bulletin* 26, no. 4:163–71.

Botha, Pieter J. J. 1998. "Houses in the World of Jesus." *Neotestamentica* 32, no. 1:37–74.

Bourdieu, Pierre. 1996. "On the Family as a Realized Category." *Theory, Culture & Society* 13, no. 3:19–26.

Bowman, John. 1965. *The Gospel of Mark: The New Christian Jewish Passover Haggadah*. Studia post-biblica 8. Leiden: Brill.

Braulik, Georg. 1985. "Die Abfolge der Gesetze in Deuteronomium 12–26 und der Dekalog." Pages 252–72 in *Das Deuteronomium: Entstehung, Gestalt und Botschaft*. Edited by Norbert Lohfink. Bibliotheca ephemeridum theologicarum lovaniensium 68. Leuven: Leuven University Press.

Brenner, Athalya. 2004–5. "Regulating 'Sons' and 'Daughters' in the Torah and in Proverbs: Some Preliminary Insights." *Journal of Hebrew Scriptures* 5 (article 10). http://www.arts.ualberta.ca/JHS/Articles/article_40.pdf.

Brichto, Herbert Chanan. 1983. "The Worship of the Golden Calf: A Literary Analysis of a Fable on Idolatry." *Hebrew Union College Annual* 54:1–44.

Brisman, Leslie. 1999. "Sacred Butchery: Exodus 32:25–29." Pages 162–81 in *Theological Exegesis*. Edited by Christopher Seitz and Kathryn Greene-McCreight. Grand Rapids: Eerdmans.

Brooke, George J. 1988. "The Temple Scroll: A Law unto Itself?" Pages 34–43 in *Law and Religion: Essays on the Place of the Law in Israel and Early Christianity*. Edited by Barnabas Lindars. Cambridge: J. Clarke.

Brooks, David L. 2007. "The Complementary Relationship between Proverbs and Moses' Law." *Criswell Theological Review* 5, no. 1:3–32.

Brown, Jeannine K. 2005. "Direct Engagement of the Reader in Matthew's Discourses: Rhetorical Techniques and Scholarly Consensus." *New Testament Studies* 51, no. 1:19–35.

Brown, William P. 2005. "The Law and the Sages: A Reexamination of *Tôrâ* in Proverbs." Pages 251–80 in *Constituting the Community: Studies on the Polity of Ancient Israel*. Edited by John T. Strong and Steven S. Tuell. Winona Lake, IN: Eisenbrauns.

———. 2008. "To Discipline without Destruction: The Multifaceted Profile of the Child in Proverbs." Pages 63–81 in *The Child in the Bible*. Edited by Marcia J. Bunge, Terence E. Fretheim, and Beverly Roberts Gaventa. Grand Rapids: Eerdmans.

Bruce, F. F. 1998 (1982). *The Epistle to the Galatians*. New International Greek Testament Commentary. Grand Rapids: Eerdmans.

Burke, Trevor J. 2003a. *Family Matters: A Socio-Historical Study of Kinship Metaphors in 1 Thessalonians*. Journal for the Study of the New Testament: Supplement Series 247. London: T&T Clark.

———. 2003b. "Paul's Role as 'Father' to his Corinthian 'Children' in Socio-Historical Context (1 Corinthians 4:14–21)." Pages 95–113 in *Paul and the Corinthians: Studies on a Community in Conflict*. Edited by Trevor J. Burke and J. Keith Elliott. Supplements to Novum Testamentum 109. Leiden: Brill.

Callaway, Phillip R. 1984. "Deuteronomy 21:18–21: Proverbial Wisdom and Law." *Journal of Biblical Literature* 103, no. 3:341–52.

Calvin, John. 1950. *Commentary on the Four Last Books of Moses Arranged in the Form of a Harmony*. Translated by Charles William Bingham. 4 vols. Grand Rapids: Eerdmans.

Camp, Claudia V. 1991. "Understanding Patriarchy: Women in Second Century Jerusalem through the Eyes of Ben Sira." Pages 1–39 in *"Women Like This": New Perspectives on Jewish Women in the Greco-Roman World*.

Edited by Amy-Jill Levine. Early Judaism and Its Literature 1. Atlanta: Scholars Press.

———. 1997a. "Honor and Shame in Ben Sira: Anthropological and Theological Reflections." Pages 171–87 in *The Book of Ben Sira in Modern Research: Proceedings of the First International Ben Sira Conference, 28–31 July 1996, Soesterberg, Netherlands*. Edited by Pancratius C. Beentjes. Beihefte zur Zeitschrift für die alttestamentliche Wissenschaft 255. Berlin: de Gruyter.

———. 1997b. "Woman Wisdom and the Strange Woman: Where Is Power to Be Found?" Pages 85–112 in *Reading Bibles, Writing Bodies: Identity and the Book*. Edited by Timothy K. Beal and David M. Gunn. Biblical Limits. London: Routledge.

Campbell, Barth. 1993. "Flesh and Spirit in 1 Cor 5:5: An Exercise in Rhetorical Criticism of the NT." *Journal of the Evangelical Theological Society* 36, no. 3:331–42.

Carmody, Timothy R. 1989. "Matt 18:15–17 in Relation to Three Texts from Qumran Literature (CD 9:2–8, 16–22; 1QS 5:25–6:1)." Pages 141–58 in *To Touch the Text*. Edited by Maurya P. Horgan and Paul J. Kobelski. New York: Crossroad.

Carter, Warren. 2005. "Constructions of Violence and Identities in Matthew's Gospel." Pages 81–108 in *Violence in the New Testament*. Edited by Shelly Matthews and E. Leigh Gibson. London: T&T Clark.

Casey, James. 1989. *The History of the Family*. New Perspectives on the Past. Oxford: Blackwell.

Causse, A. 1937. *Du groupe ethnique à la communauté religieuse: Le problème sociologique de la religion d'Israël*. Paris: Librairie Felix Alcan.

Charles, R. H. 1902. *The Book of Jubilees, or The Little Genesis*. London: A&C Black.

Chesson, Meredith S. 2003. "Households, Houses, Neighborhoods and Corporate Villages: Modeling the Early Bronze Age as a House Society." *Journal of Mediterranean Archaeology* 16, no. 1:79–102.

Ciampa, Roy E. 2007. "Deuteronomy in Galatians and Romans." Pages 99–117 in *Deuteronomy in the New Testament: The New Testament and the Scriptures of Israel*. Edited by Maarten J. J. Menken and Steve Moyise. Library of New Testament Studies 358. London: T&T Clark.

Clements, Ronald E. 1989. *Deuteronomy*. Old Testament Guides. Sheffield: JSOT Press.

Clifford, Richard J. 1993. "Woman Wisdom in the Book of Proverbs." Pages 61–72 in *Biblische Theologie und gesellschaftlicher Wandel*. Edited by Georg Braulik, Walter Gross, and Sean McEvenue. Basel: Herder.

———. 1999. *Proverbs: A Commentary*. Old Testament Library. Louisville: Westminster John Knox.

Cohen, Shaye J. D., ed. 1993. *The Jewish Family in Antiquity*. Brown Judaic Studies 289. Atlanta: Scholars Press.

———. 1999. "The Rabbi in Second-Century Jewish Society." Pages 922–90 in *The Early Roman Period*. Vol. 3 of *The Cambridge History of Judaism*. Edited by William Horbury, W. D. Davies, and John Sturdy. Cambridge: Cambridge University Press.

Cohick, Lynn H. 2009. *Women in the World of the Earliest Christians: Illuminating Ancient Ways of Life*. Grand Rapids: Baker Academic.

Cohn, Robert L. 2004. "The Second Coming of Moses: Deuteronomy and the Construction of Israelite Identity." Pages 133–46 in *The Comity and Grace of Method*. Edited by Thomas Ryba, George D. Bond, and Herman Tull. Evanston, IL: Northwestern University Press.

Collins, Adela Yarbro. 1980. "The Function of 'Excommunication' in Paul." *Harvard Theological Review* 73, nos. 1–2:251–63.

———. 1992. *The Beginning of the Gospel: Probings of Mark in Context*. Minneapolis: Fortress.

———. 1996. "The Apocalyptic Rhetoric of Mark 13 in Historical Context." *Biblical Research* 41:5–36.

———. 2007. *Mark: A Commentary*. Hermeneia. Minneapolis: Fortress.

Collins, John J. 1979. "The Jewish Apocalypses." *Semeia* 14:21–59.

———. 1984. *The Apocalyptic Imagination: An Introduction to the Jewish Matrix of Christianity*. New York: Crossroad.

———. 1997. *Jewish Wisdom in the Hellenistic Age*. Old Testament Library. Louisville: Westminster John Knox.

———. 1999. "Pseudepigraphy and Group Formation in Second Temple Judaism." Pages 43–58 in *Pseudepigraphic Perspectives: The Apocrypha and Pseudepigrapha in Light of the Dead Sea Scrolls*. Edited by Esther G. Chazon and Michael Stone. Studies on the Texts of the Desert of Judah 31. Leiden: Brill.

———. 2004. *Does the Bible Justify Violence?* Facets. Minneapolis: Fortress.

Colson, Francis H. 1937. "Appendix to *De specialibus legibus*, I." In *Philo: With an English Translation*. Loeb Classical Library 7. Cambridge, MA: Harvard University Press.

Conway, Colleen. 2003. "Gender and Divine Relativity in Philo of Alexandria." *Journal for the Study of Judaism* 34:471–91.

Conzelmann, Hans. 1975. *1 Corinthians: A Commentary on the First Epistle to the Corinthians*. Hermeneia. Philadelphia: Fortress.

Cranfield, C. E. B. 1974 (1959). *The Gospel according to Saint Mark: An Introduction and Commentary*. Cambridge Greek Testament Commentary. Cambridge: Cambridge University Press.

Crawford, Sidnie White. 2000. "The Rewritten Bible at Qumran." Pages 173–95 in *The Hebrew Bible and Qumran*. Edited by James H. Charlesworth. *The Bible and the Dead Sea Scrolls* 1. N. Richland Hills, TX: BIBAL.

———. 2008. *Rewriting Scripture in Second Temple Times*. Studies in the Dead Sea Scrolls and Related Literature. Grand Rapids: Eerdmans.

Dancy, John C. 1954. *A Commentary on 1 Maccabees*. Oxford: Blackwell.

D'Angelo, Mary Rose. 2007. "Gender and Geopolitics in the Work of Philo of Alexandria: Jewish Piety and Imperial Family Values." Pages 63–88 in *Mapping Gender in Ancient Religious Discourses*. Edited by Todd Penner and Caroline Vander Stichele. Leiden: Brill.

Davenport, Gene L. 1971. *The Eschatology of the Book of Jubilees*. Studia post-biblica. Leiden: Brill.

Davies, Margaret. 1993. *Matthew*. Readings: A New Biblical Commentary. Sheffield: JSOT Press.

Davies, Philip R. 1987. *Behind the Essenes: History and Ideology in the Dead Sea Scrolls*. Brown Judaic Studies 94. Atlanta: Scholars Press.

Davies, W. D. 1964. *The Setting of the Sermon on the Mount*. Cambridge: Cambridge University Press.

Davies, W. D., and Dale C. Allison. 1991. *Commentary on Matthew VIII–XVIII*. Vol. 2 of *A Critical and Exegetical Commentary on the Gospel according to Saint Matthew*. International Critical Commentary. Edinburgh: T&T Clark.

Davis, Ellen F. 2000. *Proverbs, Ecclesiastes, and the Song of Songs*. Westminster Bible Companion. Louisville: Westminster John Knox.

———. 2003. "Critical Traditioning: Seeking an Inner Biblical Hermeneutic." Pages 163–80 in *The Art of Reading Scripture*. Edited by Ellen F. Davis and Richard B. Hays. Grand Rapids: Eerdmans.

Davis, James F. 2005. *Lex Talionis in Early Judaism and the Exhortation of Jesus in Matthew 5.38–42*. Journal for the Study of the New Testament: Supplement Series 281. London: T&T Clark.

Dawson, David. 1992. *Allegorical Readers and Cultural Revision in Ancient Alexandria*. Berkeley: University of California Press.

Deissmann, Adolf. 1927. *Light from the Ancient East: The New Testament Illustrated by Recently Discovered Texts of the Graeco-Roman World*. Translated by Lionel R. M. Strachan. Rev. ed. New York: Harper.

Delaney, Carol. 1998. *Abraham on Trial: The Social Legacy of Biblical Myth*. Princeton: Princeton University Press.

Derrett, J. Duncan M. 1985. *From Jesus' Baptism to Peter's Recognition of Jesus as the Messiah*. Vol. 1 of *The Making of Mark: The Scriptural Bases of the Earliest Gospel*. Shipston-on-Stour, Warwickshire: Drinkwater.

DeSilva, David A. 1996. "The Wisdom of Ben Sira: Honor, Shame, and the Maintenance of the Values of a Minority Culture." *Catholic Biblical Quarterly* 58:433–55.

———. 2000. *Honor, Patronage, Kinship and Purity: Unlocking New Testament Culture*. Downers Grove, IL: InterVarsity.

Desjardins, Michel. 1997. *Peace, Violence and the New Testament*. Biblical Seminar 46. Sheffield: Sheffield Academic Press.

Dimant, Devorah. 1994. "Apocrypha and Pseudepigrapha at Qumran." *Dead Sea Discoveries* 1, no. 2:151–59.

Dion, Paul E. 1991. "Deuteronomy 13: The Suppression of Alien Religious Propaganda in Israel during the Late Monarchical Era." Pages 147–216 in *Law and Ideology in Monarchic Israel*. Edited by Baruch Halpern and Deborah W. Hobson. Journal for the Study of the Old Testament: Supplement Series 124. Sheffield: Sheffield Academic Press.

———. 1993. "La procédure d'élimination du fils rebelle (Deuteronomy 21, 18–21): Sens littéral et signes et développement juridique." Pages 73–82 in *Biblische Theologie und gesellschaftlicher Wandel*. Edited by Georg Braulik, Walter Gross, and Sean McEvenue. Basel: Herder.

Dixon, Suzanne. 1992. *The Roman Family*. Baltimore: Johns Hopkins University Press.

Dobschütz, Detlef von. 1968. *Paulus und die jüdische Thorapolizei*. [Erlangen]: J. Hogl.

Docherty, Susan. 2002. "Joseph the Patriarch: Representations of Joseph in Early Post-Biblical Literature." Pages 194–216 in *Borders, Boundaries and the Bible*. Edited by Martin O'Kane. Journal for the Study of the Old Testament: Supplement Series 313. Sheffield: Sheffield Academic Press.

Donahue, John R. 1983. *The 1983 Père Marquette Theology Lecture: The Theology and Setting of Discipleship in the Gospel of Mark*. Milwaukee: Marquette University Press.

Donfried, Karl Paul. 1976. "Justification and Last Judgment in Paul." *Interpretation* 30:140–52.

Doran, R. 1989. "The Non-Dating of Jubilees: Jub 34–38; 23.14–32 in Narrative Context." *Journal for the Study of Judaism* 20:1–11.

Dorival, Gilles. 1994. *La Bible d'Alexandrie: Les Nombres; Traduction du texte grec de la Septante, introduction et notes*. Paris: Cerf.

Duling, Dennis C. 1999. "Matthew 18:15–17: Conflict, Confrontation, and Conflict Resolution in a 'Fictive Kin' Association." *Biblical Theology Bulletin* 2, no. 1:4–22.

Dunn, James D. G. 1998. *The Theology of Paul the Apostle*. Grand Rapids: Eerdmans.

Dupont, Jacques. 1978. "La persécution comme situation missionnaire (Marc 13,9–11)." Pages 97–114 in *Die Kirche des Anfangs*. Edited by Rudolf Schnackenburg, Josef Ernst, and Joachim Wanke. Freiburg: Herder.

Durham, John I. 1987. *Exodus*. Word Biblical Commentary 3. Waco: Word Books.

Dyer, Keith D. 1998. *The Prophecy on the Mount: Mark 13 and the Gathering of the New Community*. International Theological Studies: Contributions of Baptist Scholars 2. Bern: Peter Lang.

Ellens, Deborah L. 2008. *Women in the Sex Texts of Leviticus and Deuteronomy: A Comparative Conceptual Analysis*. New York: T&T Clark.

Endres, John C. 1987. *Biblical Interpretation in the Book of Jubilees*. Catholic Biblical Quarterly Monograph Series 18. Washington, DC: Catholic Biblical Association of America.

Epstein, Louis M. 1967. *Sex Laws and Customs in Judaism*. Rev. ed. New York: Ktav.

Esler, Philip F. 1997. "Family Imagery and Christian Identity in Gal 5:13 to 6:10." Pages 121–49 in *Constructing Early Christian Families: Family as Social Reality and Metaphor*. Edited by Halvor Moxnes. London: Routledge.

Estes, Daniel J. 1997. *Hear, My Son: Teaching and Learning in Proverbs 1–9*. New Studies in Biblical Theology 4. Leicester: Apollos.

Evans, Craig A. 2001. *Mark 8:27–16:20*. Word Biblical Commentary 34B. Nashville: Thomas Nelson.

Evans, John K. 1991. *War, Women and Children in Ancient Rome*. London: Routledge.

Fairweather, W., and J. Sutherland Black, eds. 1936. *The First Book of Maccabees*. Cambridge Bible for Schools and Colleges. Cambridge: Cambridge University Press.

Feldman, Louis H. 1994. "Josephus' Portrayal of the Hasmoneans Compared with 1 Maccabees." Pages 41–68 in *Josephus and the History of the Greco-Roman Period*. Edited by Fausto Parente and Joseph Sievers. Studia postbiblica 41. Leiden: Brill.

———. 1998. *Studies in Josephus' Rewritten Bible*. Journal for the Study of Judaism: Supplement Series 58. Leiden: Brill.

———. 1999. "Josephus (CE 37–*c*. 100)." Pages 901–21 in *The Early Roman Period*. Edited by William Horbury, W. D. Davies, and John Sturdy. Vol. 3 of *The Cambridge History of Judaism*. Edited by W. D. Davies and Louis Finkelstein. Cambridge: Cambridge University Press.

———. 2000. *Judean Antiquities 1–4: Translation and Commentary*. Vol. 3 of *Flavius Josephus: Translation and Commentary*. Edited by Steve Mason. Leiden: Brill.

———. 2005. "Philo's Account of the Golden Calf Incident." *Journal of Jewish Studies* 56, no. 2:245–64.

Finkelstein, J. J. 1981. *The Ox That Gored*. Philadelphia: American Philosophical Society.

Fishbane, Michael. 1977. "Torah and Tradition." Pages 275–300 in *Tradition and Theology in the Old Testament*. Edited by Douglas A. Knight. Philadelphia: Fortress.

———. 1985. *Biblical Interpretation in Ancient Israel*. Oxford: Clarendon.

———. 1999 (1974). "Accusations of Adultery: A Study of Law and Scribal Practice in Numbers 5:11–31." Pages 487–502 in *Women in the Hebrew Bible: A Reader*. Edited by Alice Bach. New York: Routledge.

Fitzmyer, Joseph A. 1978. "Crucifixion in Ancient Palestine, Qumran Literature, and the New Testament." *Catholic Biblical Quarterly* 40:493–513.

Fleishman, Joseph. 2003. "Legal Innovation in Deuteronomy XXI 18–20." *Vetus Testamentum* 53:311–27.

———. 2008. "The Delinquent Daughter and Legal Innovation in Deuteronomy xxii 20–21." *Vetus Testamentum* 58:191–210.

Fonrobert, Charlotte Elisheva. 2000. *Menstrual Purity: Rabbinic and Christian Reconstruction of Biblical Gender*. Contraversions. Stanford, CA: Stanford University Press.

Fonrobert, Charlotte Elisheva, and Martin S. Jaffee, eds. 2007. *The Cambridge Companion to the Talmud and Rabbinic Literature*. Cambridge: Cambridge University Press.

Fontaine, Carole. 1997. "The Abusive Bible: On the Use of Feminist Method in Pastoral Contexts." Pages 84–113 in *A Feminist Companion to Reading the Bible: Approaches, Methods and Strategies*. Edited by Athalya Brenner and Carole Fontaine. Sheffield: Sheffield Academic Press.

———. 2002. *Smooth Words: Women, Proverbs and Performance in Biblical Wisdom*. Journal for the Study of the Old Testament: Supplement Series 356. Sheffield: Sheffield Academic Press.

Foster, Paul. 2004. *Community, Law and Mission in Matthew's Gospel*. Wissenschaftliche Untersuchungen zum Neuen Testament, ser. 2, vol. 177. Tübingen: Mohr Siebeck.

Fowl, Stephen E. 1998. *Engaging Scripture: A Model for Theological Interpretation*. Challenges in Contemporary Theology. Oxford: Blackwell.

Fox, Michael V. 2000. *Proverbs 1–9: A New Translation with Introduction and Commentary*. Anchor Bible 18A. New York: Doubleday.

Frankfurter, David. 2007. "The Legacy of Sectarian Rage: Vengeance Fantasies in the New Testament." Pages 114–28 in *Religion and Violence: The*

Biblical Heritage. Edited by David A. Bernat and Jonathan Klawans. Recent Research in Biblical Studies 2. Sheffield: Sheffield Phoenix.

Frymer-Kensky, Tikva. 1989. "Law and Philosophy: The Case of Sex in the Bible." *Semeia* 45:89–102.

———. 1996. "The Family in the Hebrew Bible." Pages 55–73 in *Religion, Feminism, and the Family.* Edited by Anne Carr and Mary Stewart Van Leeuwen. The Family, Religion, and Culture. Louisville: Westminster John Knox.

———. 2004 (1998). "Virginity in the Bible." Pages 79–96 in *Gender and Law in the Hebrew Bible and the Ancient Near East.* Edited by Victor H. Matthews, Bernard M. Levinson, and Tikva Frymer-Kensky. London: T&T Clark.

Fuchs, Esther. 2000. *Sexual Politics in the Biblical Narrative: Reading the Hebrew Bible as a Woman.* Journal for the Study of the Old Testament: Supplement Series 310. Sheffield: Sheffield Academic Press.

Furnish, Victor Paul. 1999. *The Theology of the First Letter to the Corinthians.* New Testament Theology. Cambridge: Cambridge University Press.

Galvao-Sobrinho, Carlos R. 2006. "Embodied Theologies: Christian Identity and Violence in Alexandria in the Early Arian Controversy." Pages 321–31 in *Violence in Late Antiquity: Perceptions and Practices.* H. A. Drake. Aldershot: Ashgate.

Gardner, Jane F. 1986. *Women in Roman Law and Society.* Bloomington: Indiana University Press.

Gaston, Lloyd. 1970. *No Stone on Another: Studies in the Significance of the Fall of Jerusalem in the Synoptic Gospels.* Novum Testamentum Supplements 23. Leiden: Brill.

Gerber, Christine. 1997. *Ein Bild des Judentums für Nichtjuden von Flavius Josephus: Untersuchungen zu seiner Schrift "Contra Apionem."* Arbeiten zur Geschichte des Antiken Judentums und des Christentums 40. Leiden: Brill.

Gevaryahu, Gilad J., and Harvey Sicherman. 2001. "What Never Was and Never Will Be: Rebellious Son—Subverted City—Infected House." *Jewish Bible Quarterly* 29, no. 4:249–54.

Gibbs, Jeffrey A., and Jeffrey Kloha. 2003. "'Following' Matthew 18: Interpreting Matthew 18:15–20 in its Context." *Concordia Journal* 29, no. 1:6–25.

Gilbert, Maurice. 1976. "Ben Sira et la Femme." *Revue théologique de Louvain* 7:426–42.

Gillespie, Susan D. 2000. "Beyond Kinship: An Introduction." Pages 1–21 in *Beyond Kinship: Social and Material Reproduction in House Societies.* Edited by Rosemary A. Joyce and Susan D. Gillespie. Philadelphia: University of Pennsylvania Press.

Girard, René. 2001. *I See Satan Fall like Lightning.* Translated by James G. Williams. Maryknoll, NY: Orbis Books.

Goldstein, Jonathan A. 1976. *1 Maccabees: A New Translation with Intro-duction and Commentary*. Anchor Bible 41. Garden City, NY: Doubleday.

———. 1983. "The Date of the Book of Jubilees." *Proceedings of the American Academy of Jewish Research* 50:63–86.

Goodenough, Erwin R. 1929. *The Jurisprudence of the Jewish Courts in Egypt: Legal Administration by the Jews under the Early Roman Empire as Described by Philo Judaeus*. New Haven: Yale University Press.

———. 1962. *An Introduction to Philo Judaeus*. 2nd ed. Oxford: Blackwell.

Goody, Jack. 1983. *The Development of the Family and Marriage in Europe*. Past and Present Publications. Cambridge: Cambridge University Press.

Grabbe, Lester L. 2008. "Sanhedrin, Sanhedriyyot, or Mere Invention?" *Journal for the Study of Judaism* 39:1–19.

Graham, Helen R. 1986. "A Passion Prediction for Mark's Community: Mark 13:9–13." *Biblical Theology Bulletin* 16, no. 1:18–22.

Green, Joel B. 1997. *The Gospel of Luke*. New International Commentary on the New Testament. Grand Rapids: Eerdmans.

———. 2001. "Crucifixion." Pages 87–101 in *The Cambridge Companion to Jesus*. Edited by Marcus Bockmuehl. Cambridge Companions to Religion. Cambridge: Cambridge University Press.

Grelot, Pierre. 1986. "Michée 7,6 dans les évangiles et dans la littérature rab-binique." *Biblica* 67, no. 3:363–77.

Gruen, Erich S. 1998. *Heritage and Hellenism: The Reinvention of Jewish Tradition*. Hellenistic Culture and Society 30. Berkeley: University of California Press.

Gundry, Robert H. 1993. *Mark: A Commentary on His Apology for the Cross*. Grand Rapids: Eerdmans.

Hadas-Lebel, Mireille. 2003. *Philon d'Alexandrie: Un penseur en diaspora*. Paris: Fayard.

Hagedorn, Anselm C. 2000. "Guarding the Parents' Honour—Deuteronomy 21.18–21." *Journal for the Study of the Old Testament* 88:101–21.

Halberstam, Chaya. 2007. "The Art of Biblical Law." *Prooftexts* 27:345–64.

Halbertal, Moshe. 1998. "Coexisting with the Enemy: Jews and Pagans in the Mishnah." Pages 159–72 in *Tolerance and Intolerance in Early Judaism and Christianity*. Edited by Graham N. Stanton and Guy G. Stroumsa. Cambridge: Cambridge University Press.

Halpern-Amaru, Betsy. 1999a. *The Empowerment of Women in the Book of Jubilees*. Journal for the Study of Judaism: Supplement Series 60. Leiden: Brill.

———. 1999b. "The Naming of Levi in the Book of Jubilees." Pages 59–69 in *Pseudepigraphic Perspectives: The Apocrypha and Pseudepigrapha in Light of the Dead Sea Scrolls.* Edited by Esther G. Chazon and Michael Stone. Studies on the Texts of the Desert of Judah 31. Leiden: Brill.

———. 2001. "Flavius Josephus and *The Book of Jubilees*: A Question of Source." *Hebrew Union College Annual* 72:15–44.

Halpern-Zylberstein, Marie-Christine. 1989. "The Archeology of Hellenistic Palestine." Pages 1–34 in *The Hellenistic Age*. Edited by W. D. Davies and Louis Finkelstein. Vol. 2 of *The Cambridge History of Judaism*. Cambridge: Cambridge University Press.

Hamilton, Jeffries M. 1998. "How to Read an Abhorrent Text: Deuteronomy 13 and the Nature of Authority." *Horizons in Biblical Theology* 20:12–32.

Hardin, James W. 2004. "Understanding Domestic Space: An Example from Iron Age Tel Halif." *Near Eastern Archaeology* 67, no. 2:71–83.

Hare, Douglas R. A. 1967. *The Theme of Jewish Persecution of Christians in the Gospel according to St. Matthew*. Society for New Testament Studies Monograph Series 6. Cambridge: Cambridge University Press.

Hartman, Lars. 1966. *Prophecy Interpreted: The Formation of Some Jewish Apocalyptic Texts and of the Eschatological Discourse Mark 13 Par.* Translated by Neil Tomkinson and Jean Gray. Coniectanea biblica: New Testament Series 1. Lund: Gleerup.

Harvey, Anthony E. 1985. "Forty Strokes Save One: Social Aspects of Judaizing and Apostasy." Pages 79–96 in *Alternative Approaches to New Testament Study*. Edited by Anthony E. Harvey. London: SPCK.

Hayes, Christine. 1999. "Intermarriage and Impurity in Ancient Jewish Sources." *Harvard Theological Review* 92, no. 1:3–36.

———. 2004. "Golden Calf Stories: The Relationship of Exodus 32 and Deuteronomy 9–10." Pages 45–93 in *The Idea of Biblical Interpretation*. Edited by Hindy Najman and Judith H. Newman. Journal for the Study of Judaism: Supplement Series 83. Leiden: Brill.

———. 2007. "The 'Other' in Rabbinic Literature." Pages 243–69 in *The Cambridge Companion to the Talmud and Rabbinic Literature*. Edited by Charlotte Elisheva Fonrobert and Martin S. Jaffee. Cambridge: Cambridge University Press.

Hays, Richard B. 1989. *Echoes of Scripture in the Letters of Paul*. New Haven: Yale University Press.

———. 1996. *The Moral Vision of the New Testament: Community, Cross, New Creation; A Contemporary Introduction to Christian Ethics*. San Francisco: Harper.

———. 2005. *The Conversion of the Imagination: Paul as Interpreter of Israel's Scripture*. Grand Rapids: Eerdmans.

Heil, Christoph. 1997. "Die Rezeption von Micha 7,6 LXX in Q und Lukas." *Zeitschrift für die neutestamentliche Wissenschaft und die Kunde der älteren Kirche* 88:211–22.

Heil, John Paul. 1992. *The Gospel of Mark as a Model for Action: A Reader-Response Commentary.* New York: Paulist Press.

Heim, Knut Martin. 2001. *Like Grapes of Gold Set in Silver: An Interpretation of Proverbial Clusters in Proverbs 10:1–22:16.* Beihefte zur Zeitschrift für die alttestamentliche Wissenschaft 273. Berlin: de Gruyter.

Hengel, Martin. 1974. *Judaism and Hellenism: Studies in Their Encounter in Palestine during the Early Hellenistic Period.* Translated by John Bowden. 2 vols. London: SCM.

———. 1985. *Studies in the Gospel of Mark.* Translated by John Bowden. London: SCM.

———. 1989a. "The Political and Social History of Palestine from Alexander to Antiochus III (333–187 B.C.E.)." Pages 35–78 in *The Hellenistic Age.* Edited by W. D. Davies and Louis Finkelstein. Vol. 2 of *The Cambridge History of Judaism.* Cambridge: Cambridge University Press.

———. 1989b. *The Zealots: Investigations into the Jewish Freedom Movement in the Period from Herod I until 70 A.D.* Translated by David Smith. Edinburgh: T&T Clark.

Henten, Jan Willem van. 2007. "Noble Death in Josephus: Just Rhetoric?" Pages 195–218 in *Making History: Josephus and Historical Method.* Edited by Zuleika Rodgers. Journal for the Study of Judaism: Supplement Series 110. Leiden: Brill.

Heskett, Randall J. 2001. "Proverbs 23:13–14." *Interpretation* 55, no. 2:181–84.

Hezser, Catherine. 1996. *The Social Structure of the Rabbinic Movement in Roman Palestine.* Texte und Studien zum antiken Judentum 66. Tübingen: Mohr Siebeck.

Himmelfarb, Martha. 1999. "Sexual Relations and Purity in the Temple Scroll and the Book of Jubilees." *Dead Sea Discoveries* 6, no. 1:11–36.

———. 2004. "Earthly Sacrifices and Heavenly Incense: The Law of the Priesthood in *Aramaic Levi* and *Jubilees.*" Pages 103–22 in *Heavenly Realms and Earthly Realities in Late Antique Religions.* Edited by Ra'anan S. Boustan and Annette Yoshiko Reed. Cambridge: Cambridge University Press.

Holladay, John S. 2009. "'Home Economics 1407' and the Israelite Family and Their Neighbors: An Anthropological/Archaeological Exploration." Pages 61–88 in *The Family in Life and Death: The Family in Ancient Israel; Sociological and Archaeological Perspectives.* Edited by Patricia Dutcher-Walls. New York: T&T Clark.

Hooker, Morna D. 1982. "Trial and Tribulation in Mark XIII." *Bulletin of the John Rylands University Library of Manchester* 65, no. 1:78–99.

————. 1991. *The Gospel according to St Mark*. Black's New Testament Commentaries. London: A&C Black.

Horbury, William. 1998. *Jews and Christians in Contact and Controversy*. Edinburgh: T&T Clark.

Horsley, Richard A. 2005. "The Politics of Cultural Production in Second Temple Judea: Historical Context and Political-Religious Relations of the Scribes Who Produced 1 Enoch, Sirach, and Daniel." Pages 123–45 in *Conflicted Boundaries in Wisdom and Apocalypticism*. Edited by Benjamin G. Wright III and Lawrence M. Wills. Society of Biblical Literature Symposium Series 35. Atlanta: Society of Biblical Literature.

Huizenga, Leroy Andrew. 2002. "The Battle for Isaac: Exploring the Composition and Function of the *Aqedah* in the Book of *Jubilees*." *Journal for the Study of the Pseudepigrapha* 13, no. 1:33–59.

Hurtado, Larry W. 1999. "Pre–70 CE Jewish Opposition to Christ-Devotion." *Journal of Theological Studies* 50, no. 1:35–58.

————. 2005. *How on Earth Did Jesus Become a God? Historical Questions about Earliest Devotion to Jesus*. Grand Rapids: Eerdmans.

Iersel, Bas M. F. van. 1996. "Failed Followers in Mark: Mark 13:12 as a Key for the Identification of the Intended Readers." *Catholic Biblical Quarterly* 58:244–63.

————. 1998. *Mark: A Reader-Response Commentary*. Translated by W. H. Bisscheroux. Journal for the Study of the New Testament: Supplement Series 164. Sheffield: Sheffield Academic Press.

Incigneri, Brian J. 2003. *The Gospel to the Romans: The Setting and Rhetoric of Mark's Gospel*. Biblical Interpretation Series 65. Leiden: Brill.

Jonge, Marinus de, and Johannes Tromp. 1998. "Jacob's Son Levi in the Old Testament Pseudepigrapha and Related Literature." Pages 203–36 in *Biblical Figures outside the Bible*. Edited by Michael E. Stone and Theodore A. Bergren. Harrisburg, PA: Trinity Press International.

Joubert, Stephan J. 1995. "Managing the Household: Paul as *Paterfamilias* of the Christian Household Group in Corinth." Pages 213–23 in *Modelling Early Christianity: Social-Scientific Studies of the New Testament in Its Context*. Edited by Philip F. Esler. London: Routledge.

Jungbauer, Harry. 2002. *Ehre Vater und Mutter: Der Weg des Elterngebots in der biblischen Tradition*. Wissenschaftliche Untersuchungen zum Neuen Testament, ser. 2, vol. 146. Tübingen: Mohr Siebeck.

Kamp, Kathryn. 2000. "From Village to Tell: Household Ethnoarchaeology in Syria." *Near Eastern Archaeology* 63:84–93.

Käsemann, Ernst. 1969. *New Testament Questions of Today*. Philadelphia: Fortress.

Kasher, Aryeh. 2005. "Josephus in Praise of Mosaic Laws on Marriage (*Contra Apionem*, II, 199–201)." Pages 95–108 in *"The Words of a Wise Man's*

Mouth Are Gracious" (Qoh 10,12). Edited by Mauro Perani. Studia judaica 32. Berlin: de Gruyter.

Kee, Howard Clark. 1999. "Jesus: A Glutton and Drunkard." Pages 311–32 in *Authenticating the Words of Jesus*. Edited by Bruce Chilton and Craig A. Evans. New Testament Tools and Studies 28.1. Leiden: Brill.

Keefe, Alicia A. 2008. "Family Metaphors and Social Conflict in Hosea." Pages 113–27 in *Writing and Reading War: Rhetoric, Gender, and Ethics in Biblical and Modern Contexts*. Edited by Brad E. Kelle and Frank Ritchel Ames. Leiden: Brill.

Keener, Craig S. 1997. *Matthew*. InterVarsity Press New Testament Commentary. Downers Grove, IL: InterVarsity.

Kensky, Allan. 1996. "The Family in Rabbinic Judaism." Pages 74–94 in *Religion, Feminism, and the Family*. Edited by Anne Carr and Mary Stewart Van Leeuwen. The Family, Religion, and Culture. Louisville: Westminster John Knox.

Kidner, Derek. 1964. *The Proverbs: An Introduction and Commentary*. Tyndale Old Testament Commentaries. Leicester: Inter-Varsity.

Kille, D. Andrew. 2007. "'The Bible Made Me Do It': Text, Interpretation, and Violence." Pages 8–24 in *The Destructive Power of Religion: Violence in Judaism, Christianity, and Islam*. Edited by J. Harold Ellens. Rev. ed. Psychology, Religion, and Spirituality. Westport, CT: Praeger.

King, Philip J., and Lawrence E. Stager. 2001. *Life in Biblical Israel*. Library of Ancient Israel. Louisville: Westminster John Knox.

Kirk-Duggan, Cheryl A. 2006. *Violence and Theology*. Horizons in Theology. Nashville: Abingdon.

Kistemaker, Simon. 1992. "'Deliver This Man to Satan' (1 Cor 5:5): A Case Study in Church Discipline." *Master's Seminary Journal* 3, no. 1:33–46.

Kister, Menahem. 1992. "Some Aspects of Qumranic Halakhah." Pages 571–88 in vol. 2 of *The Madrid Qumran Congress: Proceedings of the International Congress on the Dead Sea Scrolls Madrid 18–21 March, 1991*. Edited by Julio Trebolle Barrera and Luis Vegas Montaner. Studies on the Texts of the Desert of Judah 11.2. Leiden: Brill.

Klawans, Jonathan. 1995. "Notions of Gentile Impurity in Ancient Judaism." *Association for Jewish Studies Review* 20, no. 2:285–312.

———. 1998. "Idolatry, Incest, and Impurity: Moral Defilement in Ancient Judaism." *Journal for the Study of Judaism* 29:391–415.

Knibb, Michael A. 1989. *Jubilees and the Origins of the Qumran Community*. London: King's College Press.

Kraemer, David. 2006. "The Mishnah." Pages 299–315 in *The Late Roman-Rabbinic Period*. Edited by Steven T. Katz. Vol. 4 of *The Cambridge History of Judaism*. Edited by W. D. Davies and Louis Finkelstein. Cambridge: Cambridge University Press.

Kruse, Colin G. 1988. "The Offender and the Offence in 2 Corinthians 2:5 and 7:12." *Evangelical Quarterly* 61, no. 2:129–39.

Kuck, David W. 1992. *Judgment and Community Conflict: Paul's Use of Apocalyptic Judgment Language in 1 Corinthians 3:5–4:5.* Novum Testamentum Supplements 66. Leiden: Brill.

Kugel, James. 1993. "Levi's Elevation to the Priesthood in Second Temple Writings." *Harvard Theological Review* 86:1–64.

———. 1994. "The Jubilees Apocalypse." *Dead Sea Discoveries* 1, no. 3:322–37.

———. 1997. *The Bible as It Was.* Cambridge, MA: Harvard University Press.

Kulp, Joshua. 2006. "'Go Enjoy Your Acquisition': Virginity Claims in Rabbinic Literature Reexamined." *Hebrew Union College Annual* 77:33–65.

Kvanvig, Helge S. 2004. "Jubilees—Between Enoch and Moses: A Narrative Reading." *Journal for the Study of Judaism* 35, no. 3:243–61.

Lacey, Walter K. 1986. "Patria Potestas." Pages 121–44 in *The Family in Ancient Rome: New Perspectives.* Edited by Beryl Rawson. Ithaca, NY: Cornell University Press.

Lambert, David. 2004. "Last Testaments in the Book of Jubilees." *Dead Sea Discoveries* 11, no. 1:82–107.

———. 2006. "Did Israel Believe That Redemption Awaited Its Repentance? The Case of *Jubilees* 1." *Catholic Biblical Quarterly* 68:631–50.

Lambrecht, Jan. 1967. *Die Redaktion der Markus-Apokalypse: Literarische Analyse und Strukturuntersuchung.* Analecta biblica 28. Rome: Päpstliches Bibelinstitut.

Lampe, Geoffrey W. H. 1967. "Church Discipline and the Interpretation of the Epistles to the Corinthians." Pages 313–61 in *Christian History and Interpretation.* Edited by W. R. Farmer, C. F. D. Moule, and R. R. Niebuhr. Cambridge: Cambridge University Press.

Lassen, Eva Marie. 1997. "The Roman Family: Ideal and Metaphor." Pages 103–20 in *Constructing Early Christian Families: Family as Social Reality and Metaphor.* Edited by Halvor Moxnes. London: Routledge.

Légasse, Simon. 1995. "Paul's Pre-Christian Career according to Acts." Pages 365–90 in *The Book of Acts in Its Palestinian Setting.* Edited by Richard Bauckham. Vol. 4 of *The Book of Acts in Its First Century Setting.* Edited by Bruce W. Winter. Carlisle: Paternoster.

Levenson, Jon D. 1993. *The Death and Resurrection of the Beloved Son: The Transformation of Child Sacrifice in Judaism and Christianity.* New Haven: Yale University Press.

Levine, Daniel B. 1993. "Hubris in Josephus' *Jewish Antiquities* 1–4." *Hebrew Union College Annual* 64:51–87.

Levinson, Bernard M. 1995. "'But You Shall Surely Kill Him!' The Text-Critical and Neo-Assyrian Evidence for MT Deuteronomy 13:10." Pages 37–63 in *Bundesdokument und Gesetz: Studien zum Deuteronomium*. Edited by Georg Braulik. Freiburg: Herder.

———. 1996. "Recovering the Lost Original Meaning of תכסה עליו ולא [*tksh 'lyw wl'*] (Deuteronomy 13:9)." *Journal of Biblical Literature* 115, no. 4:601–20.

———. 1997. *Deuteronomy and the Hermeneutics of Legal Innovation*. Oxford: Oxford University Press.

———. 2001. "Textual Criticism, Assyriology, and the History of Interpretation: Deuteronomy 13:7a as a Test Case in Method." *Journal of Biblical Literature* 120, no. 2:211–43.

Lieu, Judith M. 1986. *The Second and Third Epistles of John: History and Background*. Edinburgh: T&T Clark.

———. 1991. *The Theology of the Johannine Epistles*. New Testament Theology. Cambridge: Cambridge University Press.

Lightfoot, Robert H. 1950. *The Gospel Message of St. Mark*. Oxford: Clarendon.

Loader, William. 2007. *Enoch, Levi, and Jubilees on Sexuality: Attitudes towards Sexuality in the Early Enoch Literature, the Aramaic Levi Document, and the Book of Jubilees*. Grand Rapids: Eerdmans.

Locher, Clemens. 1986. *Die Ehre einer Frau in Israel: Exegetische und rechtsvergleichende Studien zu Deuteronomium 22,13–21*. Orbis biblicus et orientalis 70. Göttingen: Vandenhoeck & Ruprecht.

Love, Stuart L. 1993. "The Household: A Major Social Component for Gender Analysis in the Gospel of Matthew." *Biblical Theology Bulletin* 23, no. 1:21–31.

Lutzky, Harriet C. 1997. "The Name 'Cozbi' (Numbers XXV 15,18)." *Vetus Testamentum* 47, no. 4:546–49.

Luz, Ulrich. 1989. *Matthew 1–7: A Continental Commentary*. Translated by Wilhelm C. Linss. Minneapolis: Fortress.

MacDonald, Nathan. 2007. "Recasting the Golden Calf: The Imaginative Potential of the Old Testament's Portrayal of Idolatry." Pages 22–39 in *Idolatry: False Worship in the Bible, Early Judaism and Christianity*. Edited by Stephen C. Barton. London: T&T Clark.

Mader, Gottfried. 2000. *Josephus and the Politics of Historiography: Apologetic and Impression Management in the "Bellum Judaicum."* Mnemosyne Supplements. Leiden: Brill.

Malbon, Elizabeth Struthers. 1996. "The Literary Context of Mark 13." Pages 105–24 in *Biblical and Humane*. Edited by Linda Bennett Elder, David L. Barr, and Elizabeth Struthers Malbon. Atlanta: Scholars Press.

Malfroy, Jean. 1965. "Sagesse et loi dans le Deutéronome." *Vetus Testamentum* 15:47–65.

Malina, Bruce J. 2001. *The New Testament World: Insights from Cultural Anthropology*. 3rd ed. Louisville: Westminster John Knox.

Malina, Bruce J., and Richard L. Rohrbaugh. 2003. *Social-Science Commentary on the Synoptic Gospels*. 2nd ed. Minneapolis: Fortress.

Marcus, Joel. 2000. *Mark 1–8: A New Translation with Introduction and Commentary*. Anchor Bible 27. New York: Doubleday.

———. 2009. *Mark 8–16: A New Translation with Introduction and Commentary*. Anchor Yale Bible 27A. New Haven: Yale University Press.

Marohl, Matthew J. 2008. *Joseph's Dilemma: "Honor Killing" in the Birth Narrative of Matthew*. Eugene, OR: Cascade.

Martola, Nils. 1984. *Capture and Liberation: A Study in the Composition of the First Book of Maccabees*. Acta Academiae Aboensis, ser. A, vol. 63.1. Åbo: Åbo Akademi.

Mason, Steve. 1998. "'Should Any Wish to Enquire Further' (*Ant.* 1.25): The Aim and Audience of Josephus's *Judean Antiquities/Life*." Pages 64–103 in *Understanding Josephus: Seven Perspectives*. Edited by Steve Mason. Journal for the Study of the Pseudepigrapha: Supplement Series 32. Sheffield: Sheffield Academic Press.

Mathew, Parackel K. 1985. "Authority and Discipline (Matt 16:17–19; 18:15–18) and the Exercise of Authority and Discipline in the Matthean Community." *Communio viatorum* 28, nos. 3–4:119–25.

Matthews, Victor H. 1994. "Female Voices: Upholding the Honor of the Household." *Biblical Theology Bulletin* 24:8–15.

———. 2004 (1998). "Honor and Shame in Gender-Related Legal Situations in the Hebrew Bible." Pages 97–112 in *Gender and Law in the Hebrew Bible and the Ancient Near East*. Edited by Victor H. Matthews, Bernard M. Levinson, and Tikva Frymer-Kensky. London: T&T Clark.

Matthews, Victor H., and Don C. Benjamin. 1991. "The Stubborn and the Fool: A Question of Labels." *Bible Today* 29, no. 4:222–26.

Mattila, Sharon Lea. 1996. "Wisdom, Sense Perception, Nature, and Philo's Gender Gradient." *Harvard Theological Review* 89:103–29.

May, David M. 1987. "Mark 3:20–35 from the Perspective of Shame/Honor." *Biblical Theology Bulletin* 17, no. 3:83–87.

———. 1990. "Leaving and Receiving: A Social-Scientific Exegesis of Mark 10:29–31." *Perspectives in Religious Studies* 17:141–51, 154.

McBride, S. Dean. 1987. "Polity of the Covenant People: The Book of Deuteronomy." *Interpretation* 41:229–44.

———. 2006. "The Essence of Orthodoxy: Deuteronomy 5:6–10 and Exodus 20:2–6." *Interpretation* 60, no. 2:133–50.

McCarthy, Dennis J. 1965. "Notes on the Love of God in Deuteronomy and the Father-Son Relationship between Yahweh and Israel." *Catholic Biblical Quarterly* 27:144–47.

McConville, J. Gordon. 2002. *Deuteronomy*. Apollos Old Testament Commentary 5. Leicester: Apollos.

McGinn, Bernard. 2005. "Apocalypticism and Violence: Aspects of their Relation in Antiquity and the Middle Ages." Pages 209–29 in *Scripture and Pluralism: Reading the Bible in the Religiously Plural Worlds of the Middle Ages and Renaissance*. Edited by Thomas J. Heffernan and Thomas E. Burman. Studies in the History of Christian Traditions 123. Leiden: Brill.

McKane, William. 1970. *Proverbs: A New Approach*. Old Testament Library. Philadelphia: Westminster.

McKnight, Scot. 2003. "Calling Jesus *Mamzer*." *Journal for the Study of the Historical Jesus* 1, no. 1:73–103.

Meeks, Wayne A. 2003 (1983). *The First Urban Christians: The Social World of the Apostle Paul*. 2nd ed. New Haven: Yale University Press.

Meier, John P. 1980. *Matthew*. New Testament Message 3. Dublin: Veritas Publications.

Meyers, Carol. 1988. *Discovering Eve: Ancient Israelite Women in Context*. Oxford: Oxford University Press.

———. 1997. "The Family in Early Israel." Pages 1–47 in *Families in Ancient Israel*. Edited by Leo G. Perdue et al. The Family, Religion, and Culture. Louisville: Westminster John Knox.

Milgrom, Jacob. 1990. *Numbers [Ba-midbar]: The Traditional Hebrew Text with the New JPS Translation*. The JPS Torah Commentary. Philadelphia: Jewish Publication Society.

———. 1999. "The Case of the Suspected Adulteress, Numbers 5:11–31: Redaction and Meaning." Pages 475–82 in *Women in the Hebrew Bible: A Reader*. Edited by Alice Bach. New York: Routledge.

Millar, J. Gary. 1998. *Now Choose Life: Theology and Ethics in Deuteronomy*. New Studies in Biblical Theology. Grand Rapids: Eerdmans.

Miller, Patrick D. 1990. *Deuteronomy*. Interpretation. Louisville: John Knox.

———. 2005. "Constitution or Instruction? The Purpose of Deuteronomy." Pages 125–41 in *Constituting the Community: Studies on the Polity of Ancient Israel*. Edited by John T. Strong and Steven S. Tuell. Winona Lake, IN: Eisenbrauns.

———. 2008. "That the Children May Know: Children in Deuteronomy." Pages 45–62 in *The Child in the Bible*. Edited by Marcia J. Bunge, Terence E. Fretheim, and Beverly Roberts Gaventa. Grand Rapids: Eerdmans.

Minkoff, Dinah. 2003. "Parental Love or Child Abuse?" *Jewish Bible Quarterly* 31, no. 1:48–52.

Moberly, R. W. L. 1983. *At the Mountain of God: Story and Theology in Exodus 32–34*. Journal for the Study of the Old Testament: Supplement Series 22. Sheffield: JSOT Press.

———. 1999. "Toward an Interpretation of the Shema." Pages 124–44 in *Theological Exegesis*. Edited by Christopher Seitz and Kathryn Greene-McCreight. Grand Rapids: Eerdmans.

Modica, Joseph B. 2008. "Jesus as Glutton and Drunkard: The 'Excesses' of Jesus." Pages 50–75 in *Who Do My Opponents Say I Am? An Investigation of the Accusations against Jesus*. Edited by Scot McKnight and Joseph B. Modica. Library of Historical Jesus Studies. Library of New Testament Studies 327. London: T&T Clark.

Mondésert, C. 1999. "Philo of Alexandria." Pages 877–900 in *The Early Roman Period*. Edited by William Horbury, W. D. Davies, and John Sturdy. Vol. 3 of *The Cambridge History of Judaism*. Edited by W. D. Davies and Louis Finkelstein. Cambridge: Cambridge University Press.

Morin, J.-Alfred. 1973. "Les deux derniers des douze: Simon le Zélote et Judas Iskariôth." *Revue biblique* 80:332–58.

Mørkholm, Otto. 1989. "Antiochus IV." Pages 278–91 in *The Hellenistic Age*. Edited by W. D. Davies and Louis Finkelstein. Vol. 2 of *The Cambridge History of Judaism*. Edited by W. D. Davies and Louis Finkelstein. Cambridge: Cambridge University Press.

Moxnes, Halvor, ed. 1997. *Constructing Early Christian Families: Family as Social Reality and Metaphor*. London: Routledge.

Moyise, Steve. 2007. "Deuteronomy in Mark's Gospel." Pages 27–41 in *Deuteronomy in the New Testament: The New Testament and the Scriptures of Israel*. Edited by Maarten J. J. Menken and Steve Moyise. Library of New Testament Studies 358. London: T&T Clark.

Murphy, Roland E. 1998. *Proverbs*. Word Biblical Commentary 22. Nashville: Thomas Nelson.

Najman, Hindy. 1999. "Interpretation as Primordial Writing: *Jubilees* and Its Authority Conferring Strategies." *Journal for the Study of Judaism* 30, no. 4:379–410.

———. 2000. "Angels at Sinai: Exegesis, Theology and Interpretive Authority." *Dead Sea Discoveries* 7, no. 3:313–33.

———. 2003. *Seconding Sinai: The Development of Mosaic Discourse in Second Temple Judaism*. Journal for the Study of Judaism: Supplement Series 77. Leiden: Brill.

Nasuti, Harry P. 1986. "Identity, Identification, and Imitation: The Narrative Hermeneutics of Biblical Law." *Journal of Law and Religion* 4, no. 1:9–23.

Nathan, Geoffrey S. 2000. *The Family in Late Antiquity: The Rise of Christianity and the Endurance of Tradition*. London: Routledge.

Neale, D. 1993. "Was Jesus a *Mesith*? Public Response to Jesus and His Ministry." *Tyndale Bulletin* 44, no. 1:89–101.

Nelson, Richard D. 1997. "*Ḥerem* and the Deuteronomic Social Conscience." Pages 39–54 in *Deuteronomy and Deuteronomic Literature*. Edited by M. Vervenne and J. Lust. Bibliotheca ephemeridum theologicarum lovaniensium 133. Leuven: Leuven University Press.

Neyrey, Jerome H. 1998. *Honor and Shame in the Gospel of Matthew*. Louisville: Westminster John Knox.

Nickelsburg, George W. E. 1972. *Resurrection, Immortality, and Eternal Life in Intertestamental Judaism*. Harvard Theological Studies 26. Cambridge, MA: Harvard University Press.

———. 1981. *Jewish Literature between the Bible and the Mishnah: A Historical and Literary Introduction*. Philadelphia: Fortress.

———. 1984. "The Bible Rewritten and Expanded." Pages 89–156 in *Jewish Writings of the Second Temple Period*. Edited by Michael E. Stone. Assen: Van Gorcum.

———. 1999. "The Nature and Function of Revelation in 1 Enoch, Jubilees, and Some Qumranic Documents." Pages 91–119 in *Pseudepigraphic Perspectives: The Apocrypha and Pseudepigrapha in Light of the Dead Sea Scrolls*. Edited by Esther G. Chazon and Michael Stone. Studies on the Texts of the Desert of Judah 31. Leiden: Brill.

Niditch, Susan. 1993. *War in the Hebrew Bible: A Study in the Ethics of Violence*. Oxford: Oxford University Press.

Niehoff, Maren R. 2001. *Philo on Jewish Identity and Culture*. Texts and Studies in Ancient Judaism 86. Tübingen: Mohr Siebeck.

Noack, Bent. 1958. "Qumran and the Book of Jubilees." *Svensk Exegetisk Årsbok* 22–23:191–207.

Noll, K. L. 2007. "Deuteronomistic History or Deuteronomistic Debate? (A Thought Experiment)." *Journal for the Study of the Old Testament* 31, no. 3:311–45.

Nongbri, Brent. 2005. "The Motivations of the Maccabees and Judean Rhetoric of Ancestral Tradition." Pages 85–111 in *Ancient Judaism in Its Hellenistic Context*. Edited by Carol Bakhos. Journal for the Study of Judaism: Supplement Series 95. Leiden: Brill.

Obenhaus, Stacy R. 2001. "Sanctified Entirely: The Theological Focus of Paul's Instructions for Church Discipline." *Restoration Quarterly* 43, no. 1:1–12.

Olyan, Saul M. 2008. *Disability in the Hebrew Bible: Interpreting Mental and Physical Differences*. Cambridge: Cambridge University Press.

Otto, Eckart. 2004 (1998). "False Weights in the Scales of Biblical Justice? Different Views of Women from Patriarchal Hierarchy to Religious Equality in the Book of Deuteronomy." Pages 128–46 in *Gender and Law in the*

Hebrew Bible and the Ancient Near East. Edited by Victor H. Matthews, Bernard M. Levinson, and Tikva Frymer-Kensky. London: T&T Clark.

Overland, Paul. 2000. "Did the Sage Draw from the Shema? A Study of Proverbs 3:1–12." *Catholic Biblical Quarterly* 62, no. 3:424–40.

Painter, John. 1997. *Mark's Gospel: Worlds in Conflict.* New Testament Readings. London: Routledge.

Park, Eung Chun. 1995. *The Mission Discourse in Matthew's Interpretation.* Wissenschaftliche Untersuchungen zum Neuen Testament, ser. 2, vol. 81. Tübingen: Mohr Siebeck.

Pásztor, J. D. 2005. "Violence in Protecting the Church and Doctrine and in Propagating the Faith in the Constantinian Era." Pages 47–56 in vol. 2 of *Christian Faith and Violence.* Edited by Dirk van Keulen and Martien E. Brinkman. Studies in Reformed Theology 11. Meinema: Zoetermeer.

Perdue, Leo G. 2000. *Proverbs.* Interpretation. Louisville: Westminster John Knox.

Perdue, Leo G., et al. 1997. *Families in Ancient Israel.* The Family, Religion, and Culture. Louisville: Westminster John Knox.

Peskowitz, Miriam B. 1993. "'Family/ies' in Antiquity: Evidence from Tannaitic Literature and Roman Galilean Architecture." Pages 9–36 in *The Jewish Family in Antiquity.* Edited by Shaye J. D. Cohen. Brown Judaic Studies 289. Atlanta: Scholars Press.

————. 1997. *Spinning Fantasies: Rabbis, Gender, and History.* Contraversions 9. Berkeley: University of California Press.

Pfitzner, Victor C. 1982. "Purified Community—Purified Sinner: Expulsion from the Community according to Matthew 18:15–18 and 1 Corinthians 5:1–5." *Australian Biblical Review* 30:34–55.

Phillips, Anthony. 1975. "*Nebalah*—A Term for Serious Disorderly and Unruly Conduct." *Vetus Testamentum* 25:237–42.

Phillips, Gary A., and Danna Nolan Fewell. 1997. "Ethics, Bible, Reading as If." *Semeia* 77:1–21.

Pilch, John J. 1993. "'Beat His Ribs While He Is Young' (Sir 30:12): A Window on the Mediterranean World." *Biblical Theology Bulletin* 23, no. 3:101–13.

————. 1997. "Family Violence in Cross-Cultural Perspective: An Approach for Feminist Interpreters of the Bible." Pages 306–23 in *A Feminist Companion to Reading the Bible: Approaches, Methods and Strategies.* Edited by Athalya Brenner and Carole Fontaine. Sheffield: Sheffield Academic Press.

Pitt-Rivers, Julian. 1968. "Kinship: Pseudo-Kinship." Pages 408–13 in vol. 8 of *International Encyclopedia of the Social Sciences.* Edited by David L. Sills. London: Macmillan.

Porter, Joshua Roy. 1967. *The Extended Family in the Old Testament.* Occasional Papers in Social and Economic Administration 6. London: Edutext Publications.

Powell, Mark Allan. 2003. "Binding and Loosing: A Paradigm for Ethical Discernment from the Gospel of Matthew." *Currents in Theology and Mission* 30, no. 6:438–45.

Pressler, Carolyn. 1993. *The View of Women Found in the Deuteronomic Family Laws.* Beihefte zur Zeitschrift für die alttestamentliche Wissenschaft 216. Berlin: de Gruyter.

Propp, William H. C. 2006. *Exodus 19–40: A New Translation with Introduction and Commentary.* Anchor Bible 2A. New York: Doubleday.

Rajak, Tessa. 1983. *Josephus: The Historian and His Society.* London: Duckworth.

———. 1990. "The Hasmoneans and the Uses of Hellenism." Pages 261–80 in *A Tribute to Géza Vermès: Essays on Jewish and Christian Literature and History.* Edited by Philip R. Davies and Richard T. White. Journal for the Study of the Old Testament: Supplement Series 100. Sheffield: Sheffield Academic Press.

Ramshaw, Elaine. 1998. "Power and Forgiveness in Matthew 18." *Word & World* 18, no. 4:397–404.

Rappaport, Uriel [Uri'el Rapaporṭ]. 1998. "A Note on the Use of the Bible in 1 Maccabees." Pages 175–79 in *Biblical Perspectives: Early Use and Interpretation of the Bible in Light of the Dead Sea Scrolls.* Edited by Michael E. Stone and Esther G. Chazon. Studies on the Texts of the Desert of Judah 28. Leiden: Brill.

Ravid, Liora. 2002. "Purity and Impurity in the Book of *Jubilees.*" *Journal for the Study of the Pseudepigrapha* 13, no. 1:61–86.

Rawson, Beryl. 1986. "The Roman Family." Pages 1–57 in *The Family in Ancient Rome: New Perspectives.* Edited by Beryl Rawson. Ithaca, NY: Cornell University Press.

Reicke, Bo. 1967. "Liturgical Traditions in Mic. 7." *Harvard Theological Review* 60:349–67.

Reinhartz, Adele. 1993. "Parents and Children: A Philonic Perspective." Pages 61–88 in *The Jewish Family in Antiquity.* Edited by Shaye J. D. Cohen. Brown Judaic Studies 289. Atlanta: Scholars Press.

Reviv, Hanoch. 1989. *The Elders in Ancient Israel: A Study of a Biblical Institution.* Translated by Lucy Plitmann. Jerusalem: Magnes.

Rofé, Alexander. 2002. *Deuteronomy: Issues and Interpretation.* Old Testament Studies. London: T&T Clark.

Rogers, Jesse. 2004. "'It Overflows like the Euphrates with Understanding': Another Look at the Relationship between Law and Wisdom in Sirach." Pages 114–21 in *Ancient Versions and Traditions.* Vol. 1 of *Of Scribes and*

Sages: Early Jewish Interpretation and Transmission of Scripture. Edited by Craig A. Evans. London: T&T Clark.

Römer, Thomas C. 2000. "Du Temple au livre: L'idéologie de la centralisation dans l'historiographie deutéronomiste." Pages 207–25 in *Rethinking the Foundations: Historiography in the Ancient World and in the Bible*. Edited by Steven L. McKenzie and Thomas Römer (in collaboration with Hans Heinrich Schmid). Beihefte zur Zeitschrift für die alttestamentliche Wissenschaft 294. Berlin: de Gruyter.

Rosner, Brian S. 1991. "Temple and Holiness in 1 Corinthians 5." *Tyndale Bulletin* 42, no. 1:137–45.

———. 1994. *Paul, Scripture and Ethics: A Study of 1 Corinthians 5–7*. Arbeiten zur Geschichte des antiken Judentums und des Urchristentums 22. Leiden: Brill.

———. 1999. "'Drive Out the Wicked Person': A Biblical Theology of Exclusion." *Evangelical Quarterly* 71, no. 1:25–36.

Rubenstein, Jeffrey L. 2007. "Social and Institutional Settings of Rabbinic Literature." Pages 58–74 in *The Cambridge Companion to the Talmud and Rabbinic Literature*. Edited by Charlotte Elisheva Fonrobert and Martin S. Jaffee. Cambridge: Cambridge University Press.

Saldarini, Anthony J. 1994. *Matthew's Christian-Jewish Community*. Chicago Studies in the History of Judaism. Chicago: University of Chicago Press.

———. 2001. "Absent Women in Matthew's Households." Pages 157–70 in *A Feminist Companion to Matthew*. Edited by Amy-Jill Levine and Marianne Blickenstaff. Feminist Companion to the New Testament and Early Christian Writings 1. Sheffield: Sheffield Academic Press.

Saller, Richard P. 1994. *Patriarchy, Property and Death in the Roman Family*. Cambridge Studies in Population, Economy and Society in Past Times 25. Cambridge: Cambridge University Press.

Sanders, James A. 2002. "The Family in the Bible." *Biblical Theology Bulletin* 32, no. 3:117–28.

Sandnes, Karl Olav. 1994. *A New Family: Conversion and Ecclesiology in the Early Church with Cross-Cultural Comparisons*. Studies in the Intercultural History of Christianity 91. Bern: Peter Lang.

Satlow, Michael L. 2001. *Jewish Marriage in Antiquity*. Princeton: Princeton University Press.

———. 2006. "Rabbinic Views on Marriage, Sexuality, and the Family." Pages 612–26 in *The Late Roman-Rabbinic Period*. Edited by Steven T. Katz. Vol. 4 of *The Cambridge History of Judaism*. Edited by W. D. Davies and Louis Finkelstein. Cambridge: Cambridge University Press.

Schloen, J. David. 2001. *The House of the Father as Fact and Symbol: Patrimonialism in Ugarit and the Ancient Near East*. Studies in the Archaeology and History of the Levant. Harvard Semitic Museum Publications. Winona Lake, IN: Eisenbrauns.

Schüssler Fiorenza, Elisabeth. 1999. *Rhetoric and Ethic: The Politics of Biblical Studies*. Minneapolis: Augsburg Fortress.

Schwartz, Daniel R. 1992. *Studies in the Jewish Background of Christianity*. Wissenschaftliche Untersuchungen zum Neuen Testament 60. Tübingen: Mohr Siebeck.

———. 1998a. "On Something Biblical about 2 Maccabees." Pages 221–32 in *Biblical Perspectives: Early Use and Interpretation of the Bible in Light of the Dead Sea Scrolls*. Edited by Michael E. Stone and Esther G. Chazon. Studies on the Texts of the Desert of Judah 28. Leiden: Brill.

———. 1998b. "The Other in 1 and 2 Maccabees." Pages 30–37 in *Tolerance and Intolerance in Early Judaism and Christianity*. Edited by Graham N. Stanton and Guy G. Stroumsa. Cambridge: Cambridge University Press.

Schwartz, Regina M. 1997. *The Curse of Cain: The Violent Legacy of Monotheism*. Chicago: University of Chicago Press.

Schwartz, Seth. 1991. "Israel and the Nations Roundabout: 1 Maccabees and the Hasmonean Expansion." *Journal of Jewish Studies* 42:16–38.

———. 2001. *Imperialism and Jewish Society, 200 B.C.E. to 640 C.E.* Jews, Christians, and Muslims from the Ancient to the Modern World. Princeton: Princeton University Press.

———. 2006. "Political, Social, and Economic Life in the Land of Israel, 66–c. 235." Pages 23–52 in *The Late Roman-Rabbinic Period*. Edited by Steven T. Katz. Volume 4 of *The Cambridge History of Judaism*. Edited by W. D. Davies and Louis Finkelstein. Cambridge: Cambridge University Press.

———. 2007. "The Political Geography of Rabbinic Texts." Pages 75–96 in *The Cambridge Companion to the Talmud and Rabbinic Literature*. Edited by Charlotte Elisheva Fonrobert and Martin S. Jaffee. Cambridge: Cambridge University Press.

Schwarz, Eberhard. 1982. *Identität durch Abgrenzung: Abgrenzungsprozesse in Israel im 2. vorchristlichen Jahrhundert und ihre traditionsgeschichtlichen Voraussetzungen; Zugleich ein Beitrag zur Erforschung des Jubiläenbuches*. Europäische Hochschulschriften 162. Frankfurt am Main: Peter Lang.

Seland, Torrey. 1995. *Establishment Violence in Philo and Luke: A Study of Non-Conformity to the Torah and Jewish Vigilante Reactions*. Biblical Interpretation Series 15. Leiden: Brill.

———. 2002. "Saul of Tarsus and Early Zealotism: Reading Gal 1,13–14 in Light of Philo's Writings." *Biblica* 83, no. 4:449–71.

———. 2003. "(Re)presentations of Violence in Philo." Pages 117–40 in *Society of Biblical Literature Seminar Papers, 2003*. Edited by Matthew Collins.

Society of Biblical Literature Seminar Papers 42. Atlanta: Society of Biblical Literature.

Sen, Amartya. 2006. *Identity and Violence: The Illusion of Destiny.* Issues of Our Time. London: Allen Lane.

Seters, John van. 1997. *In Search of History: Historiography in the Ancient World and the Origins of Biblical History.* New Haven: Yale University Press, 1983. Repr., Winona Lake, IN: Eisenbrauns.

Severy, Beth. 2003. *Augustus and the Family at the Birth of the Roman Empire.* New York: Routledge.

Shaw, Brent D. 2001. "Raising and Killing Children: Two Roman Myths." *Mnemosyne* 54, no. 1:31–77.

Sheffield, Julian. 2001. "The Father in the Gospel of Matthew." Pages 52–69 in *A Feminist Companion to Matthew.* Edited by Amy-Jill Levine and Marianne Blickenstaff. Feminist Companion to the New Testament and Early Christian Writings 1. Sheffield: Sheffield Academic Press.

Shemesh, Aharon. 1998. "4Q271.3: A Key to Sectarian Matrimonial Law." *Journal of Jewish Studies* 49:244–63.

Shillington, V. George. 1998. "Atonement Texture in 1 Corinthians 5.5." *Journal for the Study of the New Testament* 71:29–50.

Shipton, Parker. 1997. "Fictive Kinship." Pages 186–88 in *The Dictionary of Anthropology.* Edited by Thomas Barfield. Oxford: Blackwell.

Shupak, Nili. 1987. "The 'Sitz im Leben' of the Book of Proverbs in the Light of a Comparison of Biblical and Egyptian Wisdom Literature." *Revue biblique* 94, no. 1:98–119.

Sim, David C. 1998. *The Gospel of Matthew and Christian Judaism: The History and Social Setting of the Matthean Community.* Studies of the New Testament and Its World. Edinburgh: T&T Clark.

Sivan, Hagith. 2004. *Between Woman, Man and God: A New Interpretation of the Ten Commandments.* Journal for the Study of the Old Testament: Supplement Series 401. Bible in the Twenty-First Century 4. London: T&T Clark.

Sivertsev, Alexei M. 2002. *Private Households and Public Politics in 3rd–5th Century Jewish Palestine.* Texts and Studies in Ancient Judaism 90. Tübingen: Mohr Siebeck.

———. 2005. *Households, Sects, and the Origins of Rabbinic Judaism.* Journal for the Study of Judaism: Supplement Series 102. Leiden: Brill.

Skehan, Patrick W. 1974. "Sirach 30:12 and Related Texts." *Catholic Biblical Quarterly* 36:535–42.

Skehan, Patrick W., and Alexander A. DiLella. 1987. *The Wisdom of Ben Sira: A New Translation with Notes.* Anchor Bible. New York: Doubleday.

Slater, Jonathan P. 2002. "The Emergence of the Matrilineal Principle in Judaism." *Conservative Judaism* 55, no. 1:15–29.

Sly, Dorothy I. 1990. *Philo's Perception of Women*. Brown Judaic Studies 209. Atlanta: Scholars Press.

————. 1991. "Philo's Practical Application of Δικαιοσύνη." Pages 298–308 in *Society of Biblical Literature 1991 Seminar Papers*. Edited by Eugene H. Lovering. Society of Biblical Literature Seminar Papers 30. Atlanta: Scholars Press.

Smith, Carol. 2001. "Biblical Perspectives on Power." *Journal for the Study of the Old Testament* 93:93–110.

Snaith, John G. 1995. "Ecclesiasticus: A Tract for the Times." Pages 170–81 in *Wisdom in Ancient Israel*. Edited by John Day, Robert P. Gordon, and H. G. M. Williamson. Cambridge: Cambridge University Press.

Söding, Thomas. 1995. "Feindeshass und Bruderliebe beobachtungen zur essenischen Ethik." *Revue de Qumran* 16, no. 4:601–19.

Sommer, Benjamin D. 1998. *A Prophet Reads Scripture: Allusion in Isaiah 40–66*. Contraversions. Stanford, CA: Stanford University Press.

South, James T. 1993. "A Critique of the 'Curse/Death' Interpretation of 1 Corinthians 5.1–8." *New Testament Studies* 39:539–61.

Sparks, Kenton L. 1998. *Ethnicity and Identity in Ancient Israel: Prolegomena to the Study of Ethnic Sentiments and Their Expression in the Hebrew Bible*. Winona Lake, IN: Eisenbrauns.

Spilsbury, Paul. 1998. *The Image of the Jew in Flavius Josephus' Paraphrase of the Bible*. Texte und Studien zum Antiken Judentum 69. Tübingen: Mohr Siebeck.

————. 2005. "Reading the Bible in Rome: Josephus and the Constraints of Empire." Pages 209–27 in *Josephus and Jewish History in Flavian Rome and Beyond*. Edited by Joseph Sievers and Gaia Lembi. Journal for the Study of Judaism: Supplement Series 104. Leiden: Brill.

Stager, Lawrence E. 1985. "The Archaeology of the Family in Ancient Israel." *Bulletin of the American Schools of Oriental Research* 260:1–35.

Stanton, Graham N. 1992. *A Gospel for a New People: Studies in Matthew*. Edinburgh: T&T Clark.

————. 1994. "Jesus of Nazareth: A Magician and a False Prophet Who Deceived God's People?" Pages 164–80 in *Jesus of Nazareth: Lord and Christ*. Edited by Joel B. Green and Max Turner. Carlisle: Paternoster.

Steinberg, Naomi. 1991. "The Deuteronomic Law Code and the Politics of State Centralization." Pages 161–70 in *The Bible and the Politics of Exegesis*. Edited by David Jobling, Peggy L. Day, and Gerald T. Sheppard. Cleveland: Pilgrim Press.

Stern, Elsie R. 2008. "Ki Tisa [*kî tiśśa'*]: [Exod.] 30:11–34:35." Pages 495–520 in *The Torah: A Women's Commentary*. Edited by Tamara Cohen Eskenazi and Andrea L. Weiss. New York: URJ Press / Women of Reform Judaism.

Stock, Augustine. 1989. *The Method and Message of Mark*. Wilmington, DE: Michael Glazier.

Stone, Linda. 2001. "Introduction: Theoretical Implications of New Directions in Anthropological Kinship." Pages 1–20 in *New Directions in Anthropological Kinship*. Edited by Linda Stone. New York: Rowman & Littlefield.

Stone, Michael E. 1990. *A Textual Commentary on the Armenian Version of IV Ezra*. Society of Biblical Literature Septuagint and Cognate Studies 34. Atlanta: Scholars Press.

Stott, T. Lynn. 1992. "Not Merely Chattel: Women as Guardians of Holiness in the Mishnah's Society." Pages 23–37 in *Recovering the Role of Women: Power and Authority in Rabbinic Jewish Society*. Edited by Peter J. Haas. South Florida Studies in the History of Judaism 59. Atlanta: Scholars Press.

Strawn, Brent A. 2008. "'Israel, My Child': The Ethics of a Biblical Metaphor." Pages 103–40 in *The Child in the Bible*. Edited by Marcia J. Bunge, Terence E. Fretheim, and Beverly Roberts Gaventa. Grand Rapids: Eerdmans.

Strobel, August. 1980. *Die Stunde der Wahrheit: Untersuchungen zum Strafverfahren gegen Jesus*. Wissenschaftliche Untersuchungen zum Neuen Testament 21. Tübingen: Mohr Siebeck.

Stulman, Louis. 1990. "Encroachment in Deuteronomy: An Analysis of the Social World of the D Code." *Journal of Biblical Literature* 109, no. 4:613–32.

———. 1992. "Sex and Familial Crimes in the D Code: A Witness to Mores in Transition." *Journal for the Study of the Old Testament* 53:47–63.

Talstra, Eep. 2005. "Identity and Loyalty, Faith and Violence: The Case of Deuteronomy." Pages 69–85 in vol. 1 of *Christian Faith and Violence*. Edited by Dirk van Keulen and Martien E. Brinkman. Studies in Reformed Theology 10. Zoetermeer: Meinema.

Taylor, Justin. 1998. "Why Did Paul Persecute the Church?" Pages 99–120 in *Tolerance and Intolerance in Early Judaism and Christianity*. Edited by Graham N. Stanton and Guy G. Stroumsa. Cambridge: Cambridge University Press.

Taylor, Nicholas H. 1996. "Palestinian Christianity and the Caligula Crisis: Part II, The Markan Eschatological Discourse." *Journal for the Study of the New Testament* 62:13–41.

Theissen, Gerd. 1992. *The Gospels in Context: Social and Political History in the Synoptic Tradition*. Translated by Linda M. Maloney. Edinburgh: T&T Clark.

Thiselton, Anthony C. 1973. "The Meaning of Σάρξ in 1 Corinthians 5.5: A Fresh Approach in the Light of Logical and Semantic Factors." *Scottish Journal of Theology* 26, no. 2:204–28.

Thomas, Yan. 1984. "*Vitae necisque potestas*: Le père, la cité, la mort." Pages 499–548 in *Du châtiment dans la cité: Supplices corporels et peine de mort dans le monde antique*. Collection de l'École Française de Rome 79. Rome: École Française.

Thompson, John L. 2001. *Writing the Wrongs: Women of the Old Testament among Biblical Commentators from Philo through the Reformation*. Oxford Studies in Historical Theology. Oxford: Oxford University Press.

————. 2007. *Reading the Bible with the Dead: What You Can Learn from the History of Exegesis That You Can't Learn from Exegesis Alone*. Grand Rapids: Eerdmans.

Thompson, Marianne Meye. 2000. *The Promise of the Father: Jesus and God in the New Testament*. Louisville: Westminster John Knox.

Thrall, Margaret E. 1987. "The Offender and the Offence: A Problem of Detection in 2 Corinthians." Pages 65–78 in *Scripture: Meaning and Method*. Edited by Barry P. Thompson. Hull: Hull University Press.

Tigay, Jeffrey H. 1993. "Examination of the Accused Bride in 4Q159: Forensic Medicine at Qumran." *Journal of the Ancient Near Eastern Society of Columbia University* 22:129–34.

————. 1996. *Deuteronomy: The Traditional Hebrew Text with the New JPS Translation*. The JPS Torah Commentary. Philadelphia: Jewish Publication Society.

Tolbert, Mary Ann. 1989. *Sowing the Gospel: Mark's World in Literary-Historical Perspective*. Minneapolis: Fortress.

Toy, Crawford H. 1904. *A Critical and Exegetical Commentary on the Book of Proverbs*. International Critical Commentary. Edinburgh: T&T Clark.

Trenchard, Warren C. 1982. *Ben Sira's View of Women: A Literary Analysis*. Brown Judaic Studies 38. Chico, CA: Scholars Press.

Trible, Phyllis. 1984. *Texts of Terror: Literary-Feminist Readings of Biblical Narratives*. Overtures to Biblical Theology. Philadelphia: Fortress.

Unnik, W. C. Van. 1974. "Josephus' Account of the Story of the Sin with Alien Women in the Country of Midian (Num. 25:1ff)." Pages 241–61 in *Travels in the World of the Old Testament*. Edited by M. S. H. G. Heerma Van Voss, Ph. H. J. Houwink Ten Cate, and N. A. Van Uchelen. Assen: Van Gorcum.

Vander Broek, Lyle. 1994. "Discipline and Community: Another Look at 1 Corinthians 5." *Reformed Review* 48, no. 1:5–13.

VanderKam, James C. 1977. *Textual and Historical Studies in the Book of Jubilees*. Harvard Semitic Monographs 14. Missoula, MT: Scholars Press.

———. 1994. "Genesis 1 in Jubilees 2." *Dead Sea Discoveries* 1, no. 3:301–21.

———. 1999. "Isaac's Blessing of Levi and His Descendants in Jubilees 31." Pages 497–519 in *The Provo International Conference on the Dead Sea Scrolls: Technological Innovations, New Texts, and Reformulated Ideas.* Edited by Donald W. Parry and Eugene Ulrich. Studies on the Texts of the Desert of Judah 30. Leiden: Brill.

———. 2000. "Covenant and Biblical Interpretation in Jubilees 6." Pages 92–104 in *The Dead Sea Scrolls Fifty Years after Their Discovery: Proceedings of the Jerusalem Congress, July 20–25, 1997.* Edited by Lawrence H. Schiffman, Emanuel Tov, and James C. VanderKam. Jerusalem: Israel Exploration Society.

Vogt, Peter T. 2008. "Social Justice and the Vision of Deuteronomy." *Journal of the Evangelical Theological Society* 51:35–44.

Wallace-Hadrill, Andrew. 1988. "The Social Structure of the Roman House." *Papers of the British School at Rome* 56:43–97.

Waltke, Bruce K. 2005. *The Book of Proverbs: Chapters 15–31.* New International Commentary on the Old Testament. Grand Rapids: Eerdmans.

Walzer, Michael. 1968. "Exodus 32 and the Theory of Holy War: The History of a Citation." *Harvard Theological Review* 61, no. 1:1–14.

Wanamaker, Charles A. 2006. "The Power of the Absent Father: A Socio-Rhetorical Analysis of 1 Corinthians 4:14–5:13." Pages 339–64 in *The New Testament Interpreted.* Edited by Cilliers Breytenbach, Johan C. Thom, and Jeremy Punt. Novum Testamentum Supplements 124. Leiden: Brill.

Wansbrough, Henry. 1972. "Mark III.21—Was Jesus Out of His Mind?" *New Testament Studies* 18:233–35.

Washington, Harold C. 2004 (1998). "'Lest He Die in Battle and Another Man Take Her': Violence and the Construction of Gender in the Laws of Deuteronomy 20–22." Pages 185–213 in *Gender and Law in the Hebrew Bible and the Ancient Near East.* Edited by Victor H. Matthews, Bernard M. Levinson, and Tikva Frymer-Kensky. London: T&T Clark.

Wassén, Cecilia. 1994. "The Story of Judah and Tamar in the Eyes of the Earliest Interpreters." *Literature and Theology* 8:354–66.

———. 2005. *Women in the Damascus Document.* Society of Biblical Literature Academia Biblica 21. Atlanta: Society of Biblical Literature.

Weaver, Dorothy Jean. 1990. *Matthew's Missionary Discourse: A Literary Critical Analysis.* Journal for the Study of the New Testament: Supplement Series 38. Sheffield: Sheffield Academic Press.

Wegner, Judith Romney. 1988. *Chattel or Person? The Status of Women in the Mishnah.* Oxford: Oxford University Press.

———. 1991. "Philo's Portrayal of Women—Hebraic or Hellenic?" Pages 41–66 in *"Women Like This": New Perspectives on Jewish Women in the Greco-Roman World*. Edited by Amy-Jill Levine. Early Judaism and Its Literature 1. Atlanta: Scholars Press.

Wegner, Paul D. 2005. "Discipline in the Book of Proverbs: 'To Spank or Not to Spank?'" *Journal of the Evangelical Theological Society* 48, no. 4:715–32.

Weinfeld, Moshe. 1961. "The Origin of the Humanism in Deuteronomy." *Journal of Biblical Literature* 80:241–47.

———. 1983 (1972). *Deuteronomy and the Deuteronomic School*. Oxford: Clarendon.

Weitzman, Steven. 2004. "Josephus on How to Survive Martyrdom." *Journal of Jewish Studies* 55, no. 2:230–45.

Welch, John W. 2006. "Miracles, *Maleficium*, and *Maiestas* in the Trial of Jesus." Pages 349–83 in *Jesus and Archaeology*. Edited by James H. Charlesworth. Grand Rapids: Eerdmans.

Wellhausen, Julius. 1903. *Das Evangelium Marci*. Berlin: Georg Reimer.

Wells, Bruce. 2005. "Sex, Lies, and Virginal Rape: The Slandered Bride and False Accusation in Deuteronomy." *Journal of Biblical Literature* 124, no. 1:41–72.

Wenham, David. 1984. *The Rediscovery of Jesus' Eschatological Discourse*. Gospel Perspectives 4. Sheffield: JSOT Press.

Wenham, Gordon J. 1972. "*Bᵉtûlāh*: 'A Girl of Marriageable Age.'" *Vetus Testamentum* 22:326–48.

———. 1985a. "The Date of Deuteronomy: Linch-Pin of Old Testament Criticism." *Themelios* 10, no. 3:15–20.

———. 1985b. "The Date of Deuteronomy: Linch-Pin of Old Testament Criticism, Part 2." *Themelios* 11, no. 1:15–18.

Werman, Cana. 1997. "*Jubilees* 30: Building a Paradigm for the Ban on Intermarriage." *Harvard Theological Review* 90, no. 1:1–22.

Whybray, Roger N. 1994. *Proverbs*. New Century Bible Commentary. Grand Rapids: Eerdmans; London: Marshall Pickering.

Wiesenberg, Ernest. 1961. "The Jubilee of Jubilees." *Revue de Qumran* 3, no. 1:3–40.

Williams, David S. 1999. *The Structure of 1 Maccabees*. Catholic Biblical Quarterly Monograph Series 31. Washington, DC: Catholic Biblical Association.

———. 2001. "A Literary Encircling Pattern in 1 Maccabees 1." *Journal of Biblical Literature* 120, no. 1:140–42.

Willis, Timothy M. 2001. *The Elders of the City: A Study of the Elders-Laws in Deuteronomy*. Society of Biblical Literature Monograph Series 55. Atlanta: Society of Biblical Literature.

Wills, Lawrence M. 2008. *Not God's People: Insiders and Outsiders in the Biblical World*. Lanham, MD: Rowman & Littlefield.

Wilson, Robert R. 2005. "Deuteronomy, Ethnicity, and Reform: Reflections on the Social Setting of the Book of Deuteronomy." Pages 107–23 in *Constituting the Community: Studies on the Polity of Ancient Israel*. Edited by John T. Strong and Steven S. Tuell. Winona Lake, IN: Eisenbrauns.

Wink, Walter. 1998. *The Powers That Be: Theology for a New Millennium*. New York: Doubleday.

Wold, Benjamin G. 2008. "Family Ethics in 4QInstruction and the New Testament." *Novum Testamentum* 50:286–300.

Wright, Benjamin G. 1989. *No Small Difference: Sirach's Relationship to Its Hebrew Parent Text*. Society of Biblical Literature Septuagint and Cognate Studies 26. Atlanta: Scholars Press.

———. 2005. "Putting the Puzzle Together: Some Suggestions concerning the Social Location of the Wisdom of Ben Sira." Pages 89–112 in *Conflicted Boundaries in Wisdom and Apocalypticism*. Edited by Benjamin G. Wright III and Lawrence M. Wills. Society of Biblical Literature Symposium Series 35. Atlanta: Society of Biblical Literature.

Wright, Christopher J. H. 1996. *Deuteronomy*. New International Biblical Commentary. Peabody, MA: Hendrickson.

Wright, John W. 2002. "A Tale of Three Cities: Urban Gates, Squares and Power in Iron Age II, Neo-Babylonian and Achaemenid Judah." Pages 19–50 in *Second Temple Studies III: Studies in Politics, Class and Material Culture*. Edited by Philip R. Davies and John M. Halligan. Journal for the Study of the Old Testament: Supplement Series 340. Sheffield: Sheffield Academic Press.

Wright, Nicholas Thomas. 1996. *Jesus and the Victory of God*. Vol. 2 of *Christian Origins and the Question of God*. Minneapolis: Fortress.

Yoder, Christine Roy. 2005. "Forming 'Fearers of Yahweh': Repetition and Contradiction as Pedagogy in Proverbs." Pages 167–83 in *Seeking Out the Wisdom of the Ancients*. Edited by Ronald L. Troxel, Kelvin G. Friebel, and Dennis R. Magary. Winona Lake, IN: Eisenbrauns.

Young, Jeremy. 2008. *The Violence of God and the War on Terror*. New York: Seabury.

Zeitlin, Solomon. 1950. "Introduction and Commentary." In *The First Book of Maccabees*. Edited by Sidney Tedesche and Solomon Zeitlin. Jewish Apocryphal Literature. New York: Harper.

Zerbe, Gordon M. 1993. *Non-Retaliation in Early Jewish and New Testament Texts: Ethical Themes in Social Contexts*. Journal for the Study of the Pseudepigrapha: Supplement Series 13. Sheffield: Sheffield Academic Press.

Zevit, Ziony. 2007. "The Search for Violence in Israelite Culture and in the
    Bible." Pages 16–37 in *Religion and Violence: The Biblical Heritage*. Edited
    by David A. Bernat and Jonathan Klawans. Sheffield: Sheffield Phoenix.
Zlotnick, Helena. 2002. *Dinah's Daughters: Gender and Judaism from the He-
    brew Bible to Late Antiquity*. Philadelphia: University of Pennsylvania Press.

Index of Ancient Sources